A GRAMMAR OF STYLE

THE LANGUAGE LIBRARY

EDITED BY ERIC PARTRIDGE AND SIMEON POTTER

ALREADY PUBLISHED

A. E. DARBYSHIRE

A GRAMMAR OF STYLE

ANDRE DEUTSCH

FIRST PUBLISHED 1971 BY
ANDRE DEUTSCH LIMITED
105 GREAT RUSSELL STREET
LONDON WC1
COPYRIGHT © 1971 A. E. DARBYSHIRE
ALL RIGHTS RESERVED
PRINTED IN GREAT BRITAIN BY
TONBRIDGE PRINTERS LTD
TONBRIDGE, KENT
ISBN 0 233 96006 0

120757

CONTENTS

PREFACE

In the past many writers on style seem to have thought of it as a positive and rare quality in writing to which an author ought to aspire. The ideal seems to have been thought of as more important than the actual. This attitude has led to some writers on stylistics making destructive and prescriptive observations about the ways in which language is used, to be censorious towards those who, they believe, are bad writers, and to offer recipes for improvement.

No such attempt is made here. This author wants nothing to do with any holier-than-thou paranoia. He is aware that some people do sometimes say something like, for instance, 'All personnel will take cognizance of the fact of the top priority of this requisition and realize that the immediate implementation of this important policy directive is imperatively essential', that other people will simply say, 'Get 'em quick', and that the latter is admirable because of its clearness and brevity. But this book is about an aspect of linguistics; and if linguistics is the scientific study of language (the author does tend to dislike that pompous definition of an interest in what people say and the way they say it), then it does not need subjective value-judgments. All that it needs is the patient collection of facts, an ordered arrangement of them, and an effort to understand. The modern student of linguistics takes all uses of language whatever as his province, and examines them all with equal interest. Though he may privately believe that some are better than others, his concern is with the description and classification of everything, and not just with the assessment and praise of that which he likes.

In this book it is suggested that style in the use of language is a deviation from a norm and that there are good social reasons why such deviations should exist. For language is to be found only in its uses in the actuality of the world, and not in the imaginations of those who might see nothing more than its possibilities. However, the author has not been concerned to try to discover what these deviations might be. There are obviously thousands of them, ranging from *écriteaux* in the streets to the greatest works of literature. The author has been more interested in the norm. It has seemed to him reasonable to assume that unless one knows what the norm is one cannot understand the deviations. It has also seemed to him that the norm, whatever it might be, exists at the basis of that level of language-use when the substance of language becomes organized into structures which are capable of grammatical or syntactic analysis. Nor is the author very much interested, in this book, in such analysis itself. He is much more concerned with the ways in which the substance of language, the sounds of speech and their representation by the marks of a script, can develop into a condition at which such analysis becomes possible. There is, of course, no such thing as the norm to be found in actual usages. It is a concept which must be expressed by means of a formula, and it is a concept about that which is left of uses of language when all stylistic qualities have been taken away from them. For the author has taken it to be almost axiomatic that every use of language shows some kind of style or other. This has led him to think that a transformational-generative grammar is the best means of giving a description of what he thinks of as the norm. It is the main intention of this book to state what such a description might be.

The author would like to express his thanks to the following authors, authors' representatives and publishers for permission to print extracts from copyright works: to the author and Messrs Macmillan for an extract from *Principles of Electronics* by L. T. Aggar; to the poet and Messrs Faber and Faber for the first four stanzas of Trinculo's Song in 'The Sea and the Mirror' from *Collected Longer Poems* by W. H. Auden; to the author and the Longman Group Limited for an extract from *What is Language? A New Approach to Linguistic Description* by Robert M. W. Dixon; to the Editor of the *London Magazine* for an extract from 'The End of the Absurd?' by John Elsom; to the author and the Hogarth Press for an extract from *Cider with Rosie* by Laurie Lee; to the Literary Trustees of Walter de la

Mare and the Society of Authors for the poem 'The Moth' from *The Complete Poems of Walter de la Mare*; to the Council of the Faraday Society and the author for an extract from 'Vapour-phase Deposition of copper by the Iodide Process' by R. A. J. Shelton in the *Transactions of the Faraday Society,* Part I, 1966; and to the author and the Cambridge University Press for an extract from *The Dramatic Experience* by J. L. Styan.

A.E.D.

Darley Abbey
Derbyshire

March 1970

CHAPTER I

LANGUAGE AND STYLE

1 The Identity of Style

This book is an attempt at an exercise in linguistics. The purpose of writing it is to try to discover a set of linguistic principles which might be used for an examination of what is called *style* in the use of English.

That there is or can be any such concept as that of style in the use of language is an intuition which the student of linguistics can theorize about in at least two ways. From one point of view, this intuition, demonstrated in the actual use of the language which the linguist takes as his data, is simply that there are varieties of language-uses which are felt, but not made explicit, in some vaguely social and non-linguistic way, as when, for example, people who take up a pen to write feel that they must use language in a different way from that which they would use in ordinary conversation. From another point of view, that of the linguist himself who analyses the data, these varieties can be described in purely linguistic terms after they have been distinguished by means of some linguistic criteria. These criteria are features of the language-uses themselves which reside only in the language-uses, and not in any circumstances which might give rise to them, or to which they may be said to refer, or to which they might be imagined to have some kind of correlation.

It would be quite gratuitous at the beginning of the investigation to try to define the word *style*. Until we know what these linguistic features are, and whether their existence is as real as it is felt to be, we are not in a position to understand in sufficient detail, or to make valid, what we are supposed to be talking about. Nevertheless, we derive the notion of style, as well as the feeling – even if it is nothing else – that there can be a notion of style, from the observation of contrasts and from the idea that

11

using language is a form of behaviour in which the sources and purposes are not always the same. And then, having ignored the sources and purposes, we find that the results are different. To say, for example,

> Thus, hexafluorobenzene is obtained from the defluorination of perfluorocyclebenzene, perfluoroethylbenzene from perfluoroethylcyclohaxene, and perfluoroxlyenes from the corresponding isomers of perfluorodimethylcyclohaxene,

is not to behave in quite the same manner as to say

> Fain would I kiss my *Julia's* dainty leg,
> Which is as white and hair-less as an egge.

Different principles are involved. That which moves the chemist to tell other chemists about the defluorination of one or two of the carbon compounds is not the same as that which moves the poet to exclaim at the anatomy of his girl-friend; and thus, we say, different circumstances impel different people, and sometimes the same people, to use language in different ways in different circumstances, and the resulting language-uses show differences which can be accounted for by some theory of style.

In every case the resulting language-use is something physical. It is either the movement of sound waves in the atmosphere or the presence of marks of a script on something semi-durable such as paper. This physical thing started, presumably, as the creation of some central nervous system, as pure thought or pure feeling, and was then transmuted by the organs of the body containing that central nervous system into its physical substance. This physical thing, the assemblage of sound waves or ink marks, is what we study in our examination of what we call *style*. For this physical thing has elements which, in its transmutation from pure thought or pure feeling, were made ordered, formal and coherent, and various kinds of ordering, form and coherence can be looked at and compared. In the quotations give above, for instance, we can discover that the rhythm of the second is different from that of the first; that there are differences in the kinds of verbs used in each extract and therefore in the sentence structure of each; and that the concatenation of such a word as *hexafluorobenzene*, say, with such a word as *isomers* is of a different kind from that of *leg* with *egge*. Such features of the use of language as these, and many others which some one will have to describe and classify, are linguistic.

Notions such as these can give us a fairly firm starting place, so that we know at least what kinds of concepts we are talking about.

This book is called *A Grammar of Style*. I use the word *grammar* here as a name for the description of the linguistic features just referred to – those kinds of features of the organization of language substance into order, form and coherence which are recognizable by speakers of the language to which they belong, and which, indeed, make the language what it is. I also use the word *grammar* with systematic ambiguity. I use it in two senses which will have to be clearly distinguished. First, I use it to mean the internal grammar, the knowledge, that is, mostly unconscious but conscious here and there among some speakers, of the ways of organizing language substance by each individual user of the language. Second, I use it to mean the grammarian's (that is, my own) description of what such knowledge might be like. Clearly, these two meanings are distinct. The second kind of grammar is a generalization from the first. In many examples of actual usage the first will approximate to the second only at some, but by no means all, points. The first undoubtedly exists as a living reality, incontrovertible though largely inaccessible, while the second may be worthless, or at the best probably something worth arguing about.

In order to present some theory of the kind of thing I mean by *style*, I shall base what I have to say on four hypotheses. They are:

(1) that a language is, or behaves as if it were, a code;
(2) that the use of this language-code, by speakers and writers shows that a scale of competence is discernible, and that we can make a grammar of competence against which performance can be measured;
(3) that the use of language is myth-creative, and because of this it is possible to make purely linguistic statements, which are, of course, themselves myths, about the uses of language;
(4) that style is a necessary consequence of the fact – if it is a fact – that the use of language is myth-creative.

These four hypotheses are merely conceptual devices that can be used to control and operate ideas which are nowadays more or less familiar to people who have read fairly widely in the literature of modern British and American linguistics. No originality is claimed for them. Their merit, if they have any, is simply that they are convenient instruments for the management of ideas.

2 Language as a Code

One of the obvious statements that can be made about any language is that the speakers of it use it for communication and sharing experiences. The word *communication* nowadays suggests the ideas of Information Theory, and I invoke that theory here — or at least, some of the main principles of it — as a basis for further discussion. Information Theory, a branch of mathematical physics that has emerged from the examination of problems of communicating by means of telephones, radio and electronics, makes use of the concepts of codes, communication channels, signs, signals, information, redundancy and noise. These concepts are relevant to the consideration of languages.

Communication is the act of transferring messages from one system to another. The messages are transferred by means of a communication channel. Signals, however, are what are actually transferred in physical form; the signals, therefore, carry the messages and are physical embodiments of them. A communication channel is something, also physical, which can act as a vehicle to carry the signals and also be a means of their organization and control. This book, for instance, is a communication channel in this sense: the words, sentences, paragraphs, chapters, chapter headings, page numbers, and so on, are the signals which it carries, and the whole physical format of the book is a means of organizing and controlling them, so that the messages can be transferred from the central nervous system of the author to the central nervous systems of the readers.

Every act of communication consists of five parts: (1) the encoding of the message; (2) its transmission; (3) its realization as a signal; (4) its reception; and (5) its decoding. So far as communication occurs by means of language, this act is accomplished through speech and writing. The process may be illustrated by some such scheme as this:

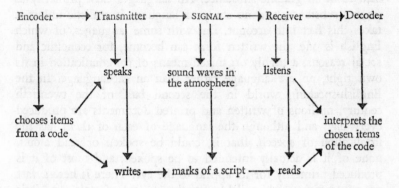

What goes on in the brains and nervous systems of individuals, or encoders, is private and cannot be examined directly; and it is in the brains and nervous systems of individuals, presumably, that messages in language originate. Thoughts, beliefs, ideas, opinions, emotions, feelings, and attitudes of mind are usually known by people other than those who experience them only when they are expressed, and this expression is always something that can be perceived by the senses.

The best that the student of language can do under these conditions is make inferences about the sorts of events he believes happen in the brains and nervous systems of individuals – such events as can be symbolized by saying 'this man feels emotion' or 'this man thinks' or 'this man reasons' – but the student of language cannot actually observe the sorts of events that do, apparently, happen.

Nevertheless, the study of signals can give him an objective way of looking at communication channels, for the signals are realizations in physical substance of signs or symbols which can be detected by the senses and interpreted. Indeed, it is only because of the existence of signals in physical substance that he knows acts of communication take place at all. Furthermore, signals can be isolated, set apart from their immediate surroundings in the hurlyburly of the universe, and then be examined, sorted out, analysed and compared.

Those language signals which exist as sound waves in the atmosphere can be said to exist in phonic substance, and those which exist as the written or printed marks of a script can be said to be in graphic substance. All languages exist primarily as phonic substance, and no study of language is realistic unless it takes this fact into account. But with some languages, of which English is one, the written form can become, for economic and social reasons, a highly organized means of communication in its own right, an eye-language rather than an ear-language. In the English-speaking world in the second half of the twentieth century, millions of written and printed documents are produced every day; and although the language of each of them has the implication of speech, that is, could be spoken or read aloud, none of it is actually intended to be spoken, and most of it is produced primarily for its appeal to the eye. There is here a vast quantity of material available for the student of style, and it is likely that stylistic studies will be concentrated more on the comparison of texts in the written medium than on those in the spoken.

When an observer watches the signals that pass across a communication channel, he notices that the items which make up the signals tend to repeat themselves, and that there is a finite, and in most cases quite restricted, number of them. There is, for instance, only a limited number of speech sounds used in the languages of the world, and not all these sounds appear in every language. Or, in the writing and printing of English, there are only the 52 letters of the alphabet (if we count both upper and lower cases), the ten numerals, and a small number of punctuation marks. This kind of restriction means that when an observer watches a communication channel he will find that certain elements which make up the signals tend to recur very often, that others recur less often, and some very rarely.

Such an observation as this enables one to make the hypothesis that a language is a sort of code. The word *code* may be defined here as a prearranged set of signs used for making signals. And the word *sign* can be defined as a discrete and measurable component of a signal that carries information. One of the properties of a communication channel is that the items which compose the signals in their physical form can be transmitted only one at a time. But there is here a difficulty in deciding what precisely one means by 'one at a time'. When people speak, for instance, they can utter only one speech sound at once, or one syllable at once, or one word at once, or one sentence at once. It is not clear that each of the items which are used to make a signal carries the same amount of importance in the structuring of that signal; and at the same time, the tendency of many codes to have built-in redundancy in the rules for making signals makes it difficult to decide what exactly the signs of some codes are.

With language this difficulty is very great. For it would seem that there is a hierarchy of levels of significance of the signs that make, say, sentences or structures of sentences such as paragraphs or paraphones, and even larger structure-bearing samples of language-use, such as, for example, whole poems or passages of prose. The observer, therefore, in his investigation of communication channels using a language, has to make various definitions of the kinds of things he calls signs; or, if he can find one comprehensive definition, the exponents of the class of things he calls signs will be different kinds of things when looked at from different points of view. Thinking in terms of language as a code, one may find it convenient to imagine a scale of signs – to think, first, of the smallest units, the individual speech sounds or phonemes, and then to note how these build up progressively into larger units – say, morphemes, words, phrases, clauses, groups, sentences or whatever, according to the technical terms of one's linguistic vocabulary. But there is no need to think that in communication in language the sentence is the largest unit at the top of the scale of signs. Notions of anaphora and coherence can lead one to thinking that there are larger structure-bearing units than the sentence. There are, in fact, many language-uses which are made up of patterns of sentences and which are more or less formalized. We have such names as chatter, gossip, conversation, talk, discussion, interview, debate, speech, oration, lecture, sermon, and the like, for those patterns of sentences where only the spoken word is used. In the written forms of the language we have institutionalized patterns of sentences in what might be called the language of information and instruction as well as in literature. In the language of information and instruction we have, for example, personal and business letters, circulars, memoranda, different kinds of newspaper and periodical items, advertisements of different sorts, textbooks of all descriptions, articles in learned journals, and specialized documents like Acts of Parliament, contracts, deeds, conveyances, and so on. In literature we make a distinction between poetry and prose. In prose we can distinguish among such forms as the short story or *conte* and the novel, the essay, *belles-lettres*, criticism, reviews, biography, and so on; and we can also make distinctions among such popular forms of fiction as romance, western, science fiction, spy-thriller, whodunit, and others; while in poetry we distinguish among such forms as lyric, ode, sonnet, ballad, epic, narrative poem, and so on. Sometimes, of course, formal distinctions such as these cut across one another, as in the language of the drama, which is written first though intended to be delivered orally in performance, and which may be in verse or prose or both. But the point is that, linguistically speaking, we can recognize a sign by its form, and a sign may be as small as a phoneme or as large as an epic.

Since a code must always have more than one sign (by definition it is a pre-arranged set of signs), the encoder of any message has to make a decision about which signs to use. With the simplest of all codes, a two-sign one, such as a doorbell which can have the two signs of ringing or not ringing, the decision is not difficult – it is a straightforward case of either/or. And when the number of signs is comparatively small, as with the script used in written English, there is again little difficulty of decision, because most users of the code have had the choices made for them by the conventions of English orthography; people learn the rules for the use of the code when they learn to write. And even as we move into larger codes, we find that although the choices of which signs to use increase in some ways they become limited in others. If we think of a language such as English as a code with a very large number of signs indeed – all words and their inflections, sentence forms, syntactic orders of elements, different literary forms, and so on – we find that here the choices are not always wide ones, and are normally circumscribed by some conventional rules which encoders are advised to obey if they want their messages to be intelligible to other people.

There are two reasons for this restraint on the uninhibited use of signs. First, a code is a pre-arranged set of signs, and this fact implies a social use of it. If we want to use a code to communicate to other people, our freedom of using it is limited by the ability of other people to understand what we are doing, and we have to obey the rules or fail to communicate. This kind of failure often occurs, of course. What is modern frequently fails to impress the traditionalist, and in art and literature new ideas are often expressed in new ways which many people are unable or unwilling to accept. Second, each of the signs of a code has its own area of applicability, and the code itself forces restrictions on the encoder by imposing on him the obligation of expressing certain kinds of messages only in certain kinds of ways. At any given time in the history of the code there are tasks which the code cannot be called upon to perform, although some codes, such as languages, can develop new attributes as they are called upon, in the social contexts of their existence, to undertake new feats. Some codes have, as it were, a built-in reluctance to attempt some acts of communications, as, for instance, the index of a library classification scheme could tell a potential reader the whereabouts on the shelves of a particular volume if it is in the library, or even where it should be on the shelves if it is not in, but it cannot tell the reader the whereabouts of the librarian, even though it could be adapted for doing so. Each sign of a code, that is to say, can carry at least one bit of information, and in any communicative act the amount of information is fixed for that particular act. A language, of course, changes in history, so that in general signs may change the kind or amount of information they carry during the development of the language, but this is not so in any one particular example of their use. Even the ambiguity of an ambiguous sign is limited.

We can define the word *information*, in its technical sense as used here, to mean the property of a sign to act as an instruction to encoders or decoders to select a particular form and reject all others. When we look for the signs of a code we are seeking a finite number of different kinds of forms. Signs are forms in the sense that they are physical things which can be recognized and distinguished by the senses, and the information of any sign is built into the kind of form that the sign is. In each of the letters of the alphabet, for instance, we recognize a form, a distinct shape, which is different from that of any of the other letters. Our awareness of this difference is the information conveyed by the sign.

A signal is composed of a number of signs. The information contained in a signal is that which gives it meaning. When a message is encoded, the encoder chooses a number of signs from the code and assembles them in a conventional arrangement to make the signal. But as the signal passes across the communication channel there is a great deal of difference between the information contained in the signal and the message itself. The signal and the message are not the same, for the signal is only the physical embodiment of the message, which is a sort of myth, an intangible creation of some central nervous system symbolized or represented by the signal. The information given by the signs that make up the signal consists of a set of instructions from the encoder to the decoder to assemble this representation of the message, and the decoder is able to do this because of his shared knowledge of the pre-arrangement of the code.

Messages in language are used to control portions of the universe, to operate things, influence other people, bring about desired ends. When they do this they have meaning. And meaning can be considered as a form of behaviour, a response to a stimulus, either on the part of the encoder or of the decoder or of both. In communication by means of language there are several layers of meaning which can be inferred from the ways in which human beings respond to different sorts of signs and different kinds of stimuli contained in the signals. But meaning extends beyond the signals themselves. Extra-linguistic signs can provoke language-activity, and this in turn can provoke other language-activity or something non-linguistic. Or within the language-activity itself the circumstances in which signs occur can give them meanings appropriate to those circumstances, as when, for instance, a capital letter at the beginning of a written sentence can mean 'sentence begins' and at the same time have its own meaning as part of a word.

The capacity of a code is all the information it is possible to convey by means of its signs and the rules for their use. These rules, or the fact of their being obeyed when the code is being used, are also signs, since they must be part of the pre-arrangement without which the code would be meaningless, that is, unable to provoke responses. It follows from the fact that every code must have more than one sign that when a message is being encoded in the signs of a very large code only a very small part of the code is being used. And with very large codes this means that some signs are likely to be used more frequently than others. Theoretically, therefore, we can speak of the total capacity of a code and the average use of the signs of the same code. Some signs will have a high probability of being used and some a low probability, with a scale of probability for other signs in between. In theory at least it should be possible to calculate what these probabilities are. The average of them would be the average use of the code, and the average amount of information conveyed by it in any given period of time or in some other measurement of use. The arithmetical difference between the theoretical total capacity of a code and the average amount of information conveyed by it is the code's *redundancy*.

It follows from this that in any use of a code with a very large number of signs there could always be more signs called upon for use than the number actually used in the making of any signal. No matter what is said in a language to make the message complete, there is, paradoxically, always something more that could be said. If a stranger to my home town, for example, asks me the way from the railway station to the nearest post office, I could tell him in a simple sentence or two. But I could also tell him the same facts in a poem of twelve Spenserian stanzas describing as well the sights he would see on the way; or I could tell him in Johnsonian prose with all verbs, nouns, adjectives and adverbs being words of more than three syllables; or I could tell him in a sonnet uttered in the Scouse dialect; and so on. No matter what use is made of the items of a very large code, there is always an unused potential of information that could be drawn upon still left in the code.

An efficient act of communication would be one that used the minimum of signs necessary for the embodiment of the message. Thus, 'No can do' is more efficient than 'I have regretfully to inform you of my inability to comply with your request'. But efficient acts of communication in language are quite rare, because very often the redundancy of the language is built into uses of it; some of the redundancy of the language becomes part of the rules for the use of signs and therefore a sign itself. The result is that in the uses of language there is often more information conveyed across the channel than the message needs. For example, in the spoken form of the question 'Why are we here?', not only is the question-form indicated by the presence of the word *why* and by the order of the words *are we*, as contrasted with the non-question-form *we are*, but also by the intonation, or tune of the words – just as, in the written form of the utterance, the final

mark of punctuation indicates the same. In attempting to convey
the message contained in the utterance, or carried by that group
of signs, the encoder has little choice of which items to use if he
wants to be as concise as possible. His originality is limited by
the built-in redundancy he must use if he wants to ask that
particular question. He could, of course, ask a different question
with more or less the same meaning, and he would have to do
so by calling upon more of the redundancy of the language, and
at the same time specify in different forms of words what he
understood by the words *we, are* and *here* – as with, say, 'For
what reason are those of us who survived the wreck stranded
upon this desert island?' or as with 'What explanation is there
for the existence of a species called *homo sapiens* to be found
on this, rather than any other, planet in this, rather than any
other, galaxy?' – And here we have the beginnings of an interesting insight into what might be understood by paraphrase.

Since the use of a code is social, involving at least two parties
if communication is to be successful, and since the parties have
made a pre-arrangement about what the signs of the code shall be,
an effective use of the code can be maintained only so long as the
rules for its use are obeyed. The presence of built-in redundance
is normally a safeguard against excessive originality on the part
of encoders, but at the same time the language allows enough
freedom to enable encoders to say something new. However,
some encoders are not always so careful about obeying the rules
as they should be. There is always the possibility of what might
be called *noise*. We can say that noise is a quality of messages
in which more or less information than is necessary for
efficient communication is given in the signals in which the
message is encoded.

Theoretically, it should be possible to measure the amount of
noise in any communication channel once one has decided how
much is the minimum of information, or how few are the signs,
needed for assembling the signal. Theoretically, too, it should
also be possible to conceive of a scale of noise, and of the
efficiency of a communication channel, as well, perhaps, of some
such notion as the productivity of styles. To speak generally,
one could say that an efficient use of a communication channel
is one which has just the right amount of information, or just the
right number of signs, to convey to the decoder just the right

number of choices to enable him to assemble the message. Any other than this would be negative or positive noise. Negative noise would be that kind of information, such as a grammatical error or a spelling mistake, which was allowed into the channel and which detracted from the efficient transmission of the message by interfering with the ability of the decoder to receive and decode it properly. Positive noise would be that which added to the amount of information needed for efficient, though not necessarily proper, transmission of the message and helped the decoder in his interpretation – that which, indeed, might enrich his experience and enlarge his understanding and pleasure in the ways in which great literature does. The presence of positive noise would therefore allow for a communication channel which demonstrated this presence to be more linguistically productive than one from which it was absent. The productivity of a style of encoding could then be regarded as a ratio of imput to output, measurable in bits of information.

It is necessary, I think, to make this distinction between noise and redundancy because of the self-consciousness about style of some encoders and because of the systematic ambiguity of the use of the word *grammar*. The meaning of some uses of language which are probably some of the most interesting, or the reason for their existence, is not so much the paraphrasable content as the use of the language itself. A great deal of imaginative literature, which intuitively we take to be of stylistic importance, is held to be literature for this very reason – it is communication that is important not in the bare statement of the myth but in the insight that arises from the way in which the myth is stated. Furthermore, no kind of grammar of style should prescribe the terms in which any user of the language should use it. A grammar of style should merely make statements, based upon some independent frame of reference, about what as a matter of observed or theoretical fact does happen in the course of actual language-use. The assumption is that in comparing two texts, say, for their stylistic features, one can describe differences, if there are any, in terms of a grammar which might be implicit in both, but which could quite easily include elements, or categories, or features, or whatever, not found in either. This grammar would be the grammarian's grammar, a description of the language which could, or should, be able to account for all possible instances, or exponents, of all possible linguistic features in the language described. However, texts could be found, I imagine, which exploited only a few, or limited range of, linguistic features, and this might be due (as in some scientific and technological writing, for example) to the built-in redundancy of the convention itself, which might also be noise from the point of view of the grammarian and his grammar.

3 Competence and Performance

The grammarian's grammar is the grammar of competence to which we referred earlier. Such a grammar is, of course, a pure fiction, a statement of generalizations about the language based on some theoretical approach to the whole mass of questions raised by the data or whatever is thought of as *the language* considered as a whole. Naturally, one cannot examine a language as a whole, for the whole must include not only all that is already said and written in it, but also all that which still remains to be said and written. So, unlike some other works of fiction, the grammarian's grammar can have a usefulness. Its generalizations can be statements of norms from which, in the actual day-to-day uses, there might or might not be deviations.

In these actual day-to-day uses of the language, communication can quite often become, if not impossible, at least very difficult, because of areas in which the encoder's knowledge of what he is doing with the language cannot always be matched by the knowledge of the decoder. On the one hand, we have just plain ignorance on the part of some decoders, and on the other the fact that in both the arts and the sciences the development of sensibility and the advancement of knowledge can lead to the use of signs in very original ways by clever and talented encoders.

This state of affairs is interesting to anyone who takes up the problems of style in the use of language. Apparently, one of the great failures of language learning and teaching in Britain at least – perhaps in the whole of the English-speaking world – has been the failure to learn, or to teach people how to learn, the proper way of being delighted by surprise. One of the difficulties of language-learning by native speakers of English seems to be the existence in many people of a kind of resistance to the acquisition of newer ways of using language than those to which they have become accustomed from their first acquaintance with it. People who suffer from this disability live in an enchanted, but not very exciting, circle of innocence and ignorance. To live thus in an age of industrial and technological democracy is to be cut off from the mainstream of civilization, and, like the girl in *Punch* who wanted her *café-au-lait* with milk, to live in exile from the glories of our culture and all that created it. This is a problem for pedagogues and psychologists, but it is undoubtedly a real one, especially when it concerns the less favoured members of our society, who, brought up and made aware of their environment only within the narrow limits of what simple stock of language they learnt in earliest childhood, have difficulties in adjusting their language habits, in official and unofficial education, to the conventions of a wider variety of styles; and this seems to separate many people from participation in the deeper intellectual, cultural and social life of the community.

The inability to be delighted by surprise is both a misfortune for the whole of society in which it occurs and a personal disaster for the individual who suffers it. In the daily uses of language, words group themselves into companies, into collocations and sets, grammatical structures and imagery, which are the expressions of the experience of the speech-community to which they belong, which are the repository and show-case of its values, and which embody in what should be the speech-community's most treasured possession the nature of its awareness of the universe around it. When any one of us, carrying with him his idiolect, which has been formed out of the patterns of his responses to his environment expressed in his language as used in his necessarily limited acquaintance with the world, comes across something difficult, like the concept of statistical entropy in thermodynamics, or comes across something surprising, like a new image in a poem, he is either baffled or confused, when he should be interested and delighted. He is baffled and confused because the style of the language he encounters is not (to put it simply) one that he has been used to.

Our knowledge of the process of language-learning is far from complete, and our way to such knowledge is made difficult, I believe, by an empirical and rationalist way of thinking which tends to describe it in terms of what is external to the language-learning subject. It is, however, possible to conceive of man in evolution as imposing something of his own neural structuring upon his environment. In this way men can be said to generate utterances as features of natural selection, and the uniqueness of man, so far as one knows, in evolving language which is different both qualitatively and quantitatively from any means of communication possessed by any other animals, is merely a part of evolution, a stage, as it were, in the evolutionary process from primitive biological states to more advanced, but not necessarily most advanced, psychosocial states in which consciousness is aware of itself and can control itself. If such a view is tenable, then the evolution of language seems a necessary condition for its existence, since only in language, and especially recorded language as we are familiar with it in our highly technological society, can man express consciousness and make it available as a means of operation and control of the whole environment as well as a source of self-understanding.

However that may be, we can make the hypothesis that in the use of language as the linguist finds it in his data there will be differences in the performance of different speakers, and even, at different times, of the same speaker. But the important question is: In the performance of what precisely? What is it that speakers and writers of the language are speaking and writing?

Given that the language in question has the features of a code, and that a code is a pre-arranged set of signs, one could perhaps say that the simplest way to answer such questions is to come to a decision about what are the signs that make up the language-code. There is no need for such a decision to be an arbitrary one. What the speakers and writers of many languages do all day long is make up sentences for other people to listen to and read. We shall have to come to some conclusions later about what we mean by the word *sentence*, but we can say here and now that a sentence is a structure of the elements of the language made in accordance with certain rules. We can further postulate that there is in any language only a limited number of sentence forms, and that what makes most sentences different from one another is not their form but their content.

One of the central questions to which any theory about language must give some of its attention is why can any speaker produce a sentence which has not been uttered before but which is perfectly intelligible to other speakers of the same language. The limited number of sentence forms of a language is part of its built-in redundancy, a control on the uninhibited exuberance and originality of speakers and writers, who, although they can produce an infinite number of sentences, can only do so in a limited number of ways. This, of course, is only another way of saying that in the use of sentences in a language by its speakers and writers the characteristics of a code are observable, and it is also a way of answering the question about why hitherto unuttered sentences are intelligible. With only a limited range, or system, of sentence forms at their disposal, the speakers and writers of a language must keep on using the same items from that range again and again, doubtless with some used more frequently than others, so that the range of sentence forms becomes a sort of classification of the kinds of things speakers and writers say about the facts, ideas, beliefs, opinions, emotions, feelings, attitudes of mind, and so on, that they talk about. Theoretically, perhaps, what they talk about is the whole of the universe with all that therein is, but the kinds of statements they make about it are limited to the kinds of sentence forms available in the language for their use. Beyond that lies the vast unuttered and unrecorded territory of the ineffable.

As a result of diligent search the grammarian can find out what these few sentence forms are, even though he cannot find out more than a small selection of all the sentences that exist in the language. The grammarian's grammar is as complete a description of these sentence forms as he can make. But his method of making is only a method of inferences from the relatively small selection that comes, or which he can bring, within the reach of his knowledge. This grammar is not of course a model of all other grammars in the brains of speakers of the language, because what goes on in those brains is theoretically unknowable, and practically inaccessible, and the fact or the supposition that anything does go on in them is itself an inference. But other people do speak and write, and what they speak and write will show grammatical similarities and peculiarities which the grammarian can assess in the terms of his own grammar.

Bound up with the postulate that a language consists of an

infinite number of sentences expressed in a limited number of forms is the theoretical notion that all these sentences are grammatical. But they are not all grammatical in the same sort of way. Some are more, or less, grammatical than others. A grammatical sentence is one which obeys the rules of some grammar, or which is generated according to the statable requirements of some range of grammatical ideas existing in a system. But since only the grammar can tell us what a grammatical sentence is, we shall not be able to recognize a grammatical sentence until we have the grammar in front of us and can refer to it. Where does it come from?

Obviously, the linguist cannot go looking for grammatical sentences among his data in a corpus of sentences from which he makes his inferences, even though his corpus may be full of them. This is because the grammaticality of a sentence is a linguistic abstraction, and the grammar displayed in the corpus is that of the speakers or writers of the language, but is not likely to be that of the linguist's description. Any particular exponent in the corpus may or may not fit in with the grammarian's generalized theory which is supposed to account for all exponents of that sort, and the fact that this may be so is not due to a failure of the grammarian's grammar, but could be due to the performance, good or bad, competent or incompetent, of the speaker or writer of the particular exponents. Nor could a grammatical sentence be identified statistically as one which conformed in certain respects with the most frequently occurring or the most probable. We might be able to find in that way sentences or utterances which were acceptable to members of the speech-community; but a condition of being acceptable is not a condition of being grammatical – as, for instance, the utterance 'No Smoking' is acceptable as the signal of an encoded message to a large number of people in the English-speaking world, even though it is a sentence of very low, perhaps zero, grammaticality. The nature of the conformity of a statistically highly probable sentence would show only that it was like other sentences in having certain characteristics, which, again, would be in the language, but not necessarily in the grammarian's description in the same sort of way. Still less could a grammatical sentence be recognized on semantic grounds as one which meant something to native speakers; for it is quite possible for a form of words to be nonsense, to be without context, to be a lie or a fiction, or to be made quite arbitrarily by random selection, and still be grammatical. In fact, there is little point, and certainly no great ultimate usefulness, in going to utterances as one finds them in the language and trying to discover whether this one is grammatical and that one is not. The best that one can do, after one has made a theory about what one's grammar is like, is to say that in terms of the grammar this sentence is more, or less grammatical than that one, or, in terms of the grammar these two sentences are equally grammatical.

The idea of grammaticality suggested here, of course, is a much wider one than that of the correct grammar of the school teacher. From one point of view, a sentence like 'Our Mam done that' is bad grammar because it does not conform to the conventions or rules of people who would normally say 'My Mummy did that', even though within its dialect it is perfectly acceptable, even grammatical. From another point of view, however, a sentence like 'Our Mam done that' is more grammatical than '*done that Mam our'. On the other hand, a sentence like

> The hearts
> That spaniel'd me at heels, to whom I gave
> Their wishes, do discandy, melt their sweets
> On blossoming Caesar

is so rich in linguistic virtuosity that its grammaticality is quite exceptional.

A grammar, of course, starts with some kind of relationship between itself and a corpus of data provided by the language. But to say that a grammar is based upon a set of observations is not to say that it is a description of what is observed. It is indeed a generalization, a theory not of what linguistic units are, but of what they are like. As a matter of fact, the grammar proposed here goes further. It states not only what a linguistic unit, such as, say, a sentence, is like; but it should also be capable of generating new sentences which, as it were, can leave the grammar and go back into the language where they will be intelligible to speakers of it. There is no need for the grammar to be able to do this, but the fact that it can do it, if called upon, is a justification of it, and from the point of view of the student of style an important justification since, if the grammar can generate intelligible sentences, there is a possibility that some of them, at least, will be paraphrases of already existing sentences. The ability of the grammar to produce paraphrases, and at the same time to demonstrate how they are produced, means that the grammar can be used as a kind of measuring instrument. A grammar such as this, in fact, can come to a decision about what is a well-formed grammatical sentence.

In theory the grammarian should have no difficulty in setting up a standard of well-formedness, or a norm, which he could apply to most of the instances in the data. This standard or norm, if it is adequately made, should measure average competence in sentence making, and this average competence will, no doubt, in most cases be higher than the performance exhibited in a great deal of the language-use which the grammarian will find in his corpus or data. There will be many speakers and writers whose performance falls below that of the most competent. Generally speaking, we can say that we shall intuitively find, and later perhaps be able to confirm, that such uses will not be of much stylistic interest or importance. But there will also be found, one intuitively believes, some speakers or writers whose performance excels that even of the competent, and from the point of view of the student of style in language such sentences will be very interesting indeed. Paradoxically, although great literature is not esteemed very highly among members of the English-speaking world except by the few who fail to see eye-to-eye with the many, some of the standards set by the great literature of the past are still having an influence upon English as a subject taught in schools and colleges; and in the teaching of writing this standard, with its associated anxiety about the plight of twentieth century civilization, is held to be quite unexceptionable. There is always the possibility that this influence will be felt strongly by some individual speaker or writer, who may promote the advancement of knowledge or the dissemination of a new sensibility by means of an outstanding competence in sentence making. A case in point in the twentieth century can be found in the criticism and poetry of T. S. Eliot which have had an effect upon subsequent literary practice.

It is therefore possible for the grammarian to set up in theory a scale of grammaticality, and his own grammar which will be neutral with regard to performances at the extreme ends of the scale, can be used in the assessment of styles as a guide. This does not mean, of course, that his grammar is prescriptive and should lay down laws about how people should speak and write. Even so, there is no reason why it should not do that, if there is some one who wants a prescriptive grammar for some purpose, such as the inculcation of decent linguistic manners and good taste among the young people of the speech-community, or for measuring inadequacy in some uses of the language, or for teaching the language to non-native speakers. Nor does it mean that the grammarian's grammar should, in theory, be so comprehensive as to be able to account for every quirk and oddity in any language-uses, although, in terms of the grammar, any quirk or oddity would show itself to be such, and could be explained as such, and might be intrinsically interesting. But to expect the grammar to demonstrate complete descriptive adequacy would be to expect the impossible of it. To condemn it, however, because it fell short in this respect would be like condemning an English carpenter's two-foot rule for not being three feet long. Nevertheless, an English carpenter's two-foot rule can be used for measuring lengths shorter or longer than two feet. In the same way, the grammarian's grammar, in the sense in which we are talking about it here, can become an instrument for measuring both what is contained in itself and what is not.

4 Myth-creativeness

In fairly recent times, but before modern linguistic science reached the academic respectability which must now be acknowledged, there grew up a theory, derived from some such ideas as those so hastily sketched in the first section of this chapter, that there were only two chief ways of using language. The first way, according to this theory, is the result of a practical and rational sort of human behaviour – a response to environment or an ordinary act of living – in which perceived phenomena become represented in language substance in such a way that the components of the signal correspond in some desirable manner to what is perceived. We thus get, it is said, a scientific or referential use of language. The second way, according to the same theory, is the result of emotional or irrational human behaviour, which is a response, not to environment directly, but to an indwelling physiological change, a feeling, an inward sensation, caused, it seems, by the perception of reality, either contemporaneously with the language-event or by recall from past experience. And we thus get, it is said, an emotive use of language, as in much of the chatter and intercourse of daily life, or as in political speeches or poetry.

The implication of all this, strongly advocated by those who have felt themselves persuaded to popularize *semantics* in our time, is that the first of these ways of using language can command the respect of those who wish for scientific accuracy and objectivity in their descriptions and accounts of the universe and all that it contains. This is because it can be relied upon, so it is claimed, to give us statements of fact, objective truths about reality (whatever that is), whereas the second way of using language merely embodies fictions or something which does not correspond to observed reality in the same way, and is only a creation of the central nervous system which has to be evaluated on its own merits, which may most often be negligible, but which may sometimes be artistic.

This dangerous doctrine depends for whatever validity it may have upon the notion that we must always examine any use of language only in order to find out what it says, and that the only value of language in human affairs is the possibility of the externalization of what is said into some sort of correlation with non-mental events. Apart from the philosophic insecurity of this position, the doctrine virtually ignores the validity, in terms of human life in human societies, of vast areas of language-use, and in the long run is linguistically trivial. Such a doctrine arises, presumably, in the history of ideas as a kind of pseudo-scientific counterblast and anti-romantic corrective to the notions of nineteenth-century idealism. Its great disadvantage is that it obscures the fact, as I think it is, that the use of language is myth-creative, or that what is said in language can just as easily impose as much reality on the external world as the external world can impose on what is said in language. The problem seems to be much more complicated than that of merely sorting out uses of language into referential and emotive, and of supposing that one kind is, by implication, better than the other, or that the chief task of literary criticism, say, is to distinguish between these two kinds and to classify emotive uses as respectable or not.

Some theory of why it is more complicated than this is necessary, and I shall begin to state it by means of the proposition that a very large number indeed, perhaps all, of the sentences of a language embody the creation of myths of some kind. I believe that this proposition is true because a sentence is something made out of language substance and symbolizes some idea, notion, concept or feeling apprehended in the central nervous system of its author. Those of us who are concerned with language as such need not always be very interested in what kinds of myths are created by the production of sentences – whether they are such myths, say, as that an acid added to a base results in salt and water, or such myths, say, as that a god named Zeus appeared in the disguise of a swan to a girl named Leda; although, of course, we are extremely interested in the myths we create for ourselves, because we believe them to be true.

Perhaps the point needs a little elaboration. Man interpenetrates with his environment, the universe. In doing so, he makes from time to time articulate sounds that enable him to communicate and share experiences with his fellows. This experience of the universe is in man and only in the universe because man is too. Given a language, men are able, as we have said, to perform the extraordinary feat of saying things which have never been said before, but which are nevertheless intelligible to other speakers of the same language. This fact, as we have also said, is central to any kind of linguistic discussion, and especially to a linguistic discussion about style, because most of the time most users of the language seem to believe that what they say has some reference to, or correlation with, their environment and their responses to it, and that what they say has some usefulness in the world. I say 'this fact' and not 'this myth', because I believe it is a myth at one end of a scale of myths. The words available in English for talking about these matters – such words as *fact, truth, belief, idea, opinion, falsehood, feeling, misconception, conviction, hope, fear, suggestion,* and so on – are, as it were, the names of calibrations on a scale that we use to measure what we think about or what we believe about different sorts of statements. All of us, I imagine, have different degrees of conviction about the truth or reasonableness, falsehood or fantasy, of what

B

we say and of what is said to us. If we are so convinced, for
instance, that water boils at 100° Celsius at sea-level that we
are ready to repel with violence all comers who are enemies to
that statement's having any reference to, or correlation with,
what we think of as reality, then we hold that belief pretty
strongly and might even be prepared to call it a fact. Usually,
however, the kinds of convictions that most people are ready
to defend with violence are far more tenuous and hypothetical
than the belief (obviously a mental construct) that water boils
at 100° Celsius at sea-level; they are the sorts of nebulous convictions with names like Freedom, Honour, Glory, Religion,
The Cause, Our Democratic Way of Life, even Science itself,
all of which, though lacking the rational authority of any
scientific evidence about why people should believe in them, are
felt by the majority of mankind to be of far greater importance
than trivial everyday facts which can be proved – as if proof
itself were not a linguistic process.

It is indeed the case that some uses of language, which are,
one supposes, believed by their authors to be of great importance
in the history and affairs of mankind, are more, or less, referential
than others. It is a question of attitude to the subject-matter of
what is said rather than to the manner of saying. I happen to
believe that the statement, which says that water boils at 100°
Celsius at sea-level, is about as referential as a statement need
be to command respect and to use in the organization of some of
the practical affairs of life. However, the statement which I
notice in a newspaper, 'The Chairman hopes to be able to give
further information at the next A.G.M.', seems to me to be not
quite so referential, because it is not likely to elicit so much near-
universal certainty, and because there may, in some quarters, be
downright scepticism about it. And no doubt statements could
be found which, though not entirely emotive, were less
referential than the one just given. At the same time, and in the
same sort of way, there is a blend from the not so referential to
the not so emotive, and also a differential of emotiveness in
emotive utterances.

One can find, as one goes up and down this scale, variations
in quality as well as in referentiality and emotiveness. No matter
what degree they are of in the scale of feeling-tone (or whatever
one likes to call it), there will be some statements which appear

to some people to be better uses of language than others, and which, therefore, will affect the sensibility of the listener or reader by means of their form as much as by means of their content. In fact, some uses of language may have for some people a distinct value because, simply, of their form and not because of what they are supposed to say. Some utterances expressed in beautiful language may be distasteful in sentiment, and acceptable to some people only because the beauty of the language cannot be denied. For myself, I find that the prayer, 'The Lord bless us and keep us and make His face to shine upon us', has a beautiful rhythm and intonation, but since I cannot share in the religious beliefs that provided a context for it, the content is meaningless to me. Exactly why the beauty of some language-uses cannot be denied, and what makes the language beautiful, are questions beyond the scope of linguistic inquiries, although some of the qualities that make uses of language beautiful could doubtless be described by the linguist when he knows what the beautiful passages are. But these qualities will be different from those which can be perceived after appeals to referentiality or emotiveness. It should be possible, in other words, to isolate what might be called purely linguistic responses to any particular impressive use of language from other kinds of responses, intellectual, emotional or aesthetic, and the pure creativeness of the language can then be examined for its own sake.

Any use of language, therefore, is creative in the sense that it is the putting together of linguistic elements which may or may not have some reference to, or correlation with, what is believed to be reality or something outside the language itself. Whether it does or does not have any such reference or correlation is nothing whatever to do with the language-use, but only what some people or other think or believe about the content or message of the signal.

This fact-fiction correlation is also a matter of scalar difference. In the past it was instinctively felt to be the case, though it was not expressed in quite that way. At one end of the scale any language-use can be creative in that it may present the listener or reader with a fact or truth, an extra-linguistic correlation, real or supposed, which is something different from the language-use itself, but which is valued, nevertheless, because people, or some people, believe that such a fact or truth is useful to them in their coping with the affairs of their lives in the universe. At the other extreme of the scale, any use of language may present the listener or reader with itself, as something valued not so much because of what it said as because of its self-creativeness or the way in which it says what it says.

Again, in the past, the concept of style was usually reserved for discussion about the uses of language as this second and more rarefied extreme of the scale. The excellence of style in works of imaginative literature, for instance, persuaded some people that style was exclusively a literary quality, and that given a few ideas about correctness derived from some such self-appointed authority as Fowler's *Modern English Usage* or what, perhaps, was said by the teacher of English at school, one had no further need to bother about style in the language of instruction and information. In the days before universal literacy, when men of letters produced literary works, whether those of imaginative literature or not, for the appreciation of the educated and the discriminating, such a view was natural, for the pursuit of elegance in prose and rhetorical excellence in poetry could be discerned and valued for its own sake among the members of an enlightened readership. But in our own industrial, democratic and technological society, distinctions between the elegant and the vulgar are blurred to an unrecognizable discoloration, and the same standards of criticism can hardly be said to apply. Our society has been taught literacy without the benefit of a classical background of the linguistic differences between English, on the one hand, and Greek and Latin on the other, so that the humanizing influences of polite letters are as remote from the commercial vulgarity of our age as the farthest galaxy. Indeed, our society has been taught how to become literate by means of an effort, not apparently entirely successful, to impose on the people at large a watered-down version of the linguistic standards of a now extinct aristocracy.

. The concept of style can be extended, theoretically, to the discussion of all possible uses of language, from merely spoken phatic communion, such as social greetings, idle chatter about the weather or gossip over the suburban garden fence, to the most important political speeches or the most exalted oratory, from the *écriteaux* in the streets to the greatest works of literature. Indeed, the proposition that almost every use of language is the creation of some kind of myth implies that almost every use of language has some kind of style. For every use of language has its own *raison d'être* for its position on the scale of grammaticality, as well as on the scale of referentiality and emotiveness, and every use of language arises in some kind of situational context in the wider non-linguistic activity of man in the universe.

5 The Sources of Style

The idea of some kind of situational context that produces a language-use in the wider non-linguistic activity of man in the universe is nowadays closely bound up, by some students of linguistics, inside the notion of register. The word *register* is not easily defined, but what it stands for can be thought of as language considered from the point of view of its use. The doctrine of register can be summed up by saying that in different kinds of language-uses, which arise to be uttered in response to different kinds of human activities, different kinds of linguistic features are found to be appropriate. The concept is due originally, I am told, to what used to be called the Edinburgh School of linguistics, and has spread among those who call themselves, or are called, the Neo-Firthians. This may be so. More important is the fact that the concept is very useful for anyone who takes an interest in the problems of style, even though it has been adversely criticized. It has been adversely criticized on the grounds that it is impossible to give an adequate linguistic definition of the word *register*; that the concept is the result of nothing more than an insight, even though a conveniently inspired one; and that, given a particular example of language-use, no one can assign it to any particular register, even if all the registers could be catalogued, on purely linguistic criteria.

Nevertheless, I shall make use of the concept, for it is useful in indicating the sources of style from a social point of view, although, of course, it cannot itself give any adequately linguistic account of style. Comprehended under the concept of register are the sub-concepts of context, sense, medium, tenor and style.

In any situation in which language is used in the wider non-linguistic activity of man in the universe, we can think of this language-use as existing, again, on a scale. Some situations need very little language-use or none at all, for there are extra-linguistic signs in the situations themselves which can make explicit the necessary myth-creation to enable the wider human activity to take place. A policeman controlling traffic, for instance, can do so by means of gestures which act as signals operating and controlling a portion of the universe, and although the significance of the gestures could be expressed in language, or paraphrased, there is rarely, in such a situation, any need to do so, and the amount of language-use in the situation is zero. In the course of a football match, however, a player may shout the word 'Here!' and hope that the ball will be passed to him. The language-use of the word *here* in that utterance is supplemented by other signs in the situation of the game, so that the player who has the ball can interpret that language-use by means of the support of those signs, and could make it implicit to himself as something like (shall we say?): 'Fred is running down the wing on my left, and wants me to pass the ball to him, so that he can pass it to Sam, who is in a position to score.' In this case the amount of language-use was near, but not at, the zero mark on the scale.

One of the advantages of language as a myth-creating activity is that its use can be separated from the immediate situation that calls it forth, and that by means of it man can range in his myth-creation all over space and time and even beyond into Heaven and Hell or wherever imagination, drug-induced enlargements of experience, or delirium may lead. Consequently, we can lay it down as a sort of law that the more a language-use is separated from the immediate situation that calls it forth the greater does its amount and intensity become, since the extra-linguistic signs in the situation, being progressively more remote, need to be specified in the language. In some kinds of myth-creation – in poems, novels, imaginative literature generally – the amount of language-use is relatively so great and intense that the immediate situation in the wider non-linguistic activity of man in the universe is completely lost. A great deal of literary criticism, uninformed by the science of linguistics and ignoring the language-use as a thing in itself, often masquerades as a quest for lost umbilical cords, instead of simply exploring the new context-free world of the purified and isolated imagination.

The situation that produces any language-use can be referred to as its *context*, if we want to proliferate technical terms. And it is easy to see that in many cases, where the amount of language-use is relatively small, the context flows, as it were, into the language-use and may even swamp it, but that as the myth-creation in the language-use grows farther and farther away from the context it becomes relatively larger, drawing more and more on the redundancy of the language, and may eventually discard context completely.

This matter is intimately connected with the *sense* of the language-use, or with what the language-use is, or is supposed to be, about. For the context is likely in most cases to dictate the sense. The linguist, whose chief pre-occupation must always be with the language, is not in his professional moments much concerned with what the sense of the language-use is, and he recognizes it as a concept which is a component of register simply because he cannot help doing so. But most speakers and writers would seem to believe that what they say and write has sense, and that the purpose of what they say and write is to embody this sense in some kind of linguistic structuring. The message they want to convey must have its physical embodiment, and the name *medium* is that by which this is identified. Both the context and the sense will tend to dictate the medium, which will in its turn have an effect upon the language-use. The most obvious distinctions in kinds of media are those of speech and writing. But each of these can be subdivided into a number of other distinctions. In speech, for instance, distinctions could be made between formal and informal, public and private, non-conversational and conversational, or whatever. The language of two friends having a talk over a drink at a bar, for example, is likely to be different from that of a talk over the radio; that of a political speech different from a sermon; that of a committee meeting different from that of a lovers' quarrel. And in the written uses of the language the sub-dividing could be even more accurate, since the written medium is normally less *ad hoc* than the spoken, and forms can become conventions, even institutionalized conventions, so that the language of a company report shows differences from that of advertisement, that of a cookery recipe differences from that of a weather forecast, that of an epic differences from that of a love poem, and so on.

Allied to the component of medium is that of *tenor*, which is a name for the way in which the social relationship between the encoder and decoder of messages influences the language-use. The kind and amount of the language-use arising out of the context will be affected not only by the sense of the myth which it embodies, but also by what the speaker or writer thinks, feels, knows or imagines about his listener or reader in relation to the context, sense and medium. Adults, for instance, do not always use the same kind of language when they are talking to children as when they are talking among themselves. Expert talking to expert may use a different kind of language from that which he would use in talking to a layman about the same topic; and in such relationships as those between lecturer and student, doctor and patient, solicitor and client, the language-uses are likely to be affected by the different states of knowledge of context and sense and the experience of the parties in relation to context and sense and the kind of language needed by particular educational, medical or legal circumstances. And where the medium is written, there are such differences as those between personal and business letters, between that of specialization and popularization in scientific and technological exposition, or between such language as that of an Act of Parliament and that of the criticism of a work of art. Under this heading, too, one could put the idiosyncrasies of particular authors, idiolectal features of particular speakers, the special training undergone by some kinds of speakers and writers, and the effects of personality on speech and writing generally.

The total of the effects of context, sense, medium and tenor in any use of language will provide it with its style, or that quality which it may have that can, in a rough and ready way, perhaps enable the investigator to distinguish it from another language use. It should be possible, though it would not necessarily be productive of any useful results, to consider language-uses in terms of these effects – if only they could be isolated in every case. The difficulty is that that cannot be isolated in every case in any significant manner. It is easy to see, for example, that some university lecturer talking to his students on, say, molecular biology is producing a language-use different from that of a wife nagging her husband. Here the effects of context, sense, medium and tenor are easily separable. But in a sentence like 'The railway stations of London were built in the nineteenth century', there is very little to distinguish it stylistically from a sentence like 'The office-blocks of Birmingham were built in the twentieth century'. In fact all that can be found is the component of sense expressed in *railway stations of London* and *office-blocks of Birmingham* and *nineteenth* and *twentieth*, and that is so tenuous and shadowy a distinction as to be almost negligible – almost, but not quite. One could conceive, in one's more imaginative moments, of an apparatus for making excessively delicate and refined distinctions; but one can also conceive, in one's more sober moments, that such an apparatus would not be of much use. It would give us very little, if any, insight into the ways in which language is used among us, and no enlightenment, so far as one can see, of any value.

More profitable, one would think, would be considerations of the effects in terms of the language-use. After all, one's intuition tells one that a very large number of language-uses can be intrinsically uninteresting, stylistically barren, and hardly worth the trouble of the work of a serious student from the point of view of whatever qualities of style there may be, even though there will undoubtedly be some, and even though all uses can be linguistically interesting to the linguist. It is only when we come to those areas of language-use where the special ability or talent of the encoders endows the language with qualities that indicate unusual performance that one's interest really awakens. Nevertheless, differences in conventions among the members of groups within the speech-community are often produced because of different contexts and senses, and these can have some kind of interest. This state of affairs has become increasingly noticeable in modern industrial and technological society, where specializations have proliferated, and where, in consequence, institutionalized conventions of language-uses have grown up. For instance, the chemist writing about chemistry is quite capable of inventing new words with a freedom not found among scientists generally; for the biologist will call upon Latin and Greek for his technical terms, and the physicist, although he may on occasion produce a new word like *meson*, is normally quite content with the common words of the language used in special ways, as with *rods* and *cones* in optics, or with such collocations as *low temperature* or *fundamental particle*. It is important for those who speak and write a language to know what they are doing with it. Specialization in science and technology in our time has done much to compartmentalize some uses of language into self-contained dialects, so that it is sometimes extremely difficult for workers in one field to know what is going on in another. The coming into existence, during the last few years, of such a branch of study as institutional linguistics is a recognition of the fact that specializations in different fields produce a large number of registers, each with its own particular context, sense and tenor. Electronics engineers do, as a matter of fact, write and talk professionally in a different way from industrial chemists; botanists use a different sort of dialect from that of bankers and financiers; and sociologists and social workers do tend to use a different linguistic frame of reference from that used by those engaged in the building trades; and so on.

The problems of style as they appear in different fields of specialization in an industrial and technological society, where language is used in so many different ways, in so many different contexts, and very often for so many different purposes in dealing with the organization and control of different aspects of the universe, are genuine problems. They do not concern trivial points of grammar or dilettantish elegances like unsplit infinitives or prepositions not put at the ends of sentences. They concern the whole use of the language. And they are problems of a deviation from a norm, but not deviations that must be regarded as aberrant or as the mistakes of ignorant people who fail to understand what they are doing; they are deviations for which there are explicable and perhaps sensible reasons. When the problems of such deviations from a norm have been stated, and various kinds of differences noted, we can have a basis for criticism, and a critical attitude towards one's native language is one that makes assessments based on facts.

As we said, the word *register* comprehends these five concepts of context, sense, medium, tenor and style within its ambit. Considerations of register, however, though they affect all uses of language, are more useful in telling us something about the ecology of style than in telling us anything about style itself. It is useful and important to know that certain styles flourish only in certain habitats, and perhaps that they would wither and die if they were removed from them. Some of us may ardently wish for the death of some styles, and the concept of register may come in handy, in an enlightened society, for pest control.

6 *The Subject-matter of Stylistic Studies*

The intuition that there is or can be such a topic of discourse as style in the use of language has led, in the previous sections, to explications of certain ideas which have tended to show, in a not very definitive way, that a language as a means of communication and sharing experiences can be used by individual writers and speakers with variations of quality. It has been hinted that these variations of quality are deviations from a norm or, at least, that they can be thought of as if they were; and various concepts such as that of noise, of performance in relation to competence, and of register, have been suggested as different aspects of accounting for and describing the existence of these deviations. It has also been suggested that some kind of grammar could be devised to describe and measure these deviations, some of which may be more interesting than others.

If this is true, then the application of the grammar could be of some use as a device in the assessment of quality in the uses of language. If these deviations from the norm actually exist in the data that are presented to the student of linguistics, then the recognition and description of them could be interesting, and could give an insight into what is happening when language is being used.

It is suggested here that the investigation of these variations in quality constitutes the general area of stylistic or lexical studies, and that the word *style* could be defined in terms of deviations from the norm – provided that we know what the norm is.

It would seem that the investigator of style would need three sets of apparatus for the carrying out of his task:

(1) He wants a grammar that will provide him with a simple but adequate description of the language, the styles of the uses of which interest him. Such a grammar would be able to state, generate, or otherwise give an account of, the norm, real or supposed, against which deviations can be measured, and it could also provide a repertoire of technical terms to name these deviations or the most interesting and important of them.

(2) He wants a contextual apparatus to relate the language-use under investigation to its registers. This, of course, need be

no more than a simple historical or sociological description, so that the language-use can be related to its period and provenance.

(3) He wants a critical apparatus which can allow him to draw from the grammar and the contextual apparatus any conclusions about the language-use in question which may be worthy of being made, such as those which might, in the terms of (1) and (2), account for the language-use in question being whatever the investigator believes that it is – for example, a good poem, a bad piece of prose, or a mediocre drama.

It is clear that only the first of these sets of apparatus is linguistic in the sense in which we speak of the science of linguistics, or cut off linguistics as a discipline from all other branches of knowledge. But, as we have said, language-uses exist in a context and create myths, and how far the period and social conditions and subject-matter of a language-use may affect its style are questions which it is helpful to have answered.

Topics suggested by the contextual and the critical apparatus, which have, probably, been the starting point of most studies of style in the past, provide information that is by no means unimportant. What is considered under these heads can range from the personal life of the writer to whole complexes of social and historical documentation. The idea, for instance, that 'Le style, c'est l'homme même' has so dominated a great deal of literary criticism, and is still so frequently found, even under such disguises as statistical studies of obsessive words or psychological revelations made through recurrent imagery, in the literature of style, that it cannot, apparently be discounted as one of those apophthegms which everybody repeats but nobody takes any notice of. And rippling outwards from l'homme même, who is cast by whatever gods into the stream of time, are circles of ever-increasing diameter that embrace not only his own personality, but the effect of a portion of history on it. Any study of an important literary text which failed to include some mention of the ways in which these matters affected the language would, one imagines, be emasculated and not very interesting.

However, the question arises: should stylistic studies be confined only to important literary texts? The answer that the writer of this book would be inclined to give is that they should not.

We have already hinted that it is possible to consider any use of language by looking only and exclusively at the linguistic features and not bothering overmuch with the message. Even so, we have also suggested that the effect of sense upon style is something to be taken into account, since without sense most speakers and writers are without incentive to produce any uses of language at all. If style can be considered as some kind of deviation from a norm, then it is the sense which is likely to be the first, and perhaps the main, cause of the deviation. Nevertheless, this deviation is a linguistic matter, for it is something which only the language can produce, and it can be explained only in linguistic terms. There is a clue here to the basis of what might be a statement about the limits of the subject-matter of stylistic studies. Obviously, a great deal of language-uses, everyday, run-of-the-mill, banal, uninspired, utilitarian chatter or gossip, triviality in the routine saying of this or that, in speech or writing, is of very little stylistic interest indeed :

Lo! thy dread Empire, CHAOS! is restor'd;
Light dies before thy uncreating word;
Thy hand, great Anarch! lets the curtain fall,
And universal darkness buries All.

No matter how linguistically interesting may be this voluble underworld babbling in anarchy – and, of course, it is linguistically interesting and an important source of our knowledge about language – there seems to be little point or profit in making a stylistic study of every kind of thing that could be said. The style of such *écriteaux* as 'Keep left' or 'Cocktail Bar', or of the numbers of policemen's uniforms or the front doors of houses may, perhaps, deserve a little essay in some obscure learned journal, and linguists engaged in their fieldwork may take tape-recorders into bus queues and pubs, suburban dining-rooms and school playgrounds, or all places where data can be found. Such work is important, for it is the whole basis of our clearly expressed knowledge about language. Stylistically, however, such data present us with an unconscionable amount of, so to speak, negatively oriented deviations from the norm. Earlier, we laid it down as a sort of law that the more the language-use was separated from the immediate situation that called it forth the greater did its amount and intensity become. We can add a corollary to this, and say that the more the language-use is separated from the immediate situation that calls it forth the greater is the stylistic interest, and the greater, probably, the need for stylistic interpretation.

This view of style, at least, makes stylistic studies endowed with some positive respectability. In such an epoch as our own the study of style in the use of language does not have to be a dilettantish matter of cosy interest in 'the romance of words', or a prescriptive method of teaching people how to write, or a pleasant way of passing the time. In an epoch such as our own, when universal literacy is expected, used and exploited, of every citizen, a vast amount of language-use in the written medium is daily produced, and, presumably, its authors expect that it will be read, even though most of them seem to try to give the public more than can ever be absorbed. The present writer, who has done some fieldwork in the mushy ground of the vast pampas of printed matter, can confirm that much that is daily written is of an almost intolerable dullness and ineptitude, and is socially very inefficient and wasteful, especially in the fields of science and technology. A very large amount of language-use has become institutionalized, so that much of its own conventions and styles needs some kind of documentation and description, if what is happening to our language is to be fully understood. Moreover, electronic aids to communication have speeded up, intensified and proliferated language-uses, both in the spoken and written media, so that, again, some kind of disinterested documentation and, possibly, criticism are needed to make explicit, and give a means of assessing the value of, the kinds of cultural influences to which people are subjected. A study of style, in this sense, is an assistance to a rational statement of what society is doing with its language.

CHAPTER II

THE GRAMMAR

1 Theoretical Preliminaries

I shall regard language generally, and in particular English as the language of exemplification, as existing at three possible levels of analysis. Fieldwork in linguistics can produce such a result, and the idea of levels of abstraction, or levels for analysis, is nowadays a familiar one in linguistic science, so that there is no need, here and now, to go into details of how these levels are arrived at. All that is needed is to say what they are and to describe them briefly.

The three levels are those of phonology, syntax and lexis. This means that from the data presented in the language to the student of linguistics inferences can be made about the language as a whole, and these inferences can be summarized in three statements:

(1) that the whole of the language exists as substance which is realized in (at least) phonic and graphic signals;
(2) that these signals have formal organizations of their parts;
(3) that these formal organizations give the signals a quality which makes them significant in the speech-community in which they have their being.

These three statements are the statements of a theory, and they show that the relationship of the observer of language-events or the student of language is rather different from that of the ordinary speaker of it. This is an important point, often overlooked, and in understanding it we must remember what was said earlier about the systematic ambiguity of the use of the word *grammar*.

We accept here the view that language is a means of communication and that any use of language provides an instance of a communication channel. In the actual day-to-day uses of the

47

language, speakers and writers of it are intimately involved with the communication channels which are thus produced, and their awareness of the language is chiefly, perhaps entirely in most cases, an awareness of the quality mentioned in statement (3) above. Their learning of the language, in fact, was largely an unconscious acquisition of the skills of operating and controlling the elements referred to in statements (1) and (2), so that such operation and control could make that quality manifest in acts of communication. That is why languages have to be learnt, and why the use of language as a form of behaviour exhibits so many conventional peculiarities which are needed to make it socially acceptable.

The observer or student of linguistics is not, however, in his professional moments, involved in quite the same kind of way. He is an observer of communication channels, and is much more concerned with understanding and solving problems of structure than with deciphering the messages which the communication channels convey. His problems, that is to day, are those of the ways in which the signs that make up the signals are deployed, of what the signs are like, and of the relationships among them. In analysing these signals, he must, in the nature of his business, destroy the total semantic content of their organization, for their semantic content is built up out of elements which it is his task to identify. For example, a fairly longish sentence can be said to mean something; but a clause in it can mean less, a word less than that, a syllable still less, and a single speech sound or letter that stands for it least of all. In this sort of analysis, the elements of language become separated from the spirit of their life which exists only in their collaboration with their fellows; they become the dry bones in the valley of linguistics, the ultimately arid science, which can display the anatomy of the language in the philological dissecting-room when the wavering breath on which the language originally lived has become oblivion or historical record. As we go down the scale, from the whole sentence, through its parts, whatever they are, to phoneme or grapheme, we descend through the three levels of abstraction. The student of linguistics sees what is indicated by the three statements above as a hierarchy of levels, with the third at the top and the others contributing upwards to it. The details of the relationship of the observer to the communication channel or language-event which he observes, together with the names of the chief concepts of analysis, can be set out schematically in some such way as this:

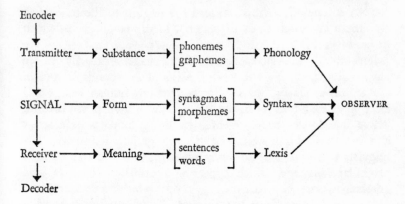

This can be interpreted as follows:

A language exists only in its use as a means of communication and sharing experiences among its speakers. In the forms in which its elements exist, anatomized and set out for display in dictionaries and books on phonetics, grammar and linguistics, there is no language in the sense in which we can speak of English, French, Russian, Urdu, Arabic, Hittite, Chinese, and so on, as being languages. The linguist has to use language to talk about language, it is true, but in doing so he introduces a metalanguage, or a set of technical terms, to help him in his job. These technical terms are necessary as devices for externalizing the concepts from the language in which he utters them. Such words as *phoneme, structure, sentence* and *lexis* are parts of the metalanguage of this book.

In observing the language in its use, the linguist can take samples of it and build up a corpus which he can analyse. If the corpus is representative enough, or if the linguist deliberately defines and states its limits, he can make inferences from it about the language as a whole, or about a specified part of the language. These inferences are hypotheses which the linguist has constantly to test by going back into the language itself, since the nature of the language is such (so one must postulate) that no matter how large or representative the corpus might be there will always exist in the language itself samples of usages giving exponents of theoretical ideas which might not be in the corpus, or giving hitherto unrecorded features, any of which might upset a hypothesis.

Such an analysis as this can lead the linguist to the conclusion that there are three kinds of material in the language on which he has to work.

The first is the substance of the language. Primarily, as we have said already, this substance consists of the sounds of speech, the sounds made by the respiratory tracts of human beings and existing as sound waves in the atmosphere in their physical form. These sounds can be represented by the graphemes of a script and preserved for a period of time in graphic substance. The linguist, therefore, has to study phonemes, or the sounds of a particular language, which appear as contrastive elements, and graphemes, or the marks of a script which represent these phonemes in some way or another. The sound system of a particular language and the means used to record it make up the subject-matter of phonology, or the study of the language at the phonological level.

Second, there is the syntax of the language. The phonemes found in language-uses are arranged normally in constantly re-curring patterns. These patterns can be said (for the moment) to be structures of different sorts, which, apparently, show a limited number of forms of methods of structuring. Although speakers of a language may have the ability to make an infinite number of such structures, they have, nevertheless, only the ability to make them in a finite number of ways. These structures are made of patterns of morphemes – that is, only some kinds of morphemes can be used, or normally are used, in given places in structures. Morphemes can be said to be 'minimal units of formal structuring', and they are made out of one or more phonemes. The study of structuring, which, so far at least as the theory of this book takes us, is also a study of the signals made out of the language-code and the disposition of the parts that make these signals. It can be referred to as syntax; so that we can speak of language-events occurring formally at the syntactic level.

It is possible, of course, for speakers to make haphazard arrangements of morphemes, but if they do so they disregard the conventions of the language and the speech-community. For languages behave as if they were codes, and by definition a code is a pre-arrangement of signs with rules for their use. A haphazard arrangement of morphemes is not a structure in the linguistic sense of the word, as a linguistic technical term. For instance, such a sentence as 'The Japanese eat plenty of fish' is a formal structure in this technical sense, but an arrangement of the same morphemes in a different order is not necessarily so. Some such arrangement as '*eat fish Japanese of plenty the' is not a formal structure in this technical sense because it does not obey the rules for the use of signs for making signals in English. Nevertheless, exactly what are the boundaries between haphazard arrangements of morphemes and formal structures could, in many cases, be difficult to determine. The matter becomes a question of the grammaticality of the particular arrangement of morphemes. Generally speaking, one can say that it is the form of structuring, and not the morphemic content, which must act as the guide, although even here, as the quotation from *Antony and Cleopatra* on page 29 shows, there can be some very doubtful cases.

The linguist finds that structures can exist, as it were, in two dimensions. They can exist in a linear dimension, in time or space, as strings of elements in a sequence, or syntagmata; and simultaneously, within such strings, there can be elements existing in depth. The notion of elements existing in depth can be expressed by saying there can be a hierarchy of structures within structures, so that different ranks of structuring carry different levels of different kinds of formal significance. For example, in such a sentence as 'Those who came to scoff remained to pray', we can have, at the top of the hierarchy, so to speak, the surface grammar of the sentence expressed by the words *Those remained* or *Those (people) remained*; and at the lower levels we have the deep grammar expressed by the words *who came* and *to scoff* and *to pray*. The combination of these two dimensions can give the strings or sequences a completeness of patterning which, in its turn, makes them recognizable, by speakers of the language when they use it, as unities, recurring in the same formal shape as other unities of the same kind, although, of course, not necessarily carrying the same content. These unities, therefore, not only have their own recursiveness of structure which it is the business of the linguist to reveal in formal patterning, but they also have, for the speakers of the language when they use it, a meaning and a significance which extend beyond their formal boundaries. At this level of abstraction, these unities can be called sentences, and, so far as English is concerned, can be said to be made up of stabilized structures of phonemes and morphemes which we call words.

Sentences could, of course, be made haphazardly out of words. The fact that this does not usually happen in ways which do violence to any great extent to the speech-community in which the language is spoken is a blessing which can make the work of the grammarian manageable. Nevertheless, it can happen – and it can happen in ways which can make the investigator of style find that his work is interesting and even exciting. The grammarian's grammar – a reflection, or, in perhaps a more accurate metaphor, a black and white photograph – is a picture of normality. It depicts the actual language in its usualness and day-to-day average competence of use. But deviations from the norm, which can be found in samples generated by other grammars of the speakers and writers of the language, can be either the inadequacies of idiots or the fortunate inspirations of genius. When the latter can be incorporated into the grammarian's grammar it gives it life and colour – it can make the black and white still photograph into a coloured moving film. The consideration of this norm and the interesting deviations from it is the consideration of language at the level of lexis.

2 Towards the Norm

We can illustate some of these ideas which we have just been looking at by a brief examination of two contrasted passages:

(1) Measurements were made at constant ambient temperatures in the range 350-525° C. and constant filament temperature from about 800 to 980° C. Filament temperatures lower than these could not be measured while higher temperatures were not used in order to avoid the evaporation of copper from the filament. For each series of measurements of the current through the filament and the voltage across it, the conductance was calculated and plotted as a function of the time.

(2) Mechanic, merchant, king,
 Are warmed by the cold clown
 Whose head is in the clouds
 And never can get down.

 Into a solitude
 Undreamed of by their fat
 Quick dreams have lifted me;
 The north wind steals my hat.

 On clear days I can see
 Green acres far below
 And the red roof where I
 Was Little Trinculo.

 There lies that solid world
 These hands can never reach;
 My history, my love,
 Is but a choice of speech.

Examining these extracts at the phonological level, we can see that they are first of all different in rhythm. In fact, the author's choices in the first extract from all the resources of the language are not concerned very much, if at all, with the sounds of the words, as the author's choices in the second extract so obviously are. The author of the first extract did not go to the trouble of arranging patterns of syllables in such a way that, with variations here and there, every second syllable was stressed; nor did he arrange a sort of counterpoint over the basic beat thus obtained, and manage nicely a variety in the length and pitch of the vowels of the syllables; nor did he see to it that every twenty-fourth syllable rhymed with the twelfth syllable before it. In fact, the author of the first extract does not seem to interest himself in sound at all; he is writing, apparently, in some institutionalized area of human communication in which the marks of the script are thought of as being able to communicate in their own right; he is using an eye-language and not an ear-language.

Even so, the author of the first extract does make deliberate linguistic choices. At the grammatical level, for instance, at the level of the formal organization of language substance, we can see that he chooses to write all his sentences in the passive voice, and that he excludes a sort of personal particularization that appears in the second extract. The kinds of verbs used in the first extract deliberately restrict the range of the kinds of things the author can say, and since verbs influence sentence structure there is less variety of sentence structure in the first extract than in the second. In fact, the verbs in the second extract move through such variety, from passive at the beginning, through active in the second and third stanzas, to a copulative verb at the end of the extract (which is not the end of the poem), that a whole gamut of human experience can be included in the differences in the kind of sentence structure that the second extract can make.

The fact that this is so in each case has an influence on the language of each at the third or lexical level of abstraction. In the first extract, the concentration of vocabulary on the restricted area of the subject-matter compels the author to use words which may be said to belong to the same sorts of sets. A *set* of words is a group of them, large or small, which is likely to be found in utterances in registers dealing with the same kinds of human experiences. Thus, in the first extract, such words as *measurement, constant, temperature,* 980° and *C*, for example, or as *filament, current, voltage,* and *conductance,* all belong to the same sets. In the second extract, this concentration is not apparent, since the second extract deals with a more far-reaching subject-matter. In the first extract, the concentration of vocabulary makes modification of the nouns and verbs by adjectives and adverbs superfluous, whereas in the second extract the greater variety of sentence structure produces the necessity of modification to give coherence to the whole, which would otherwise be so dispersed and fragmentary as to be almost incomprehensible. At the same time, this modification – '*cold* clown', 'solitude/*Undreamed of by their fat*', '*quick* dreams', for example – enriches, illuminates and gives reality to what is imagined. Along with this diversified vocabulary, which is brought about by the variety of sentence structure, we can notice the bringing together of different elements into the structure of the whole of the second extract. Thus we have words and expressions which make the poem extend outwards from its main theme, whereas the prose extract adheres closely to its own centre. We find in the poem words belonging to contrasted sets, for example, even sets that have apparently no connexion with one another, as *mechanic, merchant* and *king* are *contrasted* with *clown*, or as solitude with *fat*, or *history* with *love*, or both these last two with *choice of speech*.

These two extracts, which have not by any means been exhaustively dealt with, show deviations from the norm because both are contrived and self-conscious, and because both are examples of language-uses which are ordered and directed into the conventions of institutionalized ways of using language in which myths are created.

What then is the norm? The norm is a linguistic abstraction, an idea thought up by linguists and existing only in their minds. No actual use of the language can be said to be 'normal' in the sense that one can go to it and say that all others are deviations from it. This is because every use of language arises in its own situational context and takes on its own sense, medium, tenor and style from the circumstances of its origin. Nevertheless, we are able to recognize, in a very large number of language-uses, features which characterize each of them as deviant, for the consciousness of deviation can be valid only if there is reference to something else. For instance, the fact that the first extract quoted above has all its verbs in the passive voice is sufficiently surprising as a thing in itself to refer us to the fact that the active voice does exist and is widely used. In the second extract the phonic qualities of the rhythm and the rhyme of the verses are again sufficiently surprising as things in themselves to refer us to the fact that it is possible to make utterances without using such phonic qualities.

Thus the interesting and exciting possibilities of paraphrase are always present, and perhaps many of us are always unconsciously aware of them. Each of us has what is called his own idiolect, his particular and personal knowledge of and acquaintance with at least some of the ways of using his language. No two speakers ever learn the same language in exactly the same way, because no two speakers ever have exactly the same experiences, or ever verbalize what similar experiences they do have from exactly the same linguistic equipment. In their daily lives, therefore, when people communicate with one another by means of speech or writing, they are continually making adjustments of their own idiolects to bring them into line with the idiolects of others, and of other people's idiolects to bring them into line with their own.

In making these adjustments, users of the language find that more effort is needed on some occasions than on others. We can discover, in the ordinary day-to-day participation of ourselves in the language-uses of our personal worlds, large areas of language-use where the minimum of adjustment is necessary – among members of our own families and among personal friends or among colleagues who, as we say, 'speak the same language'. In our participation in the needs of such worlds we find a language-code that is restricted to them, that has grown up and developed with them, and which has been at least partially created by them. But when we leave these well-known and comfortable realms of experience and extend beyond them we find ourselves in contact with other codes and other forms of linguistic behaviour. Words take on different meanings, sentences are framed in ways that are not quite the same as the ways in which we would frame them, assumptions are made which we have not previously thought about. We find a conflict of idiolects, and the process of adjustment is not always easy. The situational contexts of the language-uses call forth different approaches to different media, we find ourselves being addressed in different tenors, and we become aware of different styles from those to which we have grown accustomed.

How far we are making a mental paraphrase of what we hear or read every time we make an adjustment to another idiolect, or to a new sense, a new medium, a new tenor, or a new style, it is difficult to say. If we are not to find ourselves utterly baffled, as we might be sometimes, we must, some of us, make such paraphrases now and then. If this were not true on at least some occasions we should never be able to extend our linguistic experience to be able to cope with the exigences of other language-codes than those which we learnt originally. This inability might exist very often among some people, and would account for backwardness in learning among some children and narrow-mindedness among some adults. Our idiolects, however, are our own norms; each of us has his unique idiolect, his unique linguistic equipment, good, bad, or indifferent; and each of us has to make the best of it. Even so, it would be very inconvenient for the well-being of society at large if each of us went about in the daily affairs of life always imprisoned, as it were, in the norm of his own idiolect. Language, after all, is pre-eminently social. In the end, society compensates for the idiosyncrasies of idiolects by creating institutionalized conventions of language-use. People working together in the same fields of human co-operation must be able to understand one another, to communicate with one another, and to feel the security of common knowledge and experiences shared in what they are doing. And so in these fields people learn, with greater or less actual achievement, to respond in more or less the same kinds of ways to the same linguistic signs, the same words, the same sorts of sentence structure, the same metaphors, the same feeling-tones, in the language that is used. But the specialized fields and restricted codes that they thus produce merge together in the common needs of all the speakers of the same language. Although the bus-driver may not understand the law so well as the barrister, it is possible for the bus-driver and the barrister to converse on some topics and meet somewhere in some language-code. Such a code that is available to all is the residue from all specialities, and is the norm, the language that is shared by the whole community of the individuals who speak it.

The existence of this residue depends upon two features of language-use which we have already glanced at. The first is the possibility of paraphrase – the possibility that the same facts, notions, ideas, beliefs, opinions, emotions, feelings, or whatever, can be expressed by different methods of myth-creation, or that the same kind of myth can be created in different ways. This possibility exists because of the redundancy of the language. In the making of paraphrases the unused potential of the language can be drawn upon to express what has to be said, or what could be said, in a variety of ways. For example, an utterance like 'Sorry, old chap, I can't do it' can be looked upon as a paraphrase of, let us say, 'I regret to have to transmit to you the information that I am unable to comply with your request'. It could also be a paraphrase of

'Alas, that I, most generous of men,
Must turn a deaf ear to your pleadings when
In that dire need which friendship should avow
You come to me for some assistance now.'

Indeed, were it not such a waste of time, one could go on inventing paraphrases of 'I'm sorry I can't' until one's typewriter ribbon was in shreds.

The second feature of language-use on which the residue that makes the norm depends is the distinction between surface and deep grammar in sentences. If such a sentence as 'Those who came to scoff remained to pray' can be thought of as a structure with '*Those . . . remained*' as its surface and '*who came to scoff*' and '*to pray*' as its depth, then it is possible to think of a number of structures which exist as surfaces only. Examination of a large number of structures thought of in that way would, it is presumed, be an examination of sentences largely deprived of overt meaning, but existing, nevertheless, as kinds of basic structures abstracted from all possible structures of the language, and on which all possible structures of the language are, so to speak, variations. This could mean that all the possible sentences of the language are kinds of variations on a few grammatical themes. Taken with the idea of paraphrase, this idea can make one think in terms of a limited number of grammatical forms as being a system of quite a small number of structural frames into which all possible sentences of the language can be put. In other words, there is only a quite small number of the *kinds* of things that can be said, and everything that is said is a paraphrase of one or another of this quite small number.

Indeed, the chief criterion we have for recognizing that a group of words, as a matter of fact acknowledged throughout the speech-community, is a sentence and not just a haphazard assemblage of morphemes, is our pretty strong belief amounting to a certainty that a sentence is a linguistic sign, and therefore must have some sort of form. If the number of sentence forms were infinite then the possibility of any speaker's being able to recognize a sentence form or a sentence when one was presented to him could not be guaranteed. But we do know from our daily experience that the recognition of sentences as such is possible, and that we can understand and interpret sentences which we have never met with before. That this is so is due to limitation in language of the number of sentence forms. We can say that this limited number of sentence forms can constitute a system which is the basis of the norm of the language which we are seeking. From a large number of actual sentences found in the day-to-day uses of the language which the linguist takes as his data, we can abstract the general outlines of the system, and this can become the basis for a grammar of style.

3 Transformational-generative Grammar

The kind of grammar proposed here is a simplified version of a transformational-generative grammar. A transformational grammar is one which attempts to give a description of a language, or a part of a language, by means of a set of rules. If these rules are applied in a certain fixed order specified in the grammar, then all the grammatical sentences, and only the grammatical sentences, of the language, or part of it, can be generated. It will be seen at once that if we have an apparatus that can tell us what all the grammatical sentences of a language are, then we shall have something which can be extremely useful as a measuring device, and which we can take, with some degree or other of defined arbitrariness, as a statement of a norm. The grammar which we propose here, however, is deliberately restricted in its scope because we want to apply it only to the concept of style; we don't necessarily want the grammar for its own sake.

A transformational grammar differs from other kinds of grammars hitherto widely used and invented to help linguists with their work in that it takes the sentence, theoretically defined, as the starting point. In the past there have been two chief ways of making grammatical descriptions. One that is traditionally used in the English-speaking world in the teaching of foreign languages, for instance, is based on the idea of what is called a Word and Paradigm Model. Such a grammar starts from the assumption that the words of a language are its basis, that the words can be arranged in paradigms, as in the declensions and conjugations in a traditional Latin or Greek grammar, and that the whole of the language can then be interpreted in these terms. A second sort of description, with variations which have been given such names as Item and Arrangement Model or Item and Process Model, works on the more empirical method of observing the relationships of items found in a corpus of collected data, and the linguist analyses these items into the smallest parts, such as phonemes and morphemes, and notes how from these parts structures are made.

Transformational theory draws upon both these methods of description, but goes beyond them. From the first, or traditional approach, transformational theory draws the idea of grammaticality, that is, the notion that some utterances are grammatically of different quality from others, that some are 'bad', some are 'good', and others are 'best of all'. However, it refines this idea, gets rid of the notions of subjectivity implied by such words as *good* and *bad*, and sets up a theory of scalar differences or degrees of grammaticality. From the second, or from structuralist grammars that have been so fruitful of ideas in the past forty or fifty years, transformational theory derives the concepts of constituent structures and deep structure or ranks of structural elements. But it develops such ideas into the possibility of an examination of all possible sentences in a language by means of abandoning an empirical attitude of looking only at what objectively exists, and adopting instead a theory of accountability for what could exist.

A transformational grammar is thus a kind of analogue of a process. Its only usefulness is in showing what the process is like – it cannot, of course, show what the process is – so that those who understand it may see more clearly how linguistic structures are generated, and may have a device for measuring the difference between competence and performance. A transformational grammar tries to show how fluent speakers and writers of the language make choices of the signs of the language-code when they make utterances which, given the conventions of the language or part of it in which the utterances are made, have grammatical meaning, though not necessarily any other kind of meaning, in the understanding of at least some members of the speech-community. By that is meant that such a sentence, for example, as 'The children visited the cinema' is both grammatically well-formed and semantically acceptable, but such a sentence as 'The cinema visited the children', though grammatically well-formed, is not quite so semantically acceptable if the word *cinema* is taken in one of its senses to mean 'a building in which films are exhibited' and not, say, 'the art of cinematography', or something like that.

A transformational grammar presupposes both convention and authority. It assumes that there are fluent speakers and writers of the language who produce well-formed sentences which can com-

mand respect because of their well-formedness. In this way it
shares with traditional prescriptive grammar the notion that some
speakers and writers are better at speaking and writing than
others, or at least, that some speakers and writers use their
language differently from others and that this kind of difference
is in some way approved of by some people in the speech-
community. Only a transformational grammarian can decide for
any particular transformational grammar what is a well-formed
sentence. The basis of his decision must be either intuitive judge-
ment about the nature of the language he is dealing with or else
some kind of information derived from some consensus of
opinion found somewhere or other among those who are familiar
with the language. Any such decision is quite arbitrary, and to
some people it may even seem perverse. The only justification of
it can be that it is reasonably carefully stated, that some other
people can approve of it, and that other people can find that
the same kinds of methods based on it are workable. A
transformational grammar has, obviously, to be tested, for at best
it can only be a hypothesis, which, like any hypothesis in science,
can be accepted theoretically, so long as it works, until a better
one is found.

A transformational-generative grammar would normally be
developed in at least four stages, with a separate set of rules for
each stage. The first stage would be that which generated a set of
basic sentences from which all other sentences in the language
could be derived. This stage would be a *constituent structure*
grammar, developing appropriate rules which would describe
the main structural units and their methods of structuring in the
basic sentences. The second stage would develop *morphophonemic* or *morphemic* rules which would describe the
morphology of the smaller units in the structures already
developed – the differences, for example, between the contrastive
items in such pairs as *he/him, am/is* or *walk/walked*. From
these two sets of rules a third set of *lexical* rules would have to
be developed to describe the kinds of lexical items (morphemes,
words, or perhaps in some cases groups of words – such as *The
United States* or *the Duke of Wellington*) appropriate to specific
kinds of structures. A complete statement of these lexical rules
for English could easily be as long as the *Oxford English
Dictionary*. Lastly, a set of *transformational* rules would have to

be developed to describe how new sentences, or transforms, could be derived from the set of basic sentences. These transformational rules would then need new morphophonemic or morphemic and lexical rules to account for such differences, for example, as are found in such sentences as 'Shakespeare wrote sonnets' and 'Sonnets were written by Shakespeare', or such differences as those between *laughing* and *laughs* in *the laughing man* and *the man laughs*, or to account for the presence of *is* in the difference between *the laughing man* and *the man is laughing*. As one can readily appreciate, the complete development of these rules for English would be a formidable task, and, obviously, even if they were developed, a complete statement of them would be beyond the capacity of this book. Moreover, one's theory of language, if one has one, might make it necessary for one to develop more, or fewer, than the four sets of rules just hinted at. Morphophonemic rules, for instance, should, strictly speaking, be able to account for the intonation of the spoken language; and perhaps a new set of rules may be needed to deal with the realization of these intonations, and all phonological peculiarities, in graphic substance.

The kind of restriction of scope deliberately envisaged here is, firstly, that made by concentrating more on the syntactic and lexical levels of abstraction than on the phonological, and, secondly, that made on purpose by not developing fully any rules for transformation. It will be assumed that a transform will be recognized, and easily declare itself, on account of its built-in difference from anything in the norm. There are three reasons for this deliberate restriction. First, we intend only a grammar of style, and not, by any means, a complete grammar of English. Those texts most likely to be of stylistic interest, as we have said, will be more often found in the written medium than in the spoken. In the written medium phonological conventions, though clearly very important, are fairly well fixed in the normal orthography and rules for punctuation widely observed by the printing trades, so that deviations can quickly be discovered. It is true, of course. that the language of drama and poetry, recorded in the written medium, and not residing in the memories of specially trained individuals in every instance, is nevertheless intended to have its phonic qualities displayed in performance or private reading, and this fact will have to be taken into account when the styles of dramatic or poetic language-uses are examined. But the phonic qualities of drama and poetry are easily observable, and the fact that they are so obviously deviations from the norm impresses them all the more on the sensibility of the student of style. Second, we intend only a grammar of style which is also the grammar of the norm. A grammar of the norm, by its very nature, should be non-institutionalized, for it is a grammar of a surface state of the language existing without the possibility of depth. That is to say, if we can postulate a state of affairs in which the language can be used with average competence as, so to speak, a common meeting place of all possible acts of communication, then we can also postulate a bare minimum of this language. We can think of skeletons without tissue or flesh; the smallest number of essential structural members of a building without walls, floors, ceilings or roof, a sort of substance without accidental qualities. Away from this common meeting place, which is shared by all speakers of the language, any individual speaker may have linguistic competence not found in it, and many such speakers will have idiolectal familiarity with areas of language use utterly remote from this common centre. And third, some kind of restricted scope is necessary if things are not to become excessively complicated.

4 Constituent-structure

We base our grammar of the norm on two assumptions. The first is that the English language – and perhaps other languages too, but English is our language of exemplification – consists of an infinite set of sentences which can be expressed in only a limited number of ways. The second is that this limited number of ways is in a small fixed set of forms. It follows from this, although it is not so much a linguistic fact *per se* as an inference about human behaviour, that it is the ability to recognize these forms as such that makes it possible for speakers of English to know what an English sentence is when they come across one. At any rate, it could be said that this is how we know what we are talking about.

Sentences are structures of language substance built up out of very small units. If we take the general idea of a sentence, or an abstraction of formal structural constituents derived from an examination of a very large sample indeed of the kinds of things usually called sentences in the actual day-to-day uses of the language, we can form a notion of the basic constituent structure of a set of sentences, and from this simple set of basic patterns a sort of grammar can be constructed which can be said to describe in a general way the process of sentence construction. If we accept the view that a language is a code in the sense in which we have already defined that word, it should not surprise us to find that the possible number of sentence patterns in English is limited, even though their content can be unlimited. Sentence patterns are signs of the code; each pattern carries its own sort of information; in the day-to-day uses of the language each has its own probability of occurrence, although we find that all appear in a large repertoire of variations.

That there are five basic sentence patterns in English seems to have be first pointed out by C. T. Onions at the beginning of this century[1]. He showed that these five basic sentence patterns each took their characteristic form from the structure of the predicate.

An example of a constituent-structure and generative grammar for these five basic sentence forms of English could be set out like this:

C1 $\qquad \Sigma \longrightarrow$ Subject + Predicate

C2 $\qquad$ Subject $\longrightarrow$ Nominal$_1$

C3 $\qquad$ Predicate $\longrightarrow$

$$\begin{bmatrix} V_1 \\ \\ V_2 + \text{Complement} \\ \\ V_3 + \text{Object} \\ \\ V_4 + \text{Indirect Object} + \text{Object} \\ \\ V_5 + \text{Object} + \text{Complement} \end{bmatrix}$$

[1] C. T. Onions, *An Advanced English Syntax*, London 1904

This is the basis of a constituent-structure grammar, or a phrase-structure grammar as it is sometimes called in the United States. It is also a set of rules showing how the basic sentences of English can be generated. It can be explained as follows.

The symbols C1, C2, C3 . . . Cn indicate the kind of rule and the name of the particular rule of its kind. 'C' stands for 'constituent-structure'. The numbers 1, 2, 3 . . . n symbolize both the name of the rule in its particular kind and the fixed order in which the rules must be applied. The numbers are both cardinal and ordinal.

The symbol Σ (capital S in Greek) stands for any member of the whole class of basic English sentences, whatever they are and whatever that class is, and the first rule, C1, both defines what a basic English sentence pattern is and gives instructions about how one can be generated.

The symbol ⸺⟶ can mean either 'consists of' or 're-say or rewrite as'.

The symbol + means 'with, in the company of' or 'followed by', normally the latter.

There are two kinds of rules, which we might call *categorical* and *selectional*. The form in which the rule is expressed shows to which kind it belongs. As we have seen, the act of communication implies the transmission of instructions across a communication channel. We suggested that the information conveyed by signs was an instruction to make a choice from the number of the items of a code. A sentence is a sign in this sense in that its form carries such information, and every sentence has a form which instructs decoders of it to make a choice from a small fixed number of sentence forms. Transformational-generative grammars are very much bound up with these ideas of instruction and choice.

The first two rules, C1 and C2, are categorical. Their form is indicated by the absence of square brackets on the right-hand side of the arrow. Rule C1, for instance, means that in order to produce or generate any well-formed or grammatical Σ or basic English sentence, you have to write or say a subject followed by a predicate, and there is nothing else that you or any other speaker of English can do if a well-formed or grammatical Σ is to be produced. Rule C2 says that a well-formed or grammatical

C

subject must be a Nominal$_1$ – whatever that might be – clearly it will have to be defined later.

These two rules, of course, are quite arbitrary in the sense that they define in the terms of the grammar what a well-formed basic English sentence is and what a well-formed subject of such a sentence is. If, in generating a sentence, somebody fails to obey one or another of the rules, then he has simply not produced a sentence which is well-formed in the terms of the grammar. If, for example, a sentence is found which is made of a predicate followed by a subject, it would deviate from the norm, and its deviation would be interesting for one of two reasons: it would be so badly formed that it would be just the result of incompetence, in which case it would be a matter for pedagogues or psychiatrists, and out of the hands of the linguist entirely; or it could be so well formed as to be better-formed than the average, in which case it would be of great interest to the student of style. Indeed, the celebrated sentence from *Pardise Lost*,

> Him the Almighty Power
> Hurl'd headlong flaming from th'Ethereal Sky,

is deviant in this way, and has received the attention of literary critics because it is so.

The third rule, C3, is a selectional one. It sets out to state how the predicate of any basic English sentence can be generated. The rewrite part of the rule, that on the right-hand side of the arrow, is here enclosed in square brackets. These square brackets are themselves a symbol which is an integral part of the grammar. They carry the instruction, 'Choose one, and not more than one, of the items listed inside'. A selectional rule, recognizable as such because of the square brackets, sets out to give all the choices, and only the choices, of a particular system or small fixed number of choices available to encoders in particular areas of the language-use.

The grammar given above by means of the two categorical rules and the one selectional rule is a grammar of basic English sentence forms. All it can tell anybody is that there are five ways in which basic English sentences can be constructed – that in order to construct, produce or generate a basic English sentence form one must have a subject and a predicate chosen from one

or another of the five forms give in the rule C3, which specifies
these predicates. But it says nothing about content. It tells only
of kind of content.

This fact is in itself interesting because it implies that, in
making a choice of which kind of predicate to use, an encoder
is making a choice of the kind of thing he wants to say, the
kind of message he wants to transmit, and that one particular
kind of sentence form has to be used to do this. In other words,
given that there are only five basic sentence forms in English,
one can say that there are only five kinds of messages that can be
transmitted, and that the language is limited in some manner –
or at any rate, the language of the norm is limited in some
manner which imposes a basic discipline on the users of it. It
suggests that there are only five basic methods of myth-creation,
and that all the knowledge, philosophy, literature, science, culture
and apprehension of the universe of the English-speaking people
rests upon this linguistic pentathlon. It is possible that in other
languages there may be more than these five methods of myth-
creation, or fewer. But in English, it would seem, we can make
up only five sorts of myths. We English, and those who speak
our language, live to express, as it were, only the images on a
five-image spectrum, and that beyond the infra-red and the ultra-
violet, which are so dimly guessed at, there may possibly lie
enormous regions of the unutterable, the probability of worlds in
which we must be for ever tongue-tied and silent.

5 Analysis and Function

The grammar given in the previous section is a result of abstract-
ing from the items of a corpus of a very large number of English
sentences. The opinion of C. T. Onions was confirmed by
analysing the sentences of this corpus according to the familiar
method of what is nowadays called Immediate Constituent
analysis, and sentences of the same basic patterns kept on turning up again and again. This method of analysis depends upon
two techniques: segmentation and substitution.

As a native speaker of English, one intuitively feels that
English sentences can be split up into larger or smaller units,
and that these larger or smaller units can be taken out of the
sentences under analysis, and have other larger or smaller units,

not in the sentences but in the language, substituted for them. For example, a sentence like 'The Duke of Wellington wept after the Battle of Waterloo' can have the segment *the Duke of Wellington* removed from it, and the segment *he*, which can be found in some other sentence in the language, put in its place. The resulting sentence, 'He wept after the Battle of Waterloo', could then be treated in the same way, and a large number of different sentences could thus be produced, as, for instance, 'Napoleon dined after the Battle of Marengo', or 'The Director of the Bank of England slept after a hard day's work', or 'A mouse sneezed during a performance of *The Magic Flute*', and so on, to whatever one's persistence, ingenuity, imagination and patience can lead one.

However, one of the rules of this game is that the resulting sentences must be intelligible to native speakers. And this is the crux. The interpretation of such a rule is not easy, for there can be several kinds of intelligibility. 'The dog bit the postman', for instance, is a pretty humdrum sort of sentence, but not one that is likely to strike many readers with incredulity or incomprehension. Such readers may be able to find, or at least easily imagine, a situational context in which such an event could occur. And from that sentence one could derive some other sentence such as 'The savage bloodhound devoured the dyspeptic Hermes from the G.P.O.' Although some readers might find the diction odd, the fact behind the utterance is not inherently improbable, and grammatically the sentence has nothing wrong with it. But from some such sentences one could, by means of segmentation and substitution, eventually arrive at something like 'The incalculable zero roasts the Promethean lacuna', which is not the sort of sentence for which one can readily think of a situational context or any meaning other than a grammatical one; it is a sentence which can be analysed grammatically but not semantically. Or one might produce from somewhere some such utterance as 'An elusive football plays the retired professional', which is somehow felt to be unintelligible, since a retired professional might play an elusive form of football, but football can hardly be said to play him. Even so, in the consideration of these matters, almost anything can become possible. A hundred years ago a sentence like 'Very fast films are useful in the detection of cosmic rays' would have been thought of as being without context, even though all the units in it were available then in the language; nowadays, of course, to anyone who understands physics and photography the sentence, which is an actual quotation from a book on physics, is as clear as any sentence needs to be.

Grammatical intelligibility is the only criterion. And grammatical intelligibility depends very largely, for English, on the order of the elements in what might be called the larger segments of the sentence. By this I mean that there are some segments of sentences which seem to have a structural rigidity that, generally speaking, defies tampering with. For example, the segment *after the Battle of Waterloo* could be a grammatically intelligible utterance in answer to some such question as 'When did it happen?', but *of after battle Waterloo the* could not. There is a stability of structuring which gives an intelligibility to the structure itself, even though the elements in the structure may be unusual or apparently out of place. One instinctively or intuitively, as a native speaker of English, knows that there is a difference between *the professional retired* and *the retired professional*, and one knows too that the difference is entirely due to the ordering of the words, that is, to the ordering of the smaller units within the larger structure. One knows too, in this same intuitive or unconsciously acquired way, that there are places in structures which can be filled only with certain kinds of items. The difference between *a special football* and *a football special* is a wide and remote one; the first is, presumably, a ball of a peculiar sort that is not generally found, and the second is either a railway train or a newspaper. But it is only in the ordering of the elements within the structure that this difference is revealed.

Given a very large corpus of English sentences, one should be able to catalogue the main features of the structuring of the units in sentences. It is not difficult to do this in a grammar of the norm, because anything which is deviant is only a variation on one or more of the basic normal structures.

We can say, first, that when they find themselves inside structures of whole sentences the units of structuring – morphemes, words, phrases, clauses, groups, or whatever they are – suddenly take on a life of their own. They behave. And they behave in four kinds of ways, which we can identify as nominal, adjectival, verbal and adverbial. Our traditional idea of sentences, when it is expressed roughly and crudely, and from the point of view of considering their usefulness in human affairs rather than the purity of their abstract grammatical structuring, is that sentences are about things performing actions. We have in English, for instance, the idea, first put forward, I think, by Leonard Bloomfield, that the 'actor-action' sort of sentence is the favourite sentence type, from which all other sentences which are not of this type, if there are any, can be derived. This vague and groping effort towards a more rigorous and refined analysis tends to fix in the mind the grammatical ideas of nominal and verbal elements or segments, and so we develop the further idea that some parts of sentences are located in a reference to the things and entities, the substantialities and material stuff of the universe, and that other parts are located in a reference to activity and movement, the operations and changes in posture and position of the things and entities to which we give names. It seems to be impossible for us, such is the rigid frame within which our thoughts have to move, to escape from this archetypal mode of structuring. And our traditional idea of adjectival units – adjectives themselves, adjectival phrases or clauses – is that they modify nouns in an effort to give clearer definition and more exact particularity, to place the idea, floating and elusive, firmly in some exact niche in the universe from which it cannot be readily dislodged. And our traditional idea of adverbial units – adverbs, adverbial phrases and clauses – is that they delimit the area of reference of verbs, adjectives or other adverbs in more or less the same kind of way. In one sense, and one which I claim here to be purely grammatical, and not much concerned with the greater philosophy of things beyond the range simply of grammar, this traditional concept of modification is the basis of the distinction between what I call surface and deep grammar.

The surface grammar of a sentence is the essential form of its structuring which makes it the kind of sentence it is within the small limited number of kinds available to the speakers of the language. The deep grammar is that which is obtained, by whatever means, whether of necessity or of rhetoric, from various kinds of modification.

For our purposes here, such as they are, we can say that the surface grammar of a sentence must have within it units which behave in nominal and verbal ways. The kind of grammar given on page 64 is a surface grammar. It specifies five types of sentences consisting of only nominal and verbal units. It gives no rules for modification, because it does not even pretend to become aware that any kinds of modification can exist. So far as that grammar is concerned – if we may continue to speak of it in this anthropomorphic way – it could regard a sentence with modification only as deviant and far from well-formed.

We can illustrate the way in which the grammar might work with some examples. Given the idea, derived from segmentation and substitution, that in a typical English sentence there is an ordering of segments which makes the sentence what it is, and that a different ordering of the same segments would produce a different sentence or no sentence at all, we can say, as the grammar on page 64 says, that a basic English sentence has a subject coming first in time or space and that a predicate comes after it. We can also go to the language or to the corpus and find a large number of examples of subjects. A typical one would be the word *he*. In the lexical rules of the grammar, if they existed, there would be a list of words or morphemes, as in a thesaurus or in a dictionary, and the word *he* would undoubtedly be among them. Having, then, chosen *he* as a subject, we can turn to the choices available under rule C3 and make selections from all the lexical items that could be specified under the general headings of the symbols given in the square brackets. The result would be five different sentences which all have the word *he* as a subject.

This is the sort of activity which the grammarian supposes goes on in the central nervous systems of people when they decide or are compelled to take on the roles of encoders of messages. The grammar itself is a generalized description of what it is presumed this activity is like.

Let us suppose that the activity has been done – and human brains can be looked upon as computers which can do this sort of thing with remarkable rapidity – then we could have five absurdly simple English sentences:

I   He waits.
II   He is a Frenchman.
III He eats ortolans.

IV He gives me some.
V   He makes me happy.

The kind of grammar that could generate such sentences as those of which these five are examples, it is contended, is a fundamental kind of grammar that can generate all English sentences whatsoever. These five sentences represent the surface or basic structural framework on which all English sentences that ever could be composed are variations – variations, that is, made up with infinite skills or absence of skills, infinite degrees of virtuosity, infinite fumbling, infinite authority.

The sentence system of English is built upon this quite small fixed number of sentence forms, and into these forms content is poured from the great stock of all the words in the language, arranged according to certain rules. Generally speaking, once the surface grammar of any sentence has been established in the process of generating it, these rules can be said to be transformational. That is, they can transform the surface grammar of a basic sentence into something different by the addition of depth, and the depth is derived from adjectival and/or adverbial modification. From this thought we can make the inference: Style is depth.

We can set out a method of displayed analysis of these five basic sentence types of this surface grammar as follows:

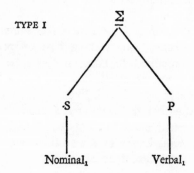

TYPE I

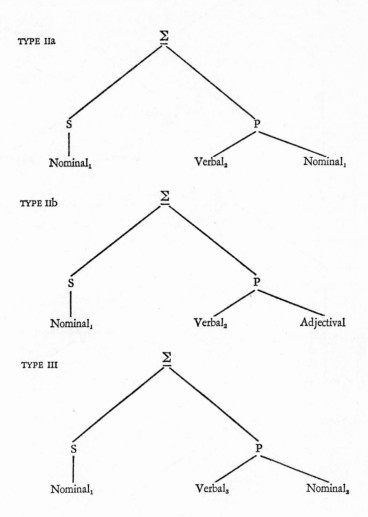

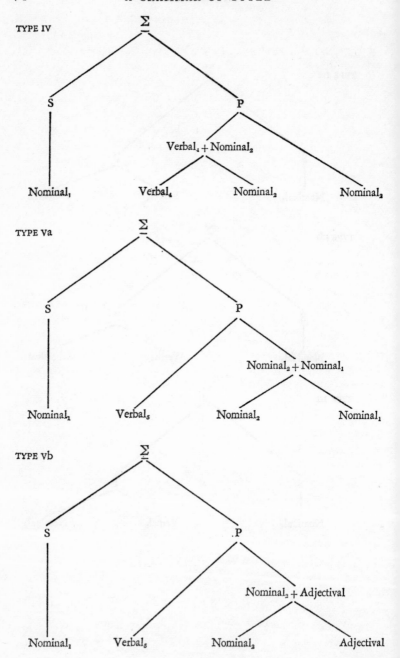

TYPE IV

Σ

S   P

Verbal₄ + Nominal₂

Nominal₁   Verbal₄   Nominal₂   Nominal₃

TYPE Va

Σ

S   P

Nominal₂ + Nominal₁

Nominal₁   Verbal₅   Nominal₂   Nominal₁

TYPE Vb

Σ

S   P

Nominal₂ + Adjectival

Nominal₁   Verbal₅   Nominal₂   Adjectival

These seven diagrams represent the fundamental structuring of the five basic sentence types of English. As can be seen, two of the basic sentence types, II and V, appear with variations in content for each, but not with any difference in form.

The symbols which appear in the bottom lines of each diagram show the kind of content of each sentence type and the normal order in which this kind of content is encoded.

The symbol, Nominal$_1$, for instance, shows that in all subjects of the basic sentence types there will be either structures of words (or morphemes) or single words (or morphemes) behaving in a nominal way.

We can define the expression *behaving in a nominal* (*verbal, adjectival*) *way* to mean 'occurring in the positions marked nominal, (verbal, adjectival) in the diagrams'. That is to say, if a sentence is analysed in accordance with any one of the diagrams, and any segment of it occurs in a position marked nominal (verbal, adjectival), then that segment is behaving in a nominal (verbal, adjectival) manner.

The subscript to Nominal$_1$ is necessary for any lexical rules that may be framed, and to show that the choice of lexical items from those listed in the lexical rules of the grammar as having the possibility of behaving in a nominal way is restricted. For example, such lexical items as *I,he,she,we,they* could be used in positions marked Nominal$_1$, but such lexical items as *me,him,her, us,them* could not – at least, not within the terms of the grammar of the norm; if they were used in sentences in the language in Nominal$_1$ positions they would be deviant, and interesting for that reason. The items *me,him,her,us,them* would normally be more likely to turn up in positions marked Nominal$_2$, and in the lexical rules of the grammar, were such a set of rules ever developed, would appear as usable in Nominal$_2$ positions.

Generally speaking, however, we can say that, except for this slight difference of restriction on the use of pronouns, the rules for the generation of nominal segments of the basic sentences are likely to be the same for both Nominal$_1$ and Nominal$_2$ positions, and that there must be, in the actual uses of the language, millions of nominal segments which can be used indiscriminately in either position.

The main interest, if there is any at all, of the diagrams lies in the analyses of the predicate parts, since these are all different and since these differences show that it is in the generation of predicates that different sorts of myth-creation can be found. In the actor-action formula which seems to determine sentence structure, it seems that we tend unconsciously to believe in, or hope for, a stable and enduring universe in which things remain always the same and have qualities of resilience which survive the hazards and adventures of their activities, their changes of posture, their forays into the worlds of deeds, or those moments or hours or years in which they neglect the comfortable permanence of their being just what they are and sally forth into the unknown hurlyburly of restless and energetic movement, in which they don't just stand there but do something. The different kinds of predicates seem to be controlled by their verbal segments, and the five subscripts to the symbol *Verbal* are supposed to show how this control works.

The control works in two ways, grammatical and lexical. In each of the five types a different kind of formal structuring is called for, and it is called for because in each case the verbal segment is of a different kind with a different area of general meaning. Some kinds of messages can be transmitted only by some kinds of sentence types, and this differentiation among predicates of the basic sentences is supposed to show in a general way what this sort of distribution is.

In the basic sentences of Type I, for instance, the main part of the verbal segment, the verb itself stripped of all adverbial modification, will always be intransitive. And this fact at once imposes a restriction on the kinds of things that can be said in sentences of this type. Relationships, for example, between two things that can be brought, as it were, together in an utterance by the mere mention of their names, much in the same kind of way in which the Egyptian god Tum is said to have created himself by saying his own name, can only be dealt with in a special kind of manner in sentences of Type I. Very commonly the verbs to be found in these sentences will be verbs of motion, or verbs of negative motion such as *to stop, to remain,* or *to wait.* Verbs of this kind, it could be said, imply, so to speak, a localization of the action denoted by them in what is denoted by their subjects, so that there is nothing else taking part in the area of the action except what is denoted by the subjects. A sentence like 'He went to Leningrad' (Type I) is different from a sentence like 'He reached Leningrad' (Type III), and the subtlety of the difference lies in the relative remoteness of Leningrad from his going thither in the first case, and the relative actuality of Leningrad in his arriving there in the second. A more vivid contrast can be seen in those kinds of verbs which can be used both transitively and intransitively. The difference between 'The sun melts the ice' (Type III) and 'The ice melts in the sun' (Type I), for instance, shows this localization of the action denoted by the verb in what is denoted by the subject of it in sentences of Type I. Sentences of Type I for the most part speak of lonely, isolated subjects performing self-oriented acts which never reach out in friendly or hostile contact in a bustling world of social relationships; they deal with the unassociated self of the subjects, immune alike to love and hate, rapt in a private existence, alone in a shell of intransitivity, the kernel of linguistic being, the first sensation or the first thought, before the initial encoded message created the first signal that roused a response, grateful and welcome we have no doubt, in the first decoder.

Sentences of Type II, although, one imagines, statistically very frequent, show a narrow range of choice indeed of verbal elements. The verbs in sentences of this type are, again, always intransitive, and always of the kind known nowadays as copulative. The most common of them are *to be, to seem* and *to become*. The sentences of Type II assert existence or alleged existence, and are, usually, highly subjective intellectualized methods of myth-creation. One might say that a very large class of them, definitions for instance, show language as myth-creation *par excellence*. The kind of relationship established, or said to be established, by sentences of this type is that of classification. To say, for instance, 'A phoneme is one of the speech sounds of a particular language' (Type IIa) is merely to create a class of things called 'speech sounds of a particular language' and then to say that a phoneme is one of them. Sometimes, sentences of this type borrow verbs from other types, so to speak, and thus manufacture subjective myths as expressions of emotional acceptance or rejection. In such a sentence as 'These strawberries taste good' (Type IIb) or 'She looks frightful in that hat' (Type IIb), the adjectival segment – *good* or *frightful in that hat* – by being adjectival, preserves the intransitive nature of the verb, and at the same time describes the class of things into which the myth-creator wishes to put that which is denoted by the subject. Sentences of this Type II have played an important part in the history of civilization, especially in the more self-conscious areas of myth-creation in science and technology, where they have been a great help in making people understand what other people as well as themselves are talking about, and where they have created myths that have changed the world for better or worse in many practical and impractical ways. They are great suppliers of the theory that lurks somewhat apprehensively behind practice. They are utterances about the mythical existential nature of gods, men and things. To the philosophers sentences of Type II have been an everlasting source of interest, confusion and bewilderment, for they have stated the axioms upon which all argument rests, and through them men have tried to grope towards the truths which are the ultimate but elusive goals of all knowledge. Even linguists find that they cannot do without them.

Sentences of Type III are more homely and down to earth. The verbs in them are always transitive, and the sentences themselves seem to express a relationship of observed actuality, or supposedly actual phenomena in what is observed; this relationship is that between what is denoted by the subject and what is denoted by the object, both of which are somehow real and reassuring in the structures of grammar and in the extra-grammatical world which these sentences are supposed to reflect. This relationship is that of a different kind from that of merely stated or alleged classification (a highbrow and intellectual process, arid with logic and absence of animal lifeblood or vegetable juices) which is expressed by sentences of Type II. It is different, and the difference is due normally to the fact that what is denoted by the subject of sentences of Type III is not the same thing or concept as that which is denoted by the object, or, if it is not actually so, it is, because of the form of the utterance, looked upon as if it were. This difference is noted in the subscripts of the symbol Nominal which appear in the Type III analysis. Sentences of this type seem to have empirical qualities which relate them to the actual world of things and events, not the world of fantasy or imagination. If we say 'Cats chase mice' (Type III) we at once transport listeners or readers into a firm region where facts are facts which cannot be easily gainsaid; and even if we say 'Dragons cook their food by breathing' (Type III) we externalize the imagination's product and put it into a place where facts are still facts. Of course, when one talks about worlds of actual things and events, one begs a very large number of philosophic questions, but that doesn't matter very much, because a great deal of the use of language in the daily life of a very large number of people does exactly the same, and we are talking here about language and what goes on inside language; even the philosophers, or most of them, those who tell us about their philosophizing and do not keep it for ever hidden from the light of day wrapped in a parcel of silence, seem to take it for granted that the talk which they talk is real talk. Whether what is said in language has any reference to, correlation with, or derivation from, anything outside itself, is not a question that the linguist, in his professional moments, is very well qualified to answer. His belief that uses of language arise in situational contexts is merely a statement that what is said comes from somewhere, and that he can recognize parts of what he thinks about as not being language.

The point is, presumably, that to say a sentence of Type III shows, or is likely to show, empirical qualities which a sentence of Type II cannot show, is only to characterize the difference between the two types. Another way of characterizing the same difference would be to say that sentences of Type II are more likely to be mental constructs of a more abstract kind than most of the sentences of Type III. But this does not mean to say that there are no sentences of Type III which are not mental constructs of a similar or nearly similar kind. Looked at from one point of view, all sentences whatever are mental constructs. But among the class of things called mental constructs, all kinds of sentences do not have the same status. Some sentences are felt by those who use them to be different kinds of mental constructs from others, to be different kinds of ways of controlling and managing what is apprehended in experience. Some sentences sort out and arrange what is apprehended by experience, others record it, and others recreate it.

The same kind of empirical quality is found in sentences of Types IV and Va. In the sentences of Type IV the verbs are again transitive, but they belong, either because of the meanings of the verbs themselves or because of the meanings they acquire when included in sentences of this type, to a restricted kind of transitivity. The sort of action denoted by sentences of this type seems to be action directed to or for what is denoted by the first of the two nominal segments that follow the verbal segment, and the kinds of verbs which express this must always have this nominal segment following them in some form or another. In some languages other than English we would simply label it 'dative', and there leave the matter. But if this first occurring nominal segment is absent, such verbs as appear in these sentences lose an aspect of their meaning. A typical verb of sentences of Type IV is the verb *to give*. Carried with the parts of this verb and many others like it are the combined notions of transference of something and of that transference to somebody or something. This double directedness apparently needs in English to be expressed by a kind of adverbial component which is nevertheless nominal in form. In such a sentence as 'She gave her husband a case of Scotch' (Type IV), the first nominal segment after the verb – *her husband* – seems to have adverbial properties, which, however, are so linked to the meaning of the verb itself that one could almost, in the rules for the generation of such sentences, specify 'nominal segment used adverbially' as a necessary component of the whole verbal segment. This, perhaps, is confirmed by an alternative way of saying many of the sentences of this type. 'She gave a case of Scotch to her husband' is an acceptable paraphrase of the example we just gave, and in it *to her husband* is without doubt adverbial. As soon as the first nominal segment after the verb is removed from sentences of Type IV, the verb takes on a different meaning – a fact which is itself of stylistic interest. This sentence from a popular novel, 'Mark gave a yell of despair as the beast snatched Helen from his grasp' (Type III), shows how this can happen, since Mark, presumably, didn't give the yell of despair as a donation to anyone in particular, but just rendered it up in the universe at large; in fact, he didn't *give* the yell (except perhaps to the vestigial gods) so much as *utter* or *produce* it.

Sentences of Type V seem statistically very infrequent. But these too have transitive verbs, even though their transitivity is, again, of a somewhat restricted sort. The semantic necessity of a complement in these sorts of sentences is the source of this restriction. Just as, in sentences of Type IV, the segment that immediately follows the verbal segment has adverbial properties, so this complement has something of a 'noun adjective' about it. An example of Type Va would be 'They elected him president', and in such an example there is a pretty strong flavour of the empirical quality which we have noted to be present in all sentences which have transitive verbs. But in an example of Type Vb, as, for instance, 'She thought me stupid', the empirical quality lies rather in her thinking as it is reported by the author and not so much in what she thought. There is another problem with sentences of this type. Normally, the grammatical category of case does not figure as a dominating element in the basic English sentences of the grammar, except, as we have already seen, when pronouns have to be considered as lexical items to form subjects or objects. In the analysis of sentences of Type Va we defined the nominal segment which occurs last in the syntagmatic order as Nominal$_1$. There may be some doubt about whether this is right. In such a sentence as 'She thought me stupid', there is no difficulty. But suppose she were to mistake me for some one else, and I report her mistake by saying 'She thought me him', would such an utterance be English? Certainly, such a sentence as 'She thought me he' sounds very odd to English ears. I do not propose to answer this question, because I don't think that 'She thought me him' is the sort of sentence very likely to be often said. (Most probably one would say 'She thought I was so-and-so' (Type III). One imagines that in the vast majority of cases some kind of noun or nominal phrase is likely to turn up in the final segment in these sorts of sentences when they occur at all.

6 Transforms

In a highly developed and sophisticated language like the Present-day English we are familiar with, the five basic sentence types which we have just indicated are apparently not enough, or do not make the signs of a sufficiently large code, to cope with all that speakers and writers seem to want to say or with all the ways in which they want to say it. There exist in English kinds of sentences which we call transforms. We can define the word *transform* in a general and not very precise way as meaning any sentence which is not a basic one, or any sentence which cannot be generated in terms of the grammar given on page 64, but which, by the addition of elements not included in that grammar, has acquired a deep grammar in addition to its surface one. This means that as soon as any kind of modification appears in a sentence of one of the basic types, as soon, that is, as encoders feel dissatisfied with original innocence and begin to taste the fruits of the exploration of wider knowledge, the basic sentence starts to become transformed. It starts to become transformed because its grammar acquires depth. How much depth it will acquire depends on the daring of encoders, and the lengths to which they are prepared to go with what they believe they want to do with the sentences they generate. Some sentences have a very shallow grammatical depth; others take on a terrifying grammatical profundity, though perhaps not a semantic one.

The point can be illustrated by an example. If we take 'He waits' as an instance of a basic sentence of Type I, we can expand it, paraphrase it, or mean, or intend to mean, the same as it, by saying (shall we suppose?) 'A very old man waits patiently in the rain'. This expanded sentence has now suddenly acquired some features of grammar which the basic sentence did not have, as we can see by comparing the analyses of both sentences:

(1)

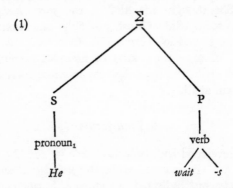

(In some circumstances, it may be necessary to analyse nouns and verbs into base and inflexions. A noun in the plural, for instance, may be of grammatical interest just because it is in the plural. In the analysis above, '*wait-s*' as distinct from '*waits*' indicates, for example, the possibility of contrast between *waits/ wait* or *waits/waited* or *waits/is waiting*, or something like that, and such contrasts may be grammatically, rhetorically or even stylistically important. Strictly speaking, I suppose, one must say that all finite verbs must have the possibility of analysis into more than one part, because in sentences they are always contrastive in at least tense, person and number.)

(2)

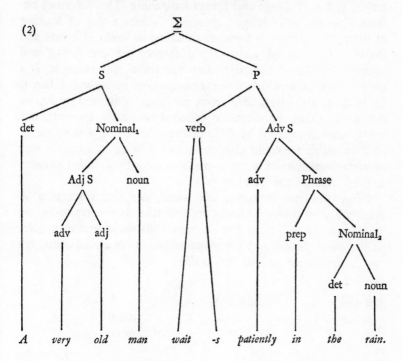

Here, *det* means 'determiner'; *Adv S* means 'adverbial segment'; *Adj S* means 'adjectival segment'; *adj* means 'adjective'; *adv* means 'adverb'; and *prep* means 'preposition'.

The point is that all the additional information given by the elements that produce the grammar in depth, all the modification, can be re-expressed in the forms of the basic sentences. In fact, the whole utterance can be regarded as if it were an extremely generalized summary of a series of basic sentences. To be able to think of it in these terms we must go backwards and forwards inside it with some agility.

Most of the information is susceptible at the grammatical level of being 'nominalized' or treated in substantival ways, if we think in the nowadays rather old-fashioned terms of noun substantive and noun adjective. That is to say, we could, if we delved deeply enough into the grammatical peculiarities of the sentence, think of a great deal of the information it conveys, perhaps all, in terms of things and events and their qualities, and not in terms of things and things happening. The difference between 'events' and 'things happening' is here a way of looking at them, the difference between thinking in terms of nouns and thinking in terms of verbs – the difference between 'being' and 'doing'. Instead of assuming that 'He waits', for example, is a unitary concept in which whatever is denoted by *waits* is inherent in, part of, and inseparable from, whatever is denoted by *he*, we can assume that the utterance contains two main concepts, one being what is denoted by *he*, and the other being a complex of notions which we could call 'the act of waiting in a certain way or certain number of ways, such as waiting by a "third person" in the "present tense", and so on'.

Given the basic sentence, 'He waits', and that a sentence 'A very old man waits patiently in the rain' is an expansion or paraphrase of it, given, that is, that both these sentences refer to the same person and the same event, or mean the same, we can think of some such scheme as this:

He		waits
is a man	(the act of)	waiting
is very old		is present tense
		is third person
		is 'patient'
		is 'in the rain'

Two points deserve to be noticed. The first is that in analysing sentences we discover that our traditional notion of what is meant by the word *word* is not very helpful. The simple truth is that there are not enough words in the language to enable us to say all that we want. Consequently we have to make structures of words inside sentences, and these structures, though comparatively loose in one sense, behave as if they were stabilized elements like those entities we traditionally call words. They behave, that is, as if they were the sorts of things we could go and look up in a dictionary. This state of affairs is particularly noticeable in the making of nominal structures. For instance, a very large number of nouns in English have to be preceded by a determiner, and in those cases where this is not so the absence of a determiner before the noun is sufficiently contrastive to mark that noun as having a different kind of meaning from that which it would have if a determiner were present. Thus in the sentences

Cake
A cake ⎱ is wanted for the wedding
The cake ⎰

we pass from the general to the particular, and note that the entire structures *a cake* and *the cake* are units which have different meanings, and that the meaning of each is different from that of the single word *cake*. In the same sort of way, in the sentence previously analysed, the structure *very old* takes on a unitary meaning of its own, and so does the structure *in the rain*. The system of analysis which we have adopted allows in its symbolism for the identification of such unitary structures which can be further analysed into words or morphemes by giving them an uppercase initial, as with the word *Phrase*. But the main point is that such unitary structures are of stylistic interest because they immediately on being included in a sentence begin to make that sentence deviate from the basic norm.

The second point which deserves to be noticed is that it is much simpler to think of adjectival modification of nouns as expressible in the form of one or another of the basic sentence types than it is to think so of abverbial modification of verbs, adjectives or other adverbs. In English we are notoriously uninhibited in our use of adverbial segments, and all manner of different shades of meaning, each of great stylistic interest, can be achieved by means of the manipulation of the adverbials in different positions in sentences. For instance, these sentences—

A very old man waits patiently in the rain
A very old man patiently waits in the rain
In the rain a very old man patiently waits
In the rain a very old man waits patiently
Patiently, a very old man waits in the rain

—all show differences of rhythm and intonation and various expressions of the feeling, tone or pathos of the situation. They can demonstrate that the place of adverbials shows subtle transformations of the basic structuring. In the last three instances, for example, bringing the adverbial to the beginning of the sentence isolates it from *waiting*, so that it applies to the whole concept of *the man waiting*, and thus creates a different sort of myth from that expressed in each of the first two sentences.

The basic sentence forms rarely appear exemplified in actual usage, for sentences, especially those in the written medium, usually occur in association with others, and in continuous discourse they have to take on qualities of meaningfulness and implication which they derive from those before and after them. A grammar of the norm excludes a great deal. The kinds of things that we want to say are the kinds of things that our society demands, positively, negatively or with assumed neutrality, that we should say. Therefore our society has made for us institutionalized and semi-institutionalized ways of saying whatever we think should be said. We also have to acknowledge a need to embellish the basic forms with modification which helps us to define and clarify, to particularize and to make specific. We need also the management of a great deal of adverbial qualification, for not only do we have to say or be told that things exist and happen, but we also want to say or be told when, where, how and why.

One of the simple kinds of transforms elaborated from the basic sentence forms is that in which the polarity of the sentence is changed, as when we make a positive sentence into a negative one. All the basic sentences of the grammar of the norm are positive; the grammar assumes that assertions will be made and that there will be no denial. The change *He waits* into *He doesn't wait* or *He does not wait* is to add three more morphemes – *do*, *-es* and *not* – which give a new dimension of depth to the original predicate. All five of the basic sentence forms, except those of Type II, need the addition of some such morphemes to make the negative. The fact that sentences of Type II need only the morpheme *not* to express their negative polarity (*I am British/I am not American*) is interesting, and could indeed single out sentences of this type for special consideration, were they not already so well qualified for distinctiveness on other grounds.

One of these other grounds is the frequent, indeed dominating, presence in basic sentences of Type II of parts of the verb *to be*. This verb has a large and controlling interest in a very important class of transforms of basic sentences of Types III, IV and V. The transitive verbs of the sentences of these types can be changed from the active to the passive voice by means of using finite parts of the verb *to be* in close association with the past participles of the transitive verbs in question.

The use of the passive voice in Present-day English is a phenomenon of considerable interest. Superficially, a sentence in the passive voice may look, when stripped of its essentials, very much like a basic sentence of Type IIb, where there is an adjectival segment in the complement position. For example, this sentence, taken from a popular article on travel, 'Snails were scattered profusely in the grass', could have, if the adverbial segments *profusely* and *in the grass* were omitted and the tense changed, the form of such exponents of basic sentences of Type IIb as 'Swallows are migratory' or 'Mermaids are amphibious' or 'They are sad'. However, this superficial appearance is deceptive. A more robust sentence in the passive voice, and one which might be taken as exemplary, is one from an article on plumbing, 'The design of a tap is dictated by the mechanism inside it'. Converted into the active, this sentence could read something like 'The mechanism inside a tap dictates its design', and there we have an expanded sentence of Type III, in which there is an undeniable empirical quality brought about by the statement made in a straightforward way that something does something to something else. But when we go back to the sentence about the snails, we find that the snails are, as it were, no one's responsibility. Who scattered the snails profusely in the grass? We shall never know, even if we actually believe that they were scattered by somebody or some god who attends to these matters. The point is that the appearance of the distribution of the snails suggested that they might have been scattered in this mysterious or even supernatural way. The great institutionaliza-tion of institutions, which is steadily going on in the society which has evolved Present-day English, has seized upon the passive voice as another way of expressing a point of view addi-tional to those which can already be expressed by the forms of the existing basic sentence types. For instance, the men who make the world of science and technology in which we live tend to fall into the habit of saying this sort of thing: 'The gasket is attached to the back-plate by six quick-action fasteners'. They say that rather than 'Six quick-action fasteners hold the back-plate' because, presumably, it is the attachment of the gasket to the back-plate that is important and not the fact that six quick-action fasteners do it. In this way the performer of the action is made to disappear entirely, for indeed, in the world of science and technology, results or end-products are what matter, and the myths of science are apparently hypotheses about what is thought to be the existential nature of the universe and not how it came about.

In addition to the ways of managing and controlling thought and environment and expressing views about the world by means of expanded basic sentences, we have also those transforms of the basic sentence types which are called questions and commands.

Questions can be looked upon as structural variants of statements, or statements can be looked upon as structural variants of questions. There is no reason in linguistic science, except the comfort and convenience of the linguist, why the basic sentences of his transformational-generative grammar should not be in question form. It is merely a matter of point of view.

As in the transformation from positive to negative polarity, there are, except in the sentence forms of Type II, which are always remarkable for their grammatical refusal to conform willingly, morphemic changes to the verb when questions are constructed. For example, *We have dinner* can become *Do we have dinner?* or *Are we having dinner?*; but it should be noted that, in addition to the inversion of the locality of the subject, the question *Are we having dinner?* could have as the basic sentence form from which it is derived the utterance *We are having dinner*, which is rather different from *We have dinner*. It may be apparent that although *We are having dinner* is a sentence of Type III it is, even so, 'more like' a sentence of Type IIb than *We have dinner* is. And we might note as well that here the influence of the part of the verb *to be* introduces subtleties which might become of interest to the student of style. Most transformations of statement to question form, however, involve the inversion of the subject and part of the verbal segment, so that the question form is signalled to be such by a special morphemic change right at the beginning – *I like Brahms: do you like Brahms?* There is, moreover, a special system of morphemes like *why, when, where, how, what, who,* etc., members of which can also signal question form when put in front of an already existing question form – *Why do you like Brahms?* – or in front of simple inversions of Type II sentences – *Why is Brahms famous?* One should note also the built-in redundancy in the rules of transformation from statement to question form.

Another type of transform, that which produces commands or imperative sentences, is made by the omission of the subject and the use of the verb in the infinitive. In transforms of this kind, as indeed also with questions, the encoder wants to manage the world outside him (unless he is giving orders to or interrogating himself) by telling people – and sometimes animals – to do things: *Go with me: Compare our prices with those in other stores: Look at the matter this way: Down, Rover.*

Lastly, we can refer to what we may call partial sentences. These are shortened versions of sentences that can be thought of as symbols for whole sentences. As we have said, in any situational context the amount of language activity is determined by the presence, number or absence of extra-linguistic signs that can or cannot make the language activity intelligible within the context. The answers *Yes* and *No* to questions are clearly symbols for whole answers expressed in whole sentences, and are only intelligible in relation to the questions to which they are answers. In other kinds of situations only one or two words may be needed as a signal to embody the message that encoders intend to transmit. The words *Bus Stop*, for example, are enough in the situation in which they are most likely to be useful, and there is no need for the sign at the edge of the public highway to give the message in full: 'This is a bus stop' or 'This is approximately the place at which buses may stop if you should ever want to board one'. The amount of language activity is a function of the information supplied by the time and the place and the circumstances in which it occurs.

This tedious discussion of minutiae was necessary – and I apologize for it – to prepare the way for what is to follow. So far as I know, the norm of the English language, or of any other language, has not previously been adumbrated in any detail in the literature of linguistics. I am afraid we shall have to examine this abstraction in a little more detail later on; but before we do that we must try to understand something of the nature of the creative process.

CHAPTER III

NORM AND DEVIATION

1 Uses of Language

When we approach language at the lexical level, that is, at the level at which the signals in language substance have a quality which makes them significant in the speech-community in which they have their being, we find we are dealing with a matter which is extremely complex. And the complexity is increased by the necessity of having to use language to talk about language. When speakers and writers use language they create myths, impositions of their thought processes on the world around them. They believe that the structures thus made out of language substance have some kind of relevance to human situations and experiences. The circumstances in which these myths are produced result in deviations from the abstract norm which we have postulated. It is the business of this chapter to try to explain in language what these deviations are and how they arise.

There can be many answers to the question, What does a language do? In general, we can say, giving one, and possibly the principal, answer, that what a language does is help its speakers and writers to operate and control their environment, to express their emotions, to give imaginative apprehensions of what they conceive to be reality, and to share experiences.

So that we ourselves, in this book, might be able to operate and control, at least in theory, the vast and inchoate mass of language-uses that we can daily find all around us, and which exists in our consciousness and our imagination as an everlasting bibblebabble of noise and an endless stream of writing and printing, it might not be a bad idea to postulate three kinds of social relationships in which language-uses might be said to occur, and which, perhaps, influence choice of human beings in making those uses by deciding for them their registers.

These three relationships are those of persons, property and power. Each of us, firstly, can exist in society, or out of it, as himself or herself, male or female, as a human being with personal feelings and sensations, hopes, fears, aspirations, anxieties, assurances and attitudes – as an individual in the midst of economic and political complexities, the partial operator and partial victim of both, striving to live a life in which the essential personality can live and be realized through them, because of them, or in spite of them. Each of us, secondly, can exist in society as producer and consumer, giver and taker, seller and buyer – he or she from whom property or rights are transferred and he or she to whom property and rights come; in this relationship we are constantly dealing with things and people, dominated by them or trying to overcome them. And each of us, thirdly, can exist as ruler or ruled, master or servant, parent or child, the giver or receiver of orders and instructions, in the realization and understanding of social status and power. In these ways we exist always as the instruments of the interpenetration of ourselves with authority and the material things and forces of the world. Sometimes we exercise economic and administrative authority over our fellows; at other times we are in postures of submission to an authority which is not our own. The limits of our freedom and free-will are defined for each of us by our being the kinds of persons we are in the midst of a network of the intimacies of our personal selves in social, political and economic arrangements.

Our language has developed with our society to enable us to deal with these social relationships and at the same time preserve a balance between originality and social order. Most of the language-uses we employ in the daily affairs of life are adapted to dealing with the relationships of property and power, since without them we should have no existence at all as biological creatures who must live and survive in society. These two relationships among men of property and power impose restrictions and taboos which hold back the unlimited appetites which each of us must confess as individual persons, uncontrolled and uncivilized by social relations and necessities. An imaginative and symbolic language, that of poetry, of timeless fictions, and of concealed metaphors, exists to express in its own way that which cannot be expressed in the language adapted to the needs of the relationships of property and power.

Reflecting these three sets of social relationships are three levels of communicative experience which can be discovered, no doubt, in the language of highly developed and sophisticated communities, such as that of the English-speaking people. These three levels of communicative experience can be looked upon as stages through which the most advanced speakers of the language normally pass through in their learning it.

As the foundation upon which all other linguistic experiences are usually built, we have a kind of vernacular which is most often only spoken, and which is the kind of language that those born with normal hearing first become acquainted with. This is the basis of each idiolect, of each individual's experience of and way of using his natural tongue. Presumably, it is a very personal and intimate possession, since it is a person's first experience of himself in intercourse with the outside world, apart from that of physical contact with his mother. This is the kind of language he learns by ear in earliest childhood, but it is hardly learnt in the sense that any teaching of it is formally organized. This first acquaintance with language is an experience of internal responses to an environment which is, for the most part, unexplored, and yet which is trusted. This personal language, so intimate at first, grows and develops with the individual, in the beginning in a world of a simple set of relationships of a few sounds, whose meaning is only an acknowledgement of innocence. But for many people it burgeons later into a linguistic efflorescence which may have no greater presumptions than those of humble wild flowers of field and hedgerow, or which, for others, may be a wild luxuriant and flamboyant vegetation indeed. This is the language of intimate and personal intercourse, of phatic communion, and most likely of the individual's expression of his linguistically structured and symbolic experience of himself, and of his daydreams and private fantasies. For without this linguistic effort – the first externalization of himself into the world of his fellows – no further learning of the language would be possible. There is, I think, no doubt that the effect of what was immediately built during childood on this foundation persists throughout life, and certainly into maturity. And we do, of course, use this vernacular on most occasions when we use the spoken language in its least formalized media and tenors, as when we engage in casual conversation, speak with our wives, children, relatives and personal friends. It is found in its social usefulness in abolishing silence when two or three people are gathered together, as in the chatter of acquaintances on informal social occasions, in the gossip of housewives in supermarkets or over garden fences, the pleasantries and exchanges of men in pubs and at football matches, and so on. It is not a language of much stylistic interest, because it is hardly ever written. Indeed, most of it would, if written, be so boring that it would be unreadable. It nevertheless exists, and it is the vocal foundation upon which all other language-uses are built. Until recently, this language has also had what might be called its literature in an oral tradition of folk tales and stories, nursery rhymes, proverbs, vulgar jokes, popular songs, ballads – the repository of the unconscious and symbolically expressed desires and wishes of the intimacies of personal relationships.

We can think of this language as *private*, that is, as an idiolectal vernacular which has been, for long ages in the past, unaffected in many ways by a higher sophistication. It is the language of each individual's participating in the speech-community, and sometimes, indeed, of much of each individual's pre-conscious crystallizations of experience before there is a more objectified structuring.

Upon this foundation we have to build, in the industrial and technological society in which we now live in the English-speaking world, a more public form of language. Thus *public* language has developed in the evolution of society especially to deal with the relationships of property and power. It is a language which shows itself more in the formalized usages of society than does the private language. It is a dialect of the language that has to be learnt – nowadays usually through some means of formally organized education, for it is a language which is primarily written, or which at least, since learning through printed books became common in the English-speaking world, is based upon a conception of what the written language should be like. This language is the main vehicle for the transmission of all facts, ideas, beliefs, opinions and attitudes of mind in the social and cultural life of society as such. It is supra-idiolectal. It is used in institutionalized aspects of community life, in education, in politics, administration, management, commerce, art, literature, criticism, and in the general dissemination of knowledge and public opinion and of all the information necessary to keep society going in national and even international relationships. In certain registers this language may even appear to have some of the characteristics of sub-dialects or jargons used by specialized groups within the larger community, and members of these groups, communicating in this language among themselves, will sometimes employ their own special technical terms and turns of phrase. But it is also a kind of language which is understood readily over large areas in society, where many people will be receivers of it but not senders, as with the language of newspapers, magazines and periodical journalism, of textbooks, of both popular and serious literature, as well as of the forms of non-personal communication, such as formal business letters, reports, minutes of meetings, and written instructions and information generally. Although it is widely written and transmitted through printing, this language quite often exists in phonic substance, especially since the invention and widespread use of electronic means of transmitting the spoken word through the telephone, radio and television. When this language does exist as speech it becomes formalized, and takes on the characteristics, or some of them, of the written language, for it is less *ad hoc* than the private language of the individual, and becomes more deliberately planned and prepared, as in sermons, political speeches, the formalized statements of parliamentary debates, board meetings or committees, radio news bulletins and talks, lectures, and so on. At one interesting level of its appearance as speech, that of the drama, as it is heard in the contemporary theatre, in the sound-tracks of films, and in radio and television plays, it is written first, very often in a mannered and self-conscious imitation of the private language, so that it becomes, as it were, very often a representation of the private language that has been filtered through itself. Indeed, in our time, a great deal of the language of imaginative literature generally is the result of an effort, deliberate and artistic, to bring the characteristics of the two sorts of language, public and private, into a close harmony, and to strip the public language of its associations with the relationships of property and power and to express personal relationships. This public language is of great stylistic interest, for it is based, in what is taught to those who in our society have to become literate, on a concept of stylistic elegance which derives from the usages of writers of the late seventeenth and early eighteenth centuries.

In the past three hundred years or so, our society has become progressively more literate, at first slowly as a result of the spread of printed books, and later more rapidly as the growth of industrialization and technology made it more and more necessary for more and more people to be able to read and write. The problem of how to teach literacy does not seem to have been very carefully thought out; but in an age in which there were both class divisions in society and a concept of *laissez-faire*, it was taken for granted that the dialect called Standard English was the one that ought to be taught. This notion suggested the notion of 'good English' or 'correct English', and the imposition of a fairly standardized dialect upon the idiolects and dialects of the personal and spoken language of those who were being taught literacy. What exactly was meant by good and correct English was discovered by the Scottish rhetoricians, Campbell, Kames and Blair, who lived in the eighteenth century and lectured at Scottish universities on the arts of rhetoric and English composition. They decided on such rules of correct English as that about not putting prepositions at the ends of sentences, not splitting infinitives, as the difference between *due to* and *owing to*, as the singularity of *every* and *none*, and so on. They came to such conclusions as these after a study of the practice of such writers as Dryden, Addison, Steele, Swift, Pope and Johnson. In the nineteenth century, when the demand for literacy became more urgent, writers of textbooks on English composition and grammar gave wide currency to these ideas, and when the establishment of public education began rapidly to increase the size of the readership of school and college textbooks, a formal style of Standard English developed, using and giving even wider currency to these ideas; their influence has extended even into the twentieth century, and is still with us perpetuated in such books as Fowler-Gowers's *Modern English Usage* or Eric Partridge's *Usage and Abusage*. Without such ideas, this public language that is so copiously received by the majority of the population could not exist. For nowadays this language is read and heard by far more people than ever initiate it. There are always more readers of books, periodicals, advertisements, and the printed word generally than there are writers; there are more listeners to drama than there are playwrights, and more who hear radio and television programmes than produce the scripts. One of the characteristics of language-use in our time in the English-speaking world is that through this public language the few address the many, even on many occasions when the few have very little to say. However, the many, who are called upon to write now and then, though not so frequently as the professionals, imitate this public language, both in phonic and graphic substance, in their own ways, and may aspire to the use (or misuse) of it on formal occasions.

Growing out of this public language, and becoming a sort of refinement of it, the third level of linguistic experience is that of preoccupation with one or more of the learned languages. A *learned* language is one that is used by a minority of specialists for exact definition, sophisticated conceptual analysis, and the recording and discussion of specialized topics at advanced levels of learning and scholarship to which the majority do not wish to aspire. There are, of course, learned languages which belong to many specialized disciplines. They are characterized by being almost exclusively available only in the written medium; they have their own vocabularies; and many, indeed, have formalized modes of sentence structure and grammatical presentation, as in the frequent use of the passive voice in contributions to scientific journals, or as in the proliferation of many qualifying clauses in the language of legal documents. Such learned languages are those of theology, law, medicine, philosophy and the sciences, and of those branches of learning where language has to be used as a precise instrument for the creation of myths that have been elevated to the status of carefully reasoned hypotheses of the greatest possible generality. Very often one or another of these learned languages will advance its myth-creativeness to such complicated and comprehensive generality that the ordinary resources of the public language will be inadequate to say all that has to be said or to be able to express the relationships one to another of the concepts involved. When this happens the vocabulary of the language and the grammatical methods of dealing with it have to be extended and refined to cope with the expression of new knowledge; and this means that a new symbolism has to be invented along with new methods of controlling and operating the symbols; such are the formulae of chemistry, the signs used in the analytical procedures of mathematics and physics, or the refinements of the general statements of symbolic logic. Because of their nature as evolved vehicles for the statement of myths about parts of the universe observed and defined from an abstract and objective point of view, the learned languages are not of much stylistic interest, except to those who use them. They become institutionalized dialects which those who strive for mastery of their subject-matter have to learn, and because they have evolved to provide a means of exact and non-figurative reference to facts, or what are imagined to be facts, and deliberately to avoid involvement in their uses with the personal feelings of the writers in relation to these facts, they acquire a conventional rigidity of structuring which has to be learnt also. Such forms of language are not likely to allow for much catholicity of choice, for many individual quirks and fancies, which are, one presumes, the main source of interest in style. This is because such forms of language develop rules which are intended to control expression of subject-matter and fix the learned language firmly in it. The way in which what is said, as in the language of law or mathematics, for example, is not so much a personal idiosyncrasy of the writer as a form of expression the writer has to adopt if he wants to express that kind of subject-matter and not any other. Indeed, one might say that at this level of language-use the language and the subject-matter become one, that the language exists only because of the subject-matter, or that it has been created deliberately to express it. In other words, at this level the myth-creation is all that matters and not necessarily the communicativeness of the myth that is created. So refined do the needs of definition and conceptual analysis become that the language has to be adjusted and adapted for this purpose. For indeed, the myth here is a special kind of myth. It is one which fixes a special set of relationships in a hypothesis which can exist only in language. To reduce the matter to a childishly simple example: if one says, for instance, that the heat of fire causes water to boil one has expressed a relationship between two events, the combustion of the burning matter and the boiling of the water, by means of a linguistic device uttered in the words *heat* and *cause*. One has in fact imposed a myth on the external world, and this myth can serve as a hypothesis which can be said to explain the relationship between the two events.

D

The very idea of explanation – the idea that the relationships between events *can* be explained – is another myth behind the myth. There is no reason to suppose, however, that once having accepted the myth of explanation, that the noun *heat* and the verb *to cause* can refer to anything except a hypothetical creation of the mind that observes the events and wishes, for some purpose or other which could be described as explanation, to relate them. In expressing relationships in as comprehensive a way as possible by means of such conceptual analysis one must strive for consistency, otherwise the control and management of such concepts become meaningless. In mastering a learned language, one has also to learn how this consistency of the inter-relatedness of concepts can be achieved, and the inter-relatedness of the elements of the learned language itself, which are precisely defined both as to meaning and method of use, is the only way in which this can become possible. A learned language therefore has its own logic which must fix it and institutionalize it.

When I say that the private language and the learned language have little to offer that is of stylistic interest, I do not mean to say that they have little or no style. For of course they have. And we have already postulated that every use of language must have some kind of style, since what we call style is always a deviation from the norm, and the norm is something abstract which does not exist in any language-use except as some sort of idealization in the background. The style of a language-use, however, can only become interesting the more it deviates – the further away it removes itself from the norm. We are back here in the midst of considerations of competence and performance. A use of language may be badly formed, well formed, or better formed, and even possibly best formed. The well formed and better formed uses of languages represent average performance, and average performance is in itself of no great interest to the student of style except that he must understand what the average is before he can recognize anything different.

2 Deviation

As we have said already, one of the central problems to which the student of linguistics can apply himself is that of the possibility of making statements which have never been made before but which are completely intelligible to speakers of the language in which the statements are made. Any use of language, the moment it comes into existence, is a new creation, a structure of language substance, which can be looked upon as a thing in itself. Since language is symbolic, such creations can actually refer, or have the appearance of referring, to things outside themselves, and also, one imagines, to things in the world external to the speaker or writer. In the affairs of the relationships of property and power, this external reference, real or supposed, provides the reason for the existence of the language-uses, which are adapted to the needs of the activities that take place within those relationships. In this way they become institutionalized in them, for the language-uses exist only in order that the activities of the relationships may be carried on, and those people who participate in such activities need definable points of reference, public and acknowledged, for understanding the conventions of the use. That is why, nowadays, one imagines, weather forecasts are presented in solidified form, repetitive and fixed, and not sometimes in heroic couplets and at other times as arias from Mozartian operas, or why company reports are not written in the same kind of language as that used for the love stories of women's magazines. Such points of reference could be said to be the *grammatical styles* of the language-uses in question, if by the expression *grammatical style* we mean the way in which a choice is made from all the resources of the language for employment in the particular circumstances of the use. And the style, as we have already suggested, arises from the situational context, the sense, the medium and the tenor.

Nevertheless, we have to understand what the average is so as to be able to recognize the below average and the above average. And the best place to look for average performance as well as average competence is clearly among the uses of the public language. This language has the advantage of being easily accessible, of having arisen to deal with a vast range of varied subject-matter, and of having a fairly comprehensive variety of the uses of the language as a whole. It can also display, one would imagine, a quite reasonable degree of well-formedness in many if not most of its samples, since it is largely the work of professionals or of those who shape the language in their daily use of it.

The grammar which we outlined briefly in the previous Chapter can be said to represent the grammarian's abstract idea of the norm of the language as a whole. It is a sort of formula of the greatest possible generality, and stands more or less in the same relationship to any sentence that can be uttered in English as the equation $ax^2 + bx + c = 0$ stands to exponents of all possible quadratic equations.

Every deviation is a result of choice, conscious or unconscious. In looking at one or two kinds of deviation from the norm we could examine single sentences, or what purport to be single sentences, and compare each with its appropriate formula in the grammar. In this manner we should observe, first, that every sentence that we came across was a deviation from the most abstract form of the norm $\Sigma \longrightarrow Subject + Predicate$. If it were an indicative sentence it would, at least, show some kind of deviation of choice by means of its predicate, which would have to be one or another of the five types displayed in the grammar or else one of the four passive transforms of three of them. If it were a question it would show its deviation in at least the peculiarities of its verb component in relation to its subject, and may also be introduced by a special question-signalling morpheme such as *why* or *when*. If it were a command it would show its deviation by means of its lack of subject. And if it were a partial sentence it would show its deviation by means of the omission of one or another of the essential parts of an indicative sentence. The general classification of sentences under the heading of *Indicative* – and by far most of the sentences in the language seem to be in the indicative mood – allows for an important opportunity of choice in making statements about anything in the universe that can have a statement made about it. Allowing for this opportunity of choice is an important part of the theory we propose in this book. It means that the very first kind of choice that can be made, the very first kind of deviation, is that a statement or sentence must deviate from the most abstract generality of the norm into either a predicative or a relational statement.

I propose to give purely grammatical definitions of predicative and relational statements. A *predicative statement* is a sentence, a structure of only one subject and one predicate, in which the finite verb is always intransitive. Thus, all the sentences of Types

I and II in the gammar given in the last Chapte
and so are all passive transforms of sentences
and V. One of the important characteristics of
ments considered as a class is that a very large
contain a finite part of the verb *to be* as an imp
in the verbal segment; many of them contain a ....
some such verb as *to become* or *to seem*; and many of them
contain verbs of motion or negative motion; while all passive
verbs, of course, must make use of some part of the verb *to be*.
There may also occur in predicative sentences some doubtful
cases of what might be called quasi-transitive verbs such as *to
resemble*. A *relational statement* is a sentence, a structure
of only one subject and one predicate, in which the finite
verb is always transitive. Thus, all the sentences of Types
III, IV and V in the grammar given in the last Chapter are
relational.

However, if the first deviation is from the abstract standard
norm of $\Sigma \longrightarrow Subject + Predicate$ into a sentence which is
either predicative or relational, it is important from the point of
view of style to be able to know why any given sentence in the
indicative mood is either one or the other. Answering this
question provides a suitable starting point for the study of deviation. For sentences do not normally exist alone. In the actual
uses of the language, speakers and writers, unless they have
utterly freed what they have to say from any situational context,
often assume that what they are talking about is something
extra-linguistic and they certainly often speak and write, and
behave in relation to what is said and written, as if this assumption had some validity. An utterly abstract, completely non-
representational, use of language, if any exists at all, is very
rare. Even surrealist works, or transcripts of delirium, or the
wildest fantasies in language substance, even, one supposes, those
'glass and concrete' poems which depend more on the typo-
graphical arrangement of words or phrases than anything else
except letters of the alphabet, have some internal cohesion which
bestows upon them a reference to themselves at least. But
normally, when one is talking or writing about something, there
are obviously millions of facts, ideas, opinions, beliefs, points of
view, emotional attitudes, feelings, or whatever, that can be said
about it, that can find some sort of way of being symbolized in

...guage substance. No speaker or writer could possibly have the time and space to utter all these millions of utterances at one go. To call upon the redundancy of the language on such a colossal scale would be to perform godlike feats. The speaker or writer therefore usually selects from all the possible millions of unsaid utterances those few which will say what, for the moment, is thought to be relevant to whatever is thought to be the subject-matter.

In this way a structure is made out of a limited number of sentences, and this structure, acquiring a particular form, can itself become a signal which embodies the message which the speaker or writer wishes to transmit. The structure itself, a thing made out of language substance, is a signal in which the sentences are component signs, and the structure may turn out to be any kind of linguistic entity which can be recognized as having some kind of form – it may be an article in a newspaper, a textbook of astronomy, a joke on the back of a matchbox, or an epic. Normally such a structure will have a theme, or a basic idea, which itself could be expressible in a single sentence, and which stands for or states the policy of the principle of selection from all other possible utterances about the subject-matter.

Such a theme, openly stated or implied, conscious or unconscious, tells the listener or reader the intention or policy of the speaker or writer. It is a means of locating in the universe the possibility of the listener's or reader's understanding of what the speaker or writer is talking about. It says such things as 'I'm now going to tell you what I saw when I witnessed Spurs beat Everton last Saturday', or 'This is how it came about that a girl named Elizabeth Bennett married a man named Fitzwilliam Darcy', or 'I am now on the point of being able to justify the ways of God to man'. These structures of language substance, whatever they are, whether they take on the form of an anecdote of a three-volume novel, a jingle of verse or a long epic, are often built up in phases of external or imaginative reference – external, that is, to the language substance itself, since the reference is to those topics which the author thinks it desirable to speak about when he makes his selection from all the utterances that could be made about the totality of the subject-matter. The speaker or writer, in constructing his speech, talk, sermon, lecture, article, essay, chapter of his book, or whatever, so organizes what he says according to this thematic principle of selection that bits can be found which have a completeness in themselves – they can be signals, that is, which are capable of delivering intelligible messages even though the messages are only parts of larger ones. These are the phases of external or imaginative reference. We could find a paragraph, say, about how the winning goal was scored, or a passage about how Mr Collins proposed to Elizabeth and was rejected, or about Satan's first view of the Garden of Eden. However, within such phases or portions, the sentences are integrated to give cohesion. In this way there arises in them a grammatical internal reference forwards and backwards within each phase. This internal reference forwards and backwards, prolepsis and anaphora, is a property of the language substance, and is a stylistic feature inherent in the sentences.

Although the speaker or writer may not be able to perform such godlike feats as calling upon the whole of the resources of the language to create a use of language which can employ all of them at one go, he is capable of more modest creation. And before creation existed there was chaos. If the construction of some language-use can be looked upon as an act of creation, and presumably it can, for it is possible to put words into the forms of grammatical sentences and make things that never existed before, then it can also be looked upon as making an order out of some kind of chaotic absence of order. Presumably there is a sort of chaos existing in the minds or in the central nervous systems of all individual encoders – existing as a vast entropic reservoir of unused energy, among the brain cells and their electrical charges, among the glandular secretions and the bio-chemic activities, of living men and women, where lie the well-springs of all linguistic motion, the murmur of all lips, the clamour of all tongues, the scratching of all pens, the tapping of all typewriters, the rumble and roar of all printing presses. Provide these vast entropic reservoirs with an impulse, stimulate them into doing something, surprise them with delight, shock them with outrage, titillate them with some ephemeral sweetmeat of living, desolate and stretch them on the racks of misery, and they will respond with speech, science, literature, philosophy. For somewhere among the atoms of the human body lurks the controller which can summon from the darkest recesses the scattered inchoate precursors of language substance which can urge the lips to speak or the hand to guide the pen.

Given, then, the impulse, which is an irritation from the outer world, a sensation in the ganglia, a necessity from acts of living, and the lips will form a sentence or the hand that guides the pen will shape an elegance or an ineptitude. The formula $\sum$———$\rightarrow$ *Subject + Predicate* sits dove-like brooding over the vast chaotic abyss, an ever-present source of inspiration in the time of need; and the speaker or writer is impelled to make the very first deviation into the created ordering of language substance. Because this first deviation is into a predicative or a relational sentence, it will also be a deviation into sense – grammatical if not semantic. From the submerged jumble of the elements of the resources of the language, stored apparently in some kind of filing system which, compared to the ultimate ordering, is chaos, just as the alphabetical list of words in a dictionary is chaos compared to all the daily language-uses that always surround us, are selected those which are most appropriate to the immediate situation. Through all the material put in the unconscious during the course of living, heaped up, one imagines, by numerous conflicting chances in all the exigences of triumphs and disasters, loves and hatreds, pleasures and pains, passions and *longueurs,* of life, and crowded into that underworld where who knows what resides, the formula finds a way. It begins to work. A grammatical subject emerges to correspond in some sort of fashion with the referential subject, or subject-matter, and then waits for its predicate, which the subject-matter decides, until speech is born and language exists. The controller has chosen, for purposes apparent or implicit in the the human situation, an utterance of some form, indicative, interrogative, imperative – a sign in the code, that flies through the atmosphere or lies sedately on the page, so that communication shall flourish among us and so that no man or woman shall be isolated and cut off from the rest of mankind.

But where there is to be continuity – and in those passages which are likely to be of stylistic interest there usually is – the initial act of creation, this first deviation into sense, will have to be followed by others. Once the creative process has started, it will most often have to go on, and take with it, or be urged forward by, some kind of logic of its own. In any discourse, an extended string of sentences will fit together in some kind of manner that is produced by the competence of the speaker or writer. These sentences will not usually be scattered haphazardly into the world by their author, nor will they move about like random molecules of gas under relaxing pressure, but each will acquire something from, and each will contribute something to, a cohesive form of the whole, according to the needs and dictates of its fellows and itself. The second kind of deviation, therefore, will be that into cohesion. For as sentence follows sentence, a language-use will be built up into some kind of form, perhaps a recognizable one. It will normally be a recognizable one, because, one would think, the principle of least effort will be more active than the effort to be original. The vast majority of speakers and writers are like the man who heard voices and said, 'It's not so much hearing the voices that worries me as what they say'. Although some of us may now and then want to create in language substance some structural truth which has not existed before in the world (such as a new form of sonnet or a revolutionary *avant-garde* novel), most of us, most of the time, say what we have to say in conventional or fairly conventional ways, because by doing so we are more likely to find that people will be more ready to listen to us or read us. We may say some new thing, but we express it in existing substantial forms. We make new journeys in old vehicles.

The conventional habit of using existing forms of the language to utter what we have to say, however, can have on occasion the property of throwing some kind of emphasis on the speaker or writer himself, so that the creator is known through his works. Once he has got his subject-matter organized, however well or ill, into its thematic mode of utterance, with the sentences all having the potential of being arrangeable into some kind of structure, the speaker or writer may find, none the less, that he has something of his own personality to put into what he is saying. The style does, for the moment, become the man, or the man becomes the style, for the two become indistinguishable. His being is in the work, and the traces of it are unmistakably his, no matter how frail, tenuous or brief. Indeed, unless he wants to behave like a parrot – and some people apparently do – things could hardly be otherwise. For in many cases the creation is his and his alone, and he may feel that it is so with an ardour whose heat may be able to hatch more chickens. Here we come across another interesting source of deviation, which is neither that of sense nor that of structural cohesion, but is one of attitude. It derives from the author's sophistication in dealing with his medium, from his point of view about his subject-matter and his love for it or his hatred of it or his indifference to it, from his notions about tenor, and from the machinations of his own idiolect or mastery of the language. It gives the language-use a not infrequently agreeable rhetorical flourish, and tends to show itself in lexical choices which are outside the necessity and dismal utility of modifications of subjects and predicates. Sometimes it leaps up into the empyrean and triumphantly stands there in the transfiguration of a brief apotheosis; at other times it dives into the ever-smouldering brimstone at the other end of the cosmos, where it can be equally interesting or amusing.

Most people, when they speak or write, but especially when they write, find themselves stuck in the public language of the relationships of property and power. The day-to-day necessities of the world can supply enough situational context to call forth the language activity of most people, who stumble along through life coping with problems of the economies of nations, of buying and selling, of getting and spending, enmeshed in conflicts and harmonies of government. management, administration, acknowledging status in society and being charmed or frustrated by it; and most people, therefore, rarely burst into song or rise to the greatest heights of imaginative literature. Undisturbed by any bardic afflatus and inhospitable to visits from the Muses, they carry on as usual. However, there are some, here and there, to whom the language itself is a source of perpetual fascination. Such people as these have a need to make structures out of the elements of language not because they have anything particularly new to say – indeed, the most important things have already long since been said – but because these people have a burning conviction that new ways of saying the old things may give a more penetrating insight into them. Here we have the best and most beautiful kinds of deviation that can be found anywhere in the uses of language – deviation into what I shall call conceits. Structures can be found which use all the resources of the language, which call upon as much redundancy as the author wishes for, which are intense with linguistic possibilities, and which turn, as it were, the light of glowing words into many places hitherto dark and inaccessible. When this happens we get imaginative literature. Sometimes we get poetry.

3 Sense

The deviation into sense from primeval chaos is the choice dictated by the kind of thing one wants to say in the situational context in which one finds oneself at the moment of starting one's utterance. But except in the most *ad hoc* and spontaneous cases, the writer or speaker has normally to establish some kind of position. Generally speaking, when we write in the public or one of the learned languages, we want to do one or another of four things, to narrate, to describe, to explain, or to persuade. Our deviation into sense starts from our localizing in the language substance a point on some frame of reference from which all that we have to say can be viewed with intelligibility. Thus, if we narrate, we start with something like 'Once upon a time, there lived a king who had a beautiful but vain and idle daughter . . .', or 'A funny thing happened to me on the way home from the office this evening . . .', or 'Ajax was sitting sulking in his tent, when . . .' Or if we come to describe we have usually to state what we are describing before the description can become a clear one: 'It was a town of red brick, or of brick that would have been red if the smoke and ashes had allowed it; but as matters stood, it was a town of unnatural red and black, like the painted face of a savage.' When we explain we have to give some sort of indication of what the explanation is about, as when some one might say: 'There are geological as well as zoological reasons for the oddity of the fauna of Australia.' And when we argue and try to convince others of the rightness, as we think it is, of our point of view, we have also to convince others that both we and they know what the subject-matter of the argument is: 'It is easy for the noble Lord, the member for Tiverton, to rise and say that I am against war under all circumstances. . . .' Of course, in long stretches of language substance, these four modes of expression may tend to get mixed up, as in a novel, say, where there can be both narrative and description, or in a work of philosophy, where there can be both explanation and argument.

But normally the first deviation into sense has a controlling influence upon what follows. Once destiny has decided, then an inevitability of the fates comes after. We might illustrate by quoting two or three passages of utilitarian prose, of no great stylistic interest, from the public language. I set out the passages not continuously, but grammatical sentence by grammatical sentence, so as to make reference to the parts more simple.

Here is the first:

1.1 Language patterns are best treated from the point of view of the listener or observer, not of the speaker.

1.2 The listener may hear a different pattern from that which the speaker directed his attention to produce;

c   and

1.3 similarly, though to much lesser extent, for a writer and his audience.

1.4 Ideally, we would like to describe patterns from the point of view of speaker *and* hearer;

c   but

1.5 whilst it is easy to take up a hearer's position it is normally impossible to know what a speaker intended.

1.6 Only if the analyst were himself one of the active participants in the conversation could he know what was meant, for some of the utterances.

In this simple little explanation, we have first the choice of a predicative sentence which is there to state the position. It is a predicative sentence because the author is imposing an idea on the universe. There is no absolute guarantee that what this first sentence says is true; it must simply be regarded, from the referential point of view, as a hypothesis which we can either accept or reject. It shows, however, a sophisticated kind of choice, for not only is it a predicative sentence of some abstraction, but it is also in the passive voice. It is a transform of something which could be found in the grammar of the last Chapter to be not in the passive voice at all. It is based on the formula of sentences of Type III. To generate the basic sentence from which it is derived, we should have to make grammatical and lexical choices from a wide range of resources of the language and say something like 'Students of linguistics can best treat language patterns from the point of view of the listener or observer, not of the speaker.' And that in itself is a pretty sophisticated kind of sentence, of great generality, and deriving itself from several others. At the same time it also shows a deviation of attitude implied in the word *best*. In fact, if we wanted to get down to the fundamental utterances which are implied in this transform, 1.1 of the text, we should have a set of basic sentences stating (1) that language patterns exist, (2) that students of linguistics exist, (3) that they treat language patterns, (4) that there are various ways of treatment, (5) that one of these ways is from the point of view of the speaker, (6) that another is from the point of view of the listener or observer, (7) that a third is from some unspecified point of view, (8) that there are at least three ways, (9) that the author has an opinion, (10) that his opinion is about these matters, (11) that that treatment from the point of view of the listener or observer is the best one, and that (12) he rejects treatment from the point of view of the speaker. These at least are some of the assumptions that lie behind sentence 1.1; there are, of course, others which the reader will be able to discover for himself.

The point is that in sentence 1.1 the writer establishes a position, makes a kind of prolepsis or prelude to what is to follow, and the sense of what follows has to be explicated – and one assumes that it will be so explicated – in terms of this established position. Thus, sentence 1.2 has to start, somehow or other, with some kind of anaphora that carries the sense back into one or another of those terms. The author chooses the obvious lexical anaphora and makes the words *The listener* the grammatical subject of sentence 1.2. Since the author has embarked on an explanation, and since what he is giving an explanation of is the hypothesis adumbrated in 1.1, the sense dictates some method by which the explanation can be expounded. The method which the author chooses is that of an appeal to experience. He proceeds to suggest the possibility of observed facts. Consequently, sentence 1.2 is relational and not predicative. The author is not so much imposing one of his own ideas on the universe – giving a hypothetical principle which may dictate or direct possible courses of action – as stating the limits which observation and experience of the world of actuality are likely to impose on the freedom of that action so as to give a reason for making the hypothesis. This sentence 1.2 is the Type III, in direct contrast to its forerunner. However, it has its own deviation from its straightforward Subject-Verb-Object prototype in its permissive modalization of the verb – the use of *may hear* and not *hears*. This is due, one imagines, to the sustained generality of the discourse. The choice *may hear* includes *hears*, so to speak, so that the reader is left with the impression that, although the listener or observer does as a matter of fact normally hear what the speaker intended, there is often the possibility, even the probability, that he might not, and this uncertainty must be taken into account. Sentence 1.3, which appears to be a partial sentence of somewhat cumbersome form, is only granted a place in the sentence string because the author wants, one imagines, to include graphic substance as well as phonic substance in his generalizations.

The explanation which the author has embarked on is, of course, finished by the end of sentence 1.3. But he can envisage possibilities which, if they were realized, would make his hypothesis appear shoddy and inadequate. Here we find ourselves back in the posture of being able to view the situation as a whole from an empyrean standpoint; and from such an exalted position we can see all the snags and difficulties. Sentence 1.4 acquires its form from the prototype of Type III for this reason. The author can speak *pro propria persona*, but because he is speaking about his longings and desires, about what we would like to do, rather than about what he did or does, the sentence takes on a deviation of attitude. It has the prelude of a sentence-adverb *Ideally*, and the verb is conditional – *would like* and not *shall like* or simply *like*.

This sentence is immediately followed by the contrasting conjunction *but*, which hurries the reader to sentence 1.5, a sentence based on the prototype of Type II. Here again we are back in the world of the author's imposition of his thought upon the universe. The sentence is one of this predicative character because of the need to sustain the generality embarked on at the beginning. This sentence has its own prelude of a different sort of sentence-adverb, this time an adverb clause, giving concessive support to the impossibility which is the complement of the main clause. But the impossibility of knowing what a speaker intends (according to the author) is not so general as the abstraction might indicate, and the adverb *normally* has to be brought in to allow for the possibility of the abnormal.

Completeness demands that what is abnormal should be referred to, and so we have in sentence 1.6 a conditional sentence which has an interesting stylistic variation. The conditionality of the analyst's being one of the active participants is carried through from the adverb clause at the beginning into the inversion *could he*, instead of *he could*, in the main clause. And still not satisfied with this reinforcement of the point, the author has to add his personal deviation of attitude in the phrase *for some of the utterances*.

The choice of sentences here, whether predicative or relational, is controlled by the subject-matter, which, of course, is also the choice of the author.

One may note, in passing, one or two other stylistic deviations which give some little linguistic interest to the passage – apart from the interest of the subject-matter. The passage shows, one imagines, signs of hasty composition, an anxiety of the author to get the thought congealed on the page before it vanishes. The partial sentence 1.3, for instance, converts or transposes the word *similarly* from its normal function as an adverb to an unusual function as a kind of pronoun or surrogate for the content of sentence 1.2. Moreover, one might be permitted to doubt, from the leisurely point of view of the critic, whether the choice of *audience* is a happy one, in view of its implied contrasting anaphora with *The listener*. Interesting, too, is the support from typography which, at the phonological level of language-use, the author brings into sentence 1.4, where the italicized *and* seems to be too easy a way of making the point. Such defects as these (as I should say they were) are examples of what might be called noise in a linguistic communication channel.

There is another way in which the chaos of the unorganized resources of the language may be made to deviate into sense. This occurs inside sentences when the universality of reference of some of the words has to be more precisely delimited by various methods of modification. The following example may illustrate:

2.1 The ancient Greek theatre had to be able to hold at least the whole male and free population of the city-state whose religious festival it housed.

2.2 To have built such a playhouse with a roof would have
been quite impossible,

c and so

2.3 the Greeks chose natural, open-air sites on conveniently
shaped hillsides,

c and

2.3 arranged the auditorium as nearly like a bowl as possible
in order that all should see and hear.

2.5 The huge London Palladium today holds 2,388 people;

2.6 it therefore staggers the imagination to learn that in Greece
the restored Theatre of Epidaurus seats 20,000 (and has
perfect acoustics), and that in classical times the Theatre of
Ephesus actually held as many as 56,000.

In its basic form sentence 2.1 could perhaps read something like
Theatre hold population. But in order to make such a general
statement intelligible in its situational context and in the language
activity to which it belongs, the author must tell his readers something about the theatre and the population and also give some
indication of the time of the holding. The answers to such
questions as 'Of what kind or species among the general class?'
or 'Where?' or 'When?', as they are revealed in the structure
made of the language substance, are normally of great importance. They are certainly needed in most uses of the public
language, and especially in the language of information and
instruction, where the referential meaning is what mostly matters.

In sentence 2.1, therefore, such additional information as that
provided by the modifications *The ancient Greek,* and *at least
the whole male and free,* and *of the city-state whose religious
festival it housed,* become vitally important to the message which
the author wants to transmit. Moreover, the tense of the verb,
where, in this case, *had* followed by a couple of infinitives makes
a past tense of the notional content of some such word as *must,*
is a deviation into sense that has to account for the time of the
event it refers to. Deviation of this kind is a necessary component
of the sense of any discourse, and normally the way in which it
starts influencing everything that follows. In the passage under
consideration, for instance, the choice of *had* as the main verb of
sentence 2.1 has an effect upon the tense of the verbs which
follow it, and even on some of the modification which also

comes afterwards. It obviously dictates the choice of *To have
built* and *would have been* in sentence 2.2, as well as *chose* in
sentence 2.3 and *arranged* and *should* in sentence 2.4. It is not
until we come to sentence 2.5 that there is a change of tense.
This in itself, given the primary deviation from unspecific
generality of the first four sentences of the passage – deviation,
that is, following the choice of *had to be able* as a deviation
itself from something like *must* – is a deviation of the deviant.
Once the discourse is started in the past tense it would normally
continue in it, and so the sudden leap to the present is surprising.
The author prepares for this surprise by the premodification of
the adverb *today* before the verb *seats*.

In this passage we can also observe other kinds of deviation
into sense which are dictated by what precedes them. Sentence
2.1 is packed with proleptic information. It is explanatory of the
kind of theatre (using that word to mean 'a place in which
plays are acted' and not 'the art of the drama in general') which
the ancient Greeks needed. Its reference is also objective
insofar as it tends to refer to actual historical events – or, at
least, to events which the author assumes to be actually historical.
The verbs in it are therefore transitive, for the first deviation into
sense, that of the choice of the predicate, leads to the choice of a
relational attitude to the subject-matter. The basic sentence from
which sentence 2.1 is derived is clearly the formula of Type III,
and as sentence 2.1 stands in the text it acquires modifications
and ramifications built on this basic formula and these reinforce
its relational nature, – in fact, it is their stylistic function to do
so. Not only is there the presence of the verb *had* as a finite
verb with an object, but there are also the transitive infinitive
to hold and the transitive verb *housed* in the dependent clause.
But the sentence 2.2 is speculative. The conditional verb *would
have been* makes the announcement that this is so. Moreover, it
is a predicative sentence; its prototypical formula is of Type II.
Nevertheless, it looks before and after. The expression *such a
playhouse with a roof* helps it do do this. The word *such* refers
back to the content of sentence 2.1 and anchors the reference
firmly in the seabed of the haven of actuality. The phrase *with a
roof* looks forward from the historical past into the historical
present and near present, at least, indeed, as far forward as
sentence 2.5. However, the conjunction *and so* immediately

dismisses the speculative nature of sentence 2.2 and leads the reader to the practical and known facts of history which we are told in the two co-ordinated sentences 2.3 and 2.4 – both of them objectively and sensibly relational – their prototype is the formula of Type III. The author, nevertheless, wishes to make a little comment on the state of affairs he has described so as to make apparent to his readers the reality of it. He does so by comparing the past with the present. The adjective *huge*, brought in as a premodification in the subject of sentence 2.5, is a choice which is a deviation into sense. It is necessary for the author to tell the reader that the London Palladium is 'huge' so as to prepare for what follows. The statistics are then introduced, but cannot, apparently, be allowed to speak for themselves. Sentence 2.6 is one of those self-deprecating utterances in which the author wants to convey information in an interesting way, yet doesn't quite know how to do it. Such utterances often start with an irreferential *it*. For what, after all, is 'it' in this case? The pronoun stands for *to learn that in Greece* ... and all the rest of the sentence. Clearly, this information – that which actually does, according to the author, stagger the imagination – is what he really wants to tell the reader. The sentence chooses its own form because of the hugeness of the London Palladium, which has, nevertheless, a mere pittance of 2,388 seats. The paradox creates itself. Although the London Palladium is huge by our present standards, it is nothing compared with the theatres of ancient Greece. The method of exposition depends on the sense, and the sense dictates the sentence form.

Such a thought as this, or perhaps the mere feeling in the bones for the subject-matter of the thought, may suggest, or may have suggested in the past, to some people, that language can actually reflect the objective and external universe. And indeed, through language thought of in this way, men have been able to control and manage what they believe is outside them. They have said, 'If you do so-and-so, something else will happen'; and people have done so-and-so, and something else has consequently or subsequently happened, and men have imagined themselves to be the Lords of Creation. The deviation into sense has made the small two-legged creature, living in a thin layer of air on a small planet bound to an insignificant star, discourse of wonders and then perform them.

In other words, the general conclusion that we may tentatively draw from all this could be that what a writer says may just as often be the choice of the language itself as of his own free-will. A writer can only say what is waiting to be said in the language. The infinite number of sentences that make up the language are, so to speak, already there, lurking in millions of central nervous systems, waiting for and seeking a mouthpiece.

4 Cohesion and Attitude

A deviation into sense is also a deviation into myth. The twin processes which we have endeavoured to suggest – the operation of the general formula $\Sigma \longrightarrow Subject + Predicate$, a misty looming shape gradually acquiring the firmer definition of being either a predicative or a relational sentence, and then taking on an even sharper definition of sense as morphemes show what the subject and predicate are in the language substance – is also a genesis of other creations which spring from it and belong to it. For a discourse has cohesion. It is a structure bonded into one piece by the integration of its own parts, which have adhesive properties, and which do not want to seem to be living alone.

What we understand by the word *cohesion*, which is a name we use for the ways in which larger linguistic structures than sentences build themselves up into integrated unities, we might illustrate by means of the following example:

3.1 *The Theatre of the Absurd* is already a period phrase, re-miniscent of those eager discussions we used to have in the fifties about *The Bald Prima Donna* and the Problems of Non-communication.

3.2 Critical phrases of this sort have the life-span of elastic.

3.3 At first they support the literary stomach admirably, giving it much needed coherence and respectability:

c but

3.4 after a time they get crammed too full, pulled in all directions

c and

3.5 the rubber starts to harden and crack,

c and

3.6 they end up more shapeless than the stomach itself.

3.7 In the early sixties, it seems as if every writer who was not obviously 'socially committed' or 'naturalistic' could be bundled in the same bag: Beckett and Milligan, Genet and Ionesco, Pirandello and Pinter.

3.8 We did not ask if these writers had anything deeply in common.

3.9 They had all rejected Ibsenite naturalism.

3.10 They were all interested in 'irrational' behaviour.

3.11 That was enough.

3.12 They were all writers of the Absurd.

  (*At this point a paragraph ends and a new one begins.*)

3.13 Nor did the definition of the Absurd, given by Martin Esslin, help very much.

3.14 Absurdity, he suggested, was man's response to a world in which the 'certitudes and unshakable basic assumptions of former ages had been swept away'.

3.15 The Second World War had exposed a decline in religious faith which had left man without clues or purpose in an increasingly menacing world.

3.16 Man had become lost, uprooted from religious and metaphysical traditions, without faith or hope:

  c and

3.17 the anguish of his conditions was reflected in the Theatre of the Absurd.

These are the first two paragraphs of a critical article. The author uses them to state a position which, in his opinion, is unsatisfactory. The rest of the article is an attack on this position and amounts, in essentials, to an explanation of why the author thinks that the definition of the Absurd given by Martin Esslin did not 'help very much'. I think it is therefore not unfair to look upon these two paragraphs as a unity, as a created myth (in the sense of the word as used in this book) which is in itself a linguistic structure.

The cohesion of a structured language-use can be looked at from the point of view of its phonology, of its syntax, and of its lexis.

From the phonological point of view one examines a piece of writing to find out how the marks of a script are deployed in the language's graphic substance to record what is primarily speech. For in every piece of writing there is always the implication of speech. What is written could be spoken; certainly it can be read aloud, and in its being read aloud can be meaningful to those who listen.

Generally speaking, one can say that nowadays the ways in which the marks of a script are used in the writing and printing of Present-day English are derived largely from the practice of the printing trades and the conventions established by typographers. Thus, there is widespread agreement about how words should be spelt, and about the main rules of punctuation, about the uses of capitals and italics, and so on.

However, in the passage under consideration we can notice one or two slight inconsistencies, which are apparently due to some inability of the conventions to come to a complete agreement among themselves. For instance, the italicization of the first five words does not, it would seem, signal information of the same kind as the italicization of the words *The Bald Prima Donna*; for the expression *The Theatre of the Absurd* is described by the author as a 'phrase', whereas the words *The Bald Prima Donna* form the title of a play. This second usage, thus italicized and capitalized, is the conventional one, while the first is not. The position is made all the more confusing because the words *The Theatre of the Absurd* also happen to form the title of a book. Nevertheless, those words do – or did – make an expression current in discussion and criticism of the theatre of the fifties and sixties of this century. Also current in the language of literary and dramatic criticism of the same period were the collocation *socially committed* and such words as *naturalistic* and *irrational,* which the author encloses in single inverted commas, as if they were quotations of the same order as that given in sentence 3.14, where the words in the single inverted commas are actually quoted from Martin Esslin's book *The Theatre of the Absurd.*

Perhaps we can see here something of the inadequacy of the written medium as a means of representing what we might call the tone of voice of the spoken medium, which, of course, is a deviation to attitude. We have, first, the same device used to signal two different kinds of information – something, it could be, comparable to the deficiencies of English spelling, where there are sometimes several letters which can represent the same sound and at others one letter has to represent several different sounds. By printing such words as *socially committed* or *irrational* in single inverted commas, the author is indicating an attitude towards them. He is presumably regarding them as clichés of literary and dramatic criticism which could, perhaps, bear further examination, or which have in some unfortunate way hardened states of mind about some modern literature and drama and made some people believe that such literature and drama is something different from what the author thinks it actually is, or which have succumbed to the fate of the elastic in his metaphor and have thus become imprecise and no longer capable of doing their job. But he can hardly be taking the same attitude to the quotation from Esslin, for in sentence 3.14 he is merely reporting a suggestion that was made as a matter of historical fact; he is not presumably wanting his readers to believe that factual reporting is the same kind of activity as thinking that certain technical terms have served their period of usefulness in critical discussion.

This same kind of double signalling of some of the signs of the written language can be seen in the use of capital letters. We use them at the beginnings of sentences, where they not only signal whatever they have to signal as parts of the words to which they belong as letters, capital or small, but where they also signal the information 'sentence begins' or 'the kind of thing I, the author, am going to call a sentence, which may actually be two or three sentences, starts now'. We also use them as the initials of a large and important class of words called proper names and of adjectives derived from these names. We might therefore be tempted to believe that *Problems of Non-communication* and *the Absurd* could be proper names of the same order as *Pirandello* or *Pinter*. The thought gives hints of fascinating areas of speculation. There is no reason why they should not be so regarded, but an interesting question, which is too metaphysical for me to answer, is 'Are they?'

Such considerations as these are clearly stylistic, since they concern deviations from the norm, even though the norm here might be shifting and unstable, and set itself up, as it were, *ad hoc*, so that we might have to establish a special norm for each text we examine. Certainly, a text could acquire its own conventions in these matters, and if it did so, it would be a stylistically interesting text at least so far as these matters were to be found in it. For what one imagines stylistic studies must ultimately aim at is a comprehension of total meaning. The achievement of that aim can be realized only if the student of style can account, in some satisfactory and consistent manner, for the existence of every sign in all the signals which is the communication channel which is the whole of the text or that portion of it considered significant. Where we have signs that sometimes carry this information and at other times that – and we do have plenty of such signs in written English – we must be ready with some kind of apparatus for making distinctions if the text is to be interpreted.

So far we have looked at one or two peculiarities of the non-cohesion of what should be cohesive. These peculiarities are exceptional in this particular example.

At the level of syntax, we have four main aspects of cohesion to consider: prolepsis, two kinds of linkage, and anaphora.

In the first paragraph of the passage above – sentences 3.1 to 3.12 – we can observe three proleptic phases. The first starts at the beginning, with the introduction of the idea of critical technical terms specified by the reference to a particular example of one, 'the Theatre of the Absurd', which is not only proleptic of critical technical terms in general, but also of the whole structure. The author wants to express a point of view about this critical technical term, and he does so by including it among 'Critical phrases of this sort' mentioned in 3.2. Sentence 3.2 begins the second proleptic phase, and the predicate of this sentence *have the life-span of elastic* is proleptic of the metaphor which he sustains and amplifies throughout sentences 3.3, 3.4, 3.5 and 3.6. These two phases are themselves proleptic of the third, that which begins in sentence 3.7, where certain writers are characterized. This characterization is given further definition in sentences 3.8, 3.9, 3.10, 3.11, until the complete definition (or the definition as complete as the author wants to make it) is rounded off in sentence 3.12. The implication of all this is that such an expression as the Theatre of the Absurd, because it is of the sort that is illustrated and typified by the metaphor of the elastic, is not very useful.

The second paragraph of the extract has but one proleptic phase. Sentence 3.13 announces itself to be about the definition of the Absurd given by Esslin, and therefore the paragraph is about that too, for sentence 3.13 is a typical example of a 'topic sentence', one that declares the subject-matter of the paragraph which it introduces. And sentences 3.14 to 3.17 are used to explain what this definition is and to do so with brief objective detail, even though the author's attitude to it, that it 'did not help very much' is made clear.

The stylistic interest of these proleptic phases, and their introductory sentences, is that they localize the myth within the structure and provide a method of organizing what has to be said so that the internal logic of the explication of the myth can proceed in its own way. In the extract under consideration, for example, a contrast between the two paragraphs is interesting because it shows two different methods of presenting this kind of internal logic. In the first of the two paragraphs there is a little flashy showmanship which has to call upon the redundancy of the language to make its point. Sentence 3.2 presents the reader with the nucleus of the metaphor, where lexical matters assist the process. We do not expect to find such words as *life-span* and *elastic* turning up in a discussion of critical technical terms, and, slightly startled, we read on. In the next sentence the collocation *literary stomach* strikes us as even more odd, partly because such an adjective is not the kind to be normally used with such a noun, and partly because we don't quite know what a literary stomach might be. The general idea of what is referred to by *elastic* becomes, as the course of the metaphor develops from sentence to sentence, to be particularized in a special form of elastic device which exists, perhaps, more for the sake of deceptive appearances than for any purpose which might reveal truth. The second paragraph, however, does not need (so the author apparently thinks) any such flamboyant exploitation of the resources of the language to create alien structures within the main structures – pearls or cancerous growths, whichever they might be, according to attitude. It proceeds with straight-forward exposition, saying what has to be said with decorum and sobriety.

Once the main features of the myth of the linguistic structure have been established in this proleptic way, the filling in of details has to go forward with different degrees of emphasis and fullness of outline. As sentence succeeds sentence, each has to be related to its fellows by some sort of linkage. There can be three ways in which this is done: co-ordination, sub-ordination, and anaphora.

Co-ordination is the setting side by side, as it were, or in juxtaposition in time, of two or more grammatical structures of the same grammatical rank. And that, of course, is normally the first rank available in the surface grammar of the utterance, for what is co-ordinated usually has the same kind of semantic reference or has reference in the same area of discourse. There are two main kinds of co-ordination, that of apposition and that of linkage by means of conjunctions. Sentences 3.1 and 3.7 provide examples of the first kind. In apposition we have a device in which, usually, the second, or second and following, linguistic structure or structures particularize the generality of the one that precedes them. Thus, in sentence 3.1, having been told that 'The Theatre of the Absurd is already a period phrase', the reader has the generality of the collocation *period piece* particularized for him by all that follows in the sentence: he is told of which period it is a phrase and of what kind of discourse it appeared in during that period. Or, in sentence 3.7, the list of the names that comes after the colon particularizes the kinds of writers referred to earlier in the sentence.

Co-ordination by means of conjunctions is a method of relating or bringing together in some fairly loose connection parts of phases of discourse, and is a means of signalling the unity of these parts. Thus, in sentences 3.3, 3.4, 3.5 and 3.6, the sustained metaphor of the elsastic is present throughout; these sentences are linked together by the words *but* and *and*, the first showing a cohesion of contrast and the second a cohesion of similarity or consequence.

Co-ordination by apposition is usually tauter and more integrated than co-ordination by means of conjunctions. It is a stylistic feature of the relativity of weight and emphasis in structural cohesion; or, to use another metaphor, co-ordination of both kinds is a feature of the texture of language-use. In sentence 3.1, for instance, the tightness of the apposition allows the author to amplify the expression *period phrase* without distracting from it with the ramifications of a more complicated or extended kind of sentence structuring. But in sentences 3.3 to 3.6, the metaphor of the elastic needs room – or the author feels that it needs room – in which to explain itself. Having grabbed it from the redundancy of the language, the author wants to show it off to the best advantage. There can, of course, be co-ordination by conjunctions of smaller units, as we can see in 3.5, *to harden and crack*, or in 3.16, *from religious and metaphysical traditions*, where the single form-classes, or parts of speech, are co-ordinated.

Subordination is a feature of structuring in which adjectival and adverbial clauses carry forward the creation of the myth by means of stating aspects of semantic reference without which the nature of the myth in its details would be unintelligible. The adjectival clause *we used to have in the fifties about . . .*, in sentence 3.1, for instance, is a necessary ingredient in the structuring of the utterance since the word *discussions* would be unintelligible without it. The same sort of thing occurs in sentences 3.7 and 3.14, where the words *writer* and *world* would respectively be meaningless in their contexts without the clauses which follow them. In fact, subordination of this kind is a form of minor myth-creation in itself. Some such whole expression as *every writer who was not obviously 'socially committed' or 'naturalistic'* shows that words have been put together to create a symbol for a concept which the author has invented. Such a symbol is a component of his total myth, and without it the myth would be incomplete. It represents a stage in the forward movement of the internal logic of the structure.

The stylistic interest of co-ordination and subordination arises because they are features of choice, but not necessarily of a re-stricted choice that is apparent in the creation of basic sentences. We can notice an example of this kind of thing in sentences 3.8, 3.9, 3.10, 3.11 and 3.12, which invite comparison with the sentences that carry the metaphor of the elastic. The *but* and the *and* which are the means of co-ordination for the sentences which carry the metaphor represent a deliberate choice of a means of exposition in which a series of statements, felt to belong together, and indeed connected because of the metaphor that runs through them, are given a stylistic unity in a phase of their own. It might also be said that sentences 3.8 to 3.12 belong to a phase of their own in the internal logic of the structure. But they are not co-ordinated in the same way. Each is allowed to stand by itself, stark and alone, grammatically isolated from the others. It is interesting to note that the showmanship of the metaphor has no place here. The redundancy of the language is not called upon to make an exhibition of any spectacular feats of any linguistic *tours de force*. All is straightforward and business-like; the author is getting near to what he really wants to talk about. Seriousness is apparent, and the language-uses chosen reflect this difference in attitude.

As we have seen, some kinds of grammatical choices are categorical and others are selectional. For instance, in sentence 3.6 the author has no option about the choice of *more* and *than*. This is a categorical choice. The moment he wrote *they end up more*, the conventions of the language made it predictable that the word *than* would follow sooner or later. But in the matter of co-ordination, and also in the matter of most kinds of subordination, the choices are selectional – they can be made or not. The language allows this choice in sentence planning, but limits choices of grammatical form once the plan has been made.

Anaphora is a lexico-grammatical device of cohesion by means of which the continuity of the internal logical structure of a language-use can be sustained. Once a writer has embarked on some discourse and made some kind of proposition, some statement introductory of his myth, he has either to accept it or fail to make order out of chaos. Usually, order is maintained and chaos is defied by means of a sort of negative entropy. Given, for instance, the opening sentence of the passage under consideration, we find that the author has set limits to a small portion of all the possible thoughts about the things and notions in the universe, and directs our attention to that small portion and to nothing else. In 3.1 the reader is given the word *phrase* and the name of one example of the sort of things that word can refer to. In sentence 3.2 the expression *Critical phrases of this sort* refers back to what we have already been told. In a similar way, throughout the phase which presents the sustained metaphor, the pronoun *they* works hard to hold together the sentences in a cohesive pattern. In the next phase the words *these writers* begins to perform the same kind of service, and the word *they* again carries it on. The transition from the first paragraph to the second is helped by the choice of *Nor*, a disjunctive conjunction which can introduce not only a new phase in the argument of the internal logic, but also convey the unity of the author's attitude to his subject-matter which has been already adumbrated. In sentence 3.14 the pronoun *he*, referring back to *Martin Esslin,* has the same grammatical purpose as *they* in the previous paragraph. The apparently parenthetical nature of *he suggested* in this sentence disguises the fact that the sentence is really one whose prototypical formula is of Type III, so that all the rest of the sentence – actually a nominal clause and the object of the verb *suggested* – is given prominence. A clause, of course, whether nominal, adjectival or adverbial, can have all the parts of a basic sentence form, and therefore can have some of the qualities of a sentence. It can, for instance, be either predicative or relational. Here we have a clause whose basic formula is of Type II, and it is therefore predicative. The fact that it is both predicative and a definition is part of the cohesion of the paragraph. This whole sentence, 3.14, has its own anaphora which is the result of its being the kind of sentence it is. It also includes the word *man's* which is proleptic of the anaphora of *man* in sentences 3.15 and 3.16 and of *his* in sentence 3.17.

This kind of grammatical cohesion is a necessity of continuous discourse rather than an ornament. It belongs to the prose of any linguistic structure and not to the poetry of it. Nevertheless, it must not be supposed that the lexical aspect of cohesion displayed by anaphora needs to be entirely whimsical or a product of the uninhibited fancy. A language-use can only be what it is; its own performance is expressive of its own competence. The lexical aspect of cohesion is seen in the choice of words. And here again the author is presented with categorical and selectional choices. Considerations of medium and tenor, constituents of the register in which he is writing, will have their effect upon his style. The register of the language-use is hinted at by the choice of some indispensable words, which must be there, even though there be only a few of them, on which the referential nature of the language-use, if it is to have one at all, must depend. These few indispensable words may gather round them other words that will make structures which are capable, perhaps, of paraphrase in a different kind of medium or a different sort of tenor – as when we can say, for instance, that such-and-such a love poem mentions the cruelty of women, or as when we can summarize the plot of a story. In the actual uses of the language in the everyday intercourse and commerce of life this sort of thing must inevitably happen. For instance, a solicitor explaining some legal problem to a client who has little or no legal knowledge may not speak in the language of an Act of Parliament, though he may have to speak about the same subject-matter as one.

In the passage under consideration, we can find words which may be said to belong to the same sets. These words are obviously necessary if the author is to talk about his subject-matter at all. Such words, we might say, in the first paragraph, are *discussion, critical, literary, writers*; and in the second paragraph are *response, certitudes, assumptions, faith, traditions, condition*. In the first paragraph, the words listed indicate to us that the register could be literary criticism, and the initial phrase of the paragraph, which contains the word *Theatre*, suggests that within the general area of literary criticism we are in that restricted portion of it devoted to the drama. In the second paragraph, the words listed tend to show that we are in the region of human experience which is concerned with the meaning of literary and dramatic works in the larger context of some such topic as the history of ideas, or something like that. However, these words gather round them accretions of attitude and definition. An inquistive reader might ask, for instance, why the discussions were *eager*, what precisely a *literary stomach* is, and what sort of writers are those who are *not obviously 'socially committed' or 'naturalistic'*.

It would seem that after the creative process has directed the first deviation from the norm into language substance which acquires sense, and while the sense takes on the apprehensible structure of form, there is always the possibility of deviation into attitude. It would seem, too, that at the lexical basis of any discourse there is a categorical choice of vocabulary, which places the discourse in its register and localizes the subject-matter among all the incohate mess of whatever it is that could be said about anything whatever in the universe. And built upon this basis, as the structure begins to develop into the thing it is to become, the unique myth which the author creates, are those items of selectional choice of vocabulary which define attitude and give the created myth its uniqueness. But beyond that there is another region, where situational context in the normality of the usual and the unexpected becomes abandoned, and the language becomes dissociated from anything except the wholeness of life itself. The register ceases to be important; roots in the real world are forgotten; the language becomes all important.

5 Conceit

Since any language-use is the result of choice on the part of some human being, it must, one presumes, reflect even in some small way the personality of the human being who made the choice. Very many people, no doubt, in their ordinary daily conversations talk in clichés and behave linguistically as if they had the choices made for them by the conventions of the language itself, for the language must have imposed on them in their daily acts of living a number of linguistic habits without which communication would be impossible. The thinking of many people has been, one imagines, influenced by the language in which are crystallized objectively certain structures representing necessities and usefulnesses that are helpful in the transactions of public business and all the affairs that are carried on in the relationships of power and property. Thus people frame their thoughts and reactions to what is going on in the world and frame them in stereotyped phrases, well-established or transient, and make do with them as best they can. Indeed, for many of the purposes of daily life, originality in the structuring and vocabulary of socially useful language-uses would hinder rather than help.

To say that the style is the man, it would seem, is only to say half the truth in the sense in which we use the word *style* in this book. For there is a distinction to be made between a writer or speaker who uses style and a writer or speaker who is a stylist. The writer or speaker who uses style is some one who fits the choices of his language-uses in a conventional accordance with the uses of the period and the milieu of his own existence. There are many writers and speakers who do this all round us every day of the week – we can read what they have written and hear what they say in most newspapers and periodicals or on the radio and television or at committee meetings and in discussions and conversations that go on in every department of life. The stylist, on the other hand, is some one who is conscious of his choices to such an extent that he makes, as it were, super choices. That is, he treats selectional choices, when he is presented with the need for them, with much greater care and discrimination than the average of writers or speakers. At this point, stylistic studies become interesting.

In the passage which we briefly discussed in the last section, this process can be seen at work. The second paragraph of the passage, sentences 3.13 to 3.17, could be described (as I don't want to sound patronizing) as a competent piece of civilized journalism which says what it sets out to say, but which is in no way distinguished among contemporary writing by its having any remarkable qualities which make it *interesting* in the sense in which I have just used the word. From the stylistic point of view, though not necessarily from the point of view of what the passage as a whole sets out to say, or of its function as a moderately ephemeral language-use, the first paragraph has features of much greater interest. This interest comes from the use of the metaphor of the elastic, and from the way in which it is handled. For here the author has attempted to make a super-choice. He has, for instance, in likening the literary clichés currently in vogue to elastic, made an imaginative leap across the categories of normal experience by calling upon the redundancy of the language in an original way to make some new kind of order out of chaos. He has created something. This becomes progressively revealed as the reader reads on, and the made thing in this phase of the whole of the language-use is given more and more precise definition. Such literary clichés as he is talking about not only have the life-span – another metaphor within the metaphor – of elastic in general, but of artefacts made of elastic which are intended, deceptively, to enhance the appearance of the human person, and which after a time fail to do so because they deteriorate in themselves and thus become unable to function. Whether one likes the metaphor or not – and for myself I am not particularly partial to it – one has to regard it as a thing in itself made out of language substance, that is, as the kind of thing I propose to call a conceit.

It would seem that there are two kinds of conceited writing nowadays current among us.

The first kind is that which shows the effect of science and technology on the use of language. In this kind the author is saying something which he believes is objective, and yet in it human individuality shows through in a very unpropitious way. The human individuality becomes submerged in the mass, and the language becomes an instrument which must always operate in a fixed and predictable manner. The choices which the writer makes are those of whole chunks of a particular register which move about as if they were mass-produced pieces of equipment. The writer becomes, as it were, a negative user of the language and the drilled, well organized mass-protagonist of an anti-style. It is said by some scientists and technologists that the craftsmanship of the past is nowadays to be found, not in the artefacts which decorate and adorn people's homes, but in the engineering and construction products in factories, cracking plant, steel works, and industrial installations in general. One can hardly believe that this is so. Mass-production is more likely to destroy the need for craftsmanship, and transfer to machines a standardization of skills that were formerly in the average competence of human hands. A similar sort of standardizing process seems to have affected a vast and important area of the language.

Consider, for example, the following extract, which is about an electronic device known as a 'variable-mu valve':

> The control which the grid exerts over the anode current is largely determined by the spacing of the wires; when these are close together, the mutual conductance is high; where they are widely spaced, it is low. In the variable-mutual conductance valve, the spacing is gradually changed along the axis of the electrode system. Thus, as the bias is made more negative, cut-off occurs, first in those parts with narrow spacing, and later where the grid-wires are widely separated. The result is an extended characteristic with remote cut-off, as shown in Figure 11. The mutual conductance, or slope of the characteristic, is varied by altering the grid bias, say, by a rheostat in the cathode lead.

The stylistic interest of this passage cannot be said to be very great. But the question, Why isn't it very great?, is one that is worth answering. The answer I would give is that the extract presents the reader with an example of anti-style. The extract shows a language-use which is quite unexciting, safe, conforming, solemn and respectable; and the author has submerged himself, in all seriousness, into the conventions of his register. In the general language of scientific and technological discussion, where the exclusion of author-involvement is almost pathological, there is a tendency for writers of necessity – as distinct from writers of inclination, temperament or talent – to merge style into the pseudo-objective and the factual. There is a notable absence of relational sentences, a predilection for the passive voice, and a selectional choice from a restricted range of clichés to perform many of the difficult linguistic jobs. These clichés lie about on the page with uninspiring lethargy: *control which ... exerts over; is largely determined by ...; the result is ...; an extended characteristic; as shown in Figure ...*

The point is that such utilitarian prose (so its writers apparently think) will be a repository in which earnest seekers after knowledge and truth will find exactly what they want, unambiguously stated, and therefore any kinds of literary frills and fancy-work have to be rigorously excluded.

Much, indeed most, of the scientific and technical prose that can be found nowadays in the language of information and instruction, in contributions to learned journals, in the textbooks intended for advanced students, and in those encyclopaedic volumes which record the vastness of modern scientific discovery, presents the reader with an anti-style. And the presentation of an anti-style shows an attitude which is timid, law-abiding and uncreative. The language which embodies the myths of modern science and technology becomes petrified, for the writers are apparently aghast with horror at the thought of straying too far from the narrow and virtuous path of orthodoxy. The reason is, of course, that the language and the myth have become one. Although the statements made by scientists and technologists in their professional moments are not oracular pronouncements of absolute truth, they tend to behave in human affairs as if they were. This is because large numbers of people accept them implicitly, act upon them, and find that they work, well or ill, promoting the happiness or misery of mankind, for the time being, until better (as some people say) or more comprehensive hypotheses are discovered. For instance, a knowledge that metals expand when heated is scientific knowledge, and technologists, designing metal artefacts, have on hand statements about the co-efficients of linear expansion of different metals which they use to help them in their work; they have to allow for the different co-efficients of linear expansion of the different metals used in the manufacture of, say, a motor-car engine; the theoretical and general statement is translated into the physical fact of the engine, which actually works, which does not seize up in action

E

or distort itself into some ungainly shape, so long as it is operated according to instructions. This kind of Fiat Lux of the scientists and technologists produces minor creations which are different expressions in different media of the same statement, paraphrases of the brain cells' motions in the hardware of technology. The myth of the theory operates through the created artefact, and the created artefact usually does what the myth of the theory tells it to do.

It could be said, I suppose, that the language of all science and technology tends to aspire to a condition of mathematics – a means of stating relationships in a rigorously codified symbolism without ambiguity; or, if that is not enough, and mathematics as we know it nowadays is nothing more than a refinement of what some philosophers call 'ordinary language', then perhaps some kind of symbolic logic is what science and technology need for making statements, not about their myths, but statements which are the myths themselves.

Ideally, this may be so. The institutionalized language of science and technology, produced by so many repetitive minds striving with almost pathological intensity to be impersonal and objective, when really, of course, they are only uttering their own or somebody else's hypotheses and deductions or inferences from them, is chiefly remarkable for its monolithic dullness. An after-noon's reading through some of the back numbers of *Nature* or some other learned scientific journal, just for the sake of savouring the monotony of the prose style of most of the con-tributions, is one of the most boring ways of wasting time that I can think of. But then, no one reads scientific contributions to learned journals just for the sake of the prose style. One reads them to find out what are called facts, or records of the possible or potential activities of non-linguistic entities as these activities are imagined to be in the minds of scientists. And I suppose that this vast institutionalized language, as we now have it in this century which has known the growth and maturity of more people with scientific training than has the whole previous history of mankind, represents a transitional stage between pre-scientific methods of exposition and a more rational and purely scientific statement than can be envisaged for the future. If the vast amount of scientific information is eventually to be coped with and encoded in a rational way, 'ordinary language' just won't do. One must look forward to a time when computers will be able to deal with all possible scientific statements of fact in computer language; when, say, not only will such an enormous corpus of knowledge as that represented by some such library of information as *Chemical Abstracts*, but also all new contributions of research, be stored in computer-controlled information centres; and one can foresee that some new styles of the learned languages will be needed for this.

As things are, however, one must assume that the tendency of most speakers and writers is towards the norm, or if not the norm as we have suggested it in this book, then towards a norm of some kind. Since more scientists and technologists in the world have been brought up in this century to write and think in this institutionalized language of myth that is translatable into fact than in the whole of the previous history of the world, they have developed as part of their training – one can hardly say education – an attitude to the language as a whole which is a result of this myth of total objectivity. I am not in any way attacking this myth, for given the kind of civilization we have to endure, it is clearly a useful and even necessary fiction which has been developed as part of scientific method. Scientific statement, though not impossible without it, would be very inconvenient if it did not exist. But the kind of writing thus produced tends to make towards, as I have said, an anti-style, or a style from which as many stylistically interesting characteristics as possible have been removed. Science, of course, is a super-myth, a series of statements, or hypotheses, imposed by scientists on what they find in the universe, or what, on one hypothesis, is said to be the reality of the universe. It is a series of statements which define relationships which the minds of some men have decided exist among perceived objects. Most of such statements must, in the nature of the case, and because the language is what it is, be predicative. Scientists, therefore, in spreading abroad the conclusions of their work, are able to utter nothing but cerebration. Since this has to be reasoned and exact, has to have, as a structuring made of language substance, its own internal logic, any kind of disturbance of its form of utterance is likely to destroy the whole aim of the expression. At the very highest levels, a few individual scientists may be allowed, perhaps, a little originality in their mode of utterance. But scientists believe – and if they did not, there would be no point in their being scientists – that facts are facts. This must be the basis of their imaginative grasp of reality. And scientists don't work nowadays in splendid isolation, cut off from one another, but in a constant interaction of training new young scientists in being able to cope with what has been discovered and in research, which can only go forward on the basis of what is already known. Therefore a very large part, probably most, of what scientists have to say in the public language, and in the language they use when talking and writing professionally among themselves, has to be as stylistically as neutral as a table of logarithms. Its attitude must be *ipso facto* a negative one of anti-style.

The second kind of conceited writing to be found among us is that which survives from an oral tradition of the past, and which has become, in the course of time, excessively refined and civilized. It can be illustrated by some sort of linguistic analysis of a poem, by considering a poem as a thing in itself made out of language substance. I have deliberately chosen a poem to which I am not entirely sympathetic, for it is sometimes a salutary exercise to try to penetrate into language-uses to which one is intellectually and emotionally opposed. The poem is one by Walter de la Mare, and is called *The Moth* :

> Isled in the midnight air,
> Musked in the dark's faint bloom,
> Out into glooming and secret haunts
>   The flame cries, 'Come!'
>
> Lovely in dye and fan,
> A-tremble in shimmering grace,
> A moth from her winter swoon
>   Uplifts her face :
>
> Stares with her glamorous eyes;
> Wafts her on plumes like mist;
> In ecstasy swirls and sways
>   To her strange tryst.

The small world encapsulated in the three stanzas of this poem is created remote and slightly mysterious by bringing together in the language substance references to unusual notions which the reader has to assent to, for the time being, if the poem is to

have any imaginative significance for him. Such a meaning, of
course, is not literal, in the sense in which scientific writing in
an anti-style is supposed to be literal, for what is referred to in
the language of the poem exists only in the language, and is
imaginatively perceived and figuratively explicated. It is like a
small dream. The way of bringing this about is by saying that in
the world of the poem the things referred to behave in ways
very different from those in which they would behave in the
'real' world, or in the general experience of mankind, outside
the poem. The very notion, for instance, of making a candle-
flame behave in the anthropomorphic way in which it does in
these lines is itself an imaginative perception, a fusion of
humanity and non-humanity, an imaginatively perceived interpenetration of opposites, of a contradiction in the nature of both
humanity and candle-flames. But this kind of contradiction is,
paradoxically, positive – it is not the mere denial of a way of
thinking or feeling, but the creation of a new way of thinking
and feeling, based on cutting across the categories of the normal
and the familiar.

To many people, such fusion, in this particular case, may seem
to be childish. My own personal view is that it is a rather great
deal of trouble over nothing very much. But a personal view is
not a negation of its validity. Nevertheless, some people might
say that it was merely silly to endow a candle-flame with vocal
organs and make it cry, 'Come!'. Such a literal and prosaic interpretation, of course, would itself be just as silly, for it would
miss the point. And the point is that such imaginative fusion,
the leaping of thought across categories of experience, is a kind
of empathy (as some people might call it), or a way of 'feeling
into' what is experienced or perceived, and that this
sort of feeling is what makes the humanity of man's being
human, for it can illuminate and enrich our experience of the
universe.

This poem *The Moth* relies for its effect, as a created thing in
language substance, on its combination of language as sound and
language as image-creating material. These two aspects of
language are in the poem so inextricably bound together that it
is almost impossible to think of one without the other. And what
binds them together is the welding of the linguistic deviations
into sense and cohesion, the essential grammar which gives

structural form to the language substance when it becomes a created thing in itself.

Reading the first stanza, we find that what is immediately striking is the rarity of such usages as *isled* and *musked*. This unusual and perhaps self-consciously 'poetical' use of words tends to obscure for the moment what might be felt at the phonological level and at the level of grammatical organization. We normally think of the words *isle* and *musk* as the names of things – rather fanciful or 'poetic' names, it is true – and not verbs with past participles. This uncommon way of using these words, a sharp deviation from the norm, creates at once the mysterious, other-world atmosphere which is the keynote of the mood of the poem. It also arouses an expectation in the dramatic movement of the poem which is one of the great differences between what is written in an anti-style and what is not – the emotional involvement of reader or audience in the time-span of the work. Obviously, we want to know what is 'isled' and what is 'musked'. At the same time, we cannot help being affected by the sounds of these words. Both are stressed long syllables (the cluster of consonants at the end of *musked* lengthens the syllable considerably), each is the nucleus of its tone-group, and both are contrasted in pitch – the first is high, the second is lower. All these features invoke and sustain the incantatory, hypnotic rhythm of the lines in which they occur, and suggest a swaying, swirling movement appropriate to the sense and the mood.

It is not until we reach the end of the first stanza that the first phase of the movement is revealed to us. This revelation is made by means of the grammar, the sentence structure. The periodicity or rhythm of the lines and the grammar are here welded into one unit, for the first stanza is one longish sentence. And this sentence is a periodic one, that is, one in which the adjectival and adverbial modifications come before the main verb. The first and second lines are each participial phrases which are adjectival premodifications of the grammatical subject *The flame,* and the third line is, presumably, an adverbial phrase which modifies the main verb *cries.* Each of these three modifying phrases fits neatly into the form of the stanza; there is no enjambment, or non-completion of the grammatical sense in a single line. This is an important factor in the integration of the sound and the sense, for the rhythm of the sound moves inexorably with the building up of the images of the sense, and the rhythm thus embodies the movement of the inevitability of the drama with feelings and overtones of remorseless insistence.

The first three lines establish the locale of the events and the décor, as well as invoke the mood. To say that something – we don't yet know what – is 'isled in the midnight air' is at once to suggest its lonely isolation and to do violence to the usual connotation (if there is one) of the word *isle*. But this violence at one stroke removes the tone of the sense from actuality; it is essential for the 'mystery' of the poem. Anything that was 'isled' would normally, one supposes, be remote in a sea or ocean. But this something here – whatever it is – stands by itself in the midnight air, alone in the darkness. The second line is ambiguous – what is 'musked', the midnight air or the as yet unspecified something which is also 'isled'? And what is the meaning of *musked*, anyhow? Is it smelling of musk, or is it white like a musk-rose? The bringing together of the notions of 'dark' and 'faint bloom' is also mysterious, for it is not quite clear what the 'dark's faint bloom' might be. Is it a petal-like evanescence, or a dim glow, or a suggestion of some delicate surface texture as of, say, a just-ripe peach, or is it merely a vague evocation of the combined notions of aura and aurora? Or is it, perhaps, something of a suggestion of all of these? This indefiniteness can only increase the mystery and make the locale of the events become some strange world known only to the poem itself. That this is indeed the point is made clear by the third line, where whatever it is that has so far been described, but is still unnamed, penetrates into and fades among the ultimately unknowable places in the darkness. These places are unknowable because they are *glooming*, that is, gradually fading into the darkness, and because they are *secret haunts*, belonging not to the clear light of day, but to an undefined twilight where nothing is clearly visible, and they are places whose exact locality is not going to be revealed by the suggested ghost-like inhabitants who know about them.

The first three lines, each starting with a stressed syllable followed by two syllables of lighter stress, maintain the incantatory swaying and swirling rhythm, which, as we have said, is so appropriate to the mood of the poem and the sense of its subject-matter. But the last line of the first stanza suddenly and with subtlety brings a change. The hesitation of the first unstressed syllable of this fourth line surprises the reader's already lulled senses, and the three following longish stressed syllables sound like the heavy footsteps of one bearing an implacable message of doom. However, what these three syllables say, 'flame cries, "Come!" ', is ironically contrasted with their sound and rhythm. Consequently, the reader feels, as it were, a smile on the face of the candle-flame, a suggestion of inevitable menace, of satanically prepared disaster, a necessary evil. Although different in rhythm and sense from the first three lines, this fourth line is linked to them, and integrated into the sentence structure of the stanza, by the cohesion of the grammar and by the rhyme.

The first stanza establishes the mood and sense, and it prepares the drama. It does this by a combination of the unusualness of the chief words and by the incantatory rhythm. It states the initial action of the drama, which is strange enough in itself: 'The flame cries'. That is, the flame calls out imperiously; it commands. Yet it does so with some agony, for men cry out in pain, anguish, despair, frustration. This candle-flame, a powerful, burning male symbol cries out in its own way, and it insists. In the real world of objectively observed scientific fact, flames don't cry out – they have no apparatus for making noises. But in the imaginatively apprehended world of the poem, there mere shining of the flame in a universe of darkness is an imperative act in itself, an order which cannot be disobeyed. It reaches out into the darkest corners of the universe, even into places where supernatural beings, or creatures not of this world, try to keep secrets from it, and it is a beacon which speaks but one word in a voice of undeniable authority, even though the sound of that word, whose initial consonant is a choke in the throat and whose final consonant is a pressure of the lips, may be an acknowledgement of selfhood and pain. This word is the climax of the terrible first act in the tragedy of innocence. We know that it is a climax pregnant with the certain catastrophe of the nature of things, because of the sudden change in rhythm and because of the grammatical finality.

At the beginning of the second stanza, the moth, unable to disobey the summons, is forced, nevertheless, to make an entrance worthy of a ballerina assoluta. Again, there is the now familiar pattern of the grammatical modification of periodic sentence preparing the way. At the level of language as sound, the pitch

and length of the stressed syllables of this second stanza echo
those of the first three lines of the first stanza, but that is only to
give impact to the drama of the entrance by means of an ironic
contrast between the great unknown and unknowable places of
the universe and the narrower and bedecked personality of the
moth. At the level of image-making, the drama is reinforced by
the exotic vocabulary of the first line. The words *dye* and *fan*,
standing for 'colours' and 'wings', by means of their reference
to man's artefacts and not to natural objects, intensify the
artificiality of the state of affairs, the dressed and made-up geisha-
like appearance of the heroine.

But once the conflict of the total drama is joined, the pace
has to be quickened. At the level of language as sound, this is
achieved by the short stressed syllables of the remaining part of
the stanza, and by the assonance of the short front vowels in the
stressed syllables of *shimmering, winter* and *uplifts* : though,
again, the consonant cluster at the end of the last of these does
for a moment slow down the pace, as the moth, with whose
appearance we are now no longer pre-occupied, but whose actions
become important, begins to stare in wonder and make her own
contribution to the action of the drama. These short syllables
contrast with the longer ones of the first stanza, so that the
agitated movement of the moth, and her transient life foredoomed
to a pitiful destiny, is set against the steady, permanent and everlasting dominance of the candle-flame. At the grammatical level,
the quickening pace is achieved by shortening the modifications,
so that, although the same general pattern is preserved as in
the first stanza, this patterning is carried forward more swiftly
into the drama. At the level of image-making, the quickening
pace is achieved by means of a more informative vocabulary which
concentrates on the heroine and her activities rather than on
descriptions of the setting.

And, of course, once awakened from 'her winter swoon' –
which expression is only an imaginatively poetic way of talking
about the moth's hibernation, and which becomes a means of
fusing that idea to a means of uttering the moth's realization of
her own destiny – the moth finds that the steady and deadly
glow of the candle-flame is irresistibly fascinating. When she has,
after the mild bravura of her beautifully contrived entrance,
'uplifted' her face and seen the candle-flame with eyes that do

little more than reveal their own beauty and stare without apparent understanding – hence, one imagines, the deliberate choice of the adjective *glamorous*, suggesting the surface only of beauty and not any depth – events begin to move with great rapidity.

The tragic fate of the moth is so compelling that the sentences of the third stanza become shorter and the modification is cut down to a minimum. In this last stanza, there are really four grammatical sentences, but they are telescoped into one another to give the impression of speed. The four sentences are represented by the four finite verbs, *stares, wafts, swirls* and *sways*; their grammatical subject is not in this third stanza at all, but in the second. In each of the two previous stanzas, there was only one finite verb, and this state of affairs enabled the poet to make the sentences longer by the addition of descriptive material – for the drama could not exist without the setting, and before there could be narrative there had to be deviation into sense. But in the last three lines of the third stanza we can see the merging of the grammatical and the image-making components into the interests of the dramatic action. Three of the four finite verbs are here, and the modification is distributed both before and after that which it modifies, but mostly after, so that the headlong movement, expressed by the verbs, rushes forward without, as it were, understanding where it is going, and not knowing where it is until it arrives. The movement, too, becomes erratic. This erratic motion is embodied in the language by the contrasts of pitch and length in the syllables of *wafts, plumes, mist* and *ecstasy*, and in the alliteration of *swirls and sways*.

The final mystery of the whole little mysterious world of this poem is realized with a sudden slowing down of the pace of the movement in the grammatical phrase which constitutes the last line. This line is different in its pattern of intonation from the last lines of the other two stanzas. It begins with two medium stressed syllables and ends with two heavily stressed. Since these last two heavily stressed syllables are also long and cluttered with consonants, they have to be pronounced slowly. The high pitch of *strange* invokes again, along with the ordinary dictionary meaning of the word, the unreality and the mystery; and the lower pitch of *tryst*, along with the slightly archaic flavour of the word, gives the poem and its reader the impetus of a sensation

of fading away – perhaps into the incomprehensible nowhere of
the darkness – but a sensation, too, of nothing definite, nothing
conclusive in the mystery of it all.

What, in plain language outside the world of the poem and
the creative imagination, the poem says is simply that a moth
flies into a candle-flame. But looked at from another point of
view – one inside the world of the creative imagination where
the act of creation can be examined – the poem says nothing of
the sort. It takes it for granted, as part of the general experience
of mankind, that moths do fly into candle-flames; and given that,
it explores an interesting and even exciting facet of this state of
affairs. The poem says that a moth flying into a candle-flame is
like the life of man and woman, male and female, in lonely
isolation on a planet shining with light in the dark vastness of
an incomprehensible universe, and that the beautiful connexion
between man and woman can be contemplated with pity and
terror even in the smallest and most insignificant of things, as it
is seen in the cruelty of the dominating male who, nevertheless,
fascinates the female who makes herself beautiful only for him
so that she can be destroyed by him.

Whether this is the correct interpretation of this little poem,
or whether it is a relevant illusion generated by the reading of
it, is not a very important question. In fact, the question of
whether a poem is to be interpreted at all, except insofar as the
making of some kind of paraphrase of it may give satisfaction
to somebody who cannot be pleased enough with its impact and
the experience of it while it is being read and appreciated, is
not a very important one either. People do what they have to do
if they can. And there can obviously be as many responses to a
poem as there are readers; for a poem is not necessarily so
much what it says as what it does, or as what interpretation is
put upon it by individual readers, or what its emotional effect
might be.

The point is that in this section we have looked at two extremes
of the conceited use of language. In the first, a special kind of
the use of language evolved for a special purpose, there was a
conscious whittling away of all but an exclusively demarked area
of the language's redundancy; in the second, there was an effort
to call upon as much of the language's redundancy as possible.
It is clear, I think, that we have here an indication of what I

shall call the control and management of language activity, an indication of an impulse to give orders and directions to the smaller units in their manner of combining to build up larger structures which have a total meaning made of the information of their parts. This control and this management of the resources of the language are the topic of the next chapter.

CHAPTER IV

CONTROL AND MANAGEMENT

1 Meaning and Information

I wish to make a distinction between the words *meaning* and *information* as technical terms used in the discussion of the grammar of style. To speak generally, one might say that information is provided by the encoders of messages in order to give the messages meaning, and that meaning, therefore, is a totality of the experiences of responding to a given amount of information. The encoder of a message may know, or may not know completely, what he intends or means by the message he hopes to convey when the signals pass across the communication channel. But when the decoder receives and interprets the signals in order to assess the meaning of the message, he has only the information provided in the signal to guide him, and he must respond to this information as best he can if he wants to know what message the encoder intended the signals to convey. Although encoder and decoder have come to some agreement about the items of the code, and the rules for their use, this agreement can hardly, in most cases, be absolute; nor can the encoder expect utter and total sympathy from the decoder; and with those kinds of messages in which the styles of encoding draw upon a large amount of the redundancy of the code, in which, that is, there are marked and original deviations from the norm, the difficulties of the decoder are likely to be increased. Nevertheless, messages do get sent and received, and as a result of their being sent and received events do happen in the world – or, at least, one assumes that the events happen because of the message and are not completely independent of them. We can say, therefore, that some kind of interpretation does take place, whether it is of the right kind or not, and that very large numbers of people understand with sufficient clarity the messages they receive to be able positively to act upon them, and, even, that sometimes very difficult and obscure writers, not at all comprehensible to the majority, have their disciples.

If we assume that stylistic peculiarities are the results of deviations from a norm, and that interpretation of these peculiarities is possible, it would seem that a message can only be understood by means of an act of comparison which notes and takes account of differences. In some way or another a decoder knows that the norm is there, and is able to appreciate deviant signals as such because this is so. The differences, it could be said, are differences in the amount of meaning. As soon as the abstract formula $\Sigma \longrightarrow Subject + Predicate$, for instance, takes on its first deviation into sense in being either a predicative or a relational statement it begins to have some meaning; as it grows into a structural unity or part of one it acquires more, and then if its creator endows it with some sort of attitude and conceited distinctiveness it acquires most of all. We might indeed go on from this idea to construct a linguistic law, and say that the farther away from the norm an utterance deviates then the greater is the amount of meaning it contains. This can happen because to make an utterance deviant an author has to put information into it that is not in its basic prototypical form; the utterance has to have the information of the norm as well as of its deviances; and the more information the author puts in, the more meaning it will have. This idea also accords with one of the main notions of mathematical Information Theory, which says that a signal of very great probability – such as 'Good morning' – will have very little information-content, and that a signal of very low probability – such as *Hamlet, Prince of Denmark* – will have a large amount of information-content; all of which is only what reasonable people would expect.

However, when we come to consider the doctrine of interpreting signals – and we must come so to consider if we want to understand about style – we encounter difficulties. For we want to know what information means, so that we can discriminate among different sorts of information. And we have also to decide, if we can, what sort of a question we are asking when we ask what information means, otherwise we shall miss the significance of the differences that make what is deviant not the same as the norm. To say that the farther away from the norm an utterance deviates the greater the amount of meaning is

to raise problems of interpretation and of meanir
are presupposing that an author, when he makes
deviant, put the right information into it to do
that he understood perfectly what he was doir
suppositions may not always be reliable. For instar
like the following, taken from a technical journal, is abundantly
deviant: 'Motorways involve a varied number of structures
over their length, ranging from major bridge structures to minor
culverts.' The interpretation of this sentence, if it is decoded
according to the rules, could lead to flights of odd and unusual
fancy – such as, of motorways curling up like clockwork springs
in order spirally to enwrap structures whose quantities varied
from time to time, or of motorways constantly changing their
size as they become transmogrified into bridges and culverts, or
of both of these wonders happening simultaneously. Yet we
know that this is not the correct interpretation of the message.
We know that the participle phrase starting with *ranging* was
not really intended to modify the noun *motorways*; we know that
a varied number of structures really means 'many different
structures', and that *over their length* really means 'across them'.
We know, in other words, that the writer did not intend the
fantastical, and we either hold up the sentence as an example of
how to commit solecisms, or, if we are civil engineers not concerned with grammar, we assume that what he says is true. On
the other hand, when we come across an utterance like the following, we expect to be transported to regions where imagination
can be allowed to do almost what it likes:

> And from the other opening in the wood
> Rushes, with loud and whirlwind harmony,
> A sphere, which is as many thousand spheres,
> Solid as crystal, yet through all its mass
> Flow, as through empty space, music and light:
> Ten thousand orbs involving and involved,
> Purple and azure, white, and green, and golden,
> Sphere within sphere; and every space between
> Peopled with unimaginable shapes,
> Such as ghosts dream dwell in the lampless deep ...

To go from incompetence in the use of the language to a portion
of what many have considered to be among the highest reaches

of it is to try to understand the range of possible deviations. We have, therefore, if we want to understand fully all the processes of deviation, to come to some sort of decision about what is the meaning of the norm in relations to possible deviations from it. The purpose of this chapter is to inquire into this problem. We have to ask, and try to answer, the question, not what is the norm, but what is the meaning of the norm and how does it control and manage meaning.

The name *semantics* has in this century been given to the study of the concept of meaning, and semantics is at once a science, a philosophy, and a kind of discipline of thought which has many applications in sciences outside linguistics. A dangerous assumption of semantics and of those who profess the discipline is that meaning can exist apart from its ontogenesis as an analytical concept, and that we can talk about some such notion as the meaning of the word *meaning* in a meaningful way. There are many people who seem to believe that because a word exists in a language there must be something outside the language for it to refer to. Indeed, without fictions to believe in many people would be lost, and certainly thousands of writers would have nothing to write about. And when we come to apply the word *semantic* to communication by means of language, and say that by the word we intend to mean 'having to do with meaning', confusions are likely to occur. Apart from the well known emotional connotations of some words for some people and the problems of the insubstantial nature of symbols, there are many other difficulties. Chief among them for our purposes are the confusions that could arise over which meaning, of several possible meanings of the word *meaning* and kinds of meaning there might be, we are supposed to be talking about. Especially in dealing with language do these confusions arise, because, I suppose, we tend often to think of language-uses as dead and petrified, and then proceed to examine them in that false unnatural condition, as if we were believing that the biography of a man could be deduced from his corpse.

But if we think of language-uses in their contexts as living acts of communication, we can observe, I think, several different aspects of meaning, or even different kinds of meaning, attached to them. In one sense, the spoken word has no meaning unless it is heard and understood, and in the same sort of sense the written word is meaningless unless it is read and the message deciphered. Certainly, without interpretation there is no communication, and one could argue that an attempted act of communication which does not succeed in communicating is meaningless. On the other hand, there is, for the encoder of the message, some sort of meaning in the attempt. The man on the desert island who put the message in a bottle and hurled it into the ocean certainly meant, or intended to mean, something, even though the bottle and the message were never washed up on a distant shore. From another point of view, Alfred de Vigny's poem *La Bouteille à la Mer* is just the opposite; de Vigny believed, or pretended to believe, that his poem had meaning which could not be understood by his contemporaries, but he published it nevertheless, and some people, apparently, did understand it. Just the opposite of de Vigny, at the remotest pole away from him, was the man who wrote about the motorways – the words he put down on the paper did not say what he meant, though he thought they did; the words actually mean something different from what he intended them to mean, although we, his readers, know what he meant in spite of the words he did as a matter of fact write. At the encoding end of the communication channel there can be the extremes of competence and incompetence, and all the places on the scale in between, which can be regarded as an intention to mean something or other. When these different degrees of competence are translated into the performance of the signal they are reflected in its form and in the kind and amount of information that the signal contains. If the signal finds decoders, there can be the same sort of range from woeful incompetence to extraordinary skill in the act of interpreting it. Something is observable here of the grand and careless, uneconomic, inefficient prodigality of nature, as in the hit-and-miss attempts to ensure the survival of species, in which among many millions of potential acts of fertilization only a comparatively few succeed.

To try to make things as simple as can be, we have, I think, to try to distinguish among three main kinds of meaning, and then concentrate on one of them. First, there is a meaning of intention in language-uses. This is what the encoder intends to mean, or thinks he intends to mean, when he encodes the message and puts the information in the signal. Clearly, his performance is likely to vary with his competence. Second, there is the meaning of interpretation of language-uses. This is what decoders of the signal think the message is and what they think it means, for decoders have, of course, only the signal itself and the circumstances in which it reaches them to go on. The communication channel may not be a direct route, either in space or in time, from encoder to decoder, but may have, over a period, gone through many winding ways and devious paths, as when, for instance, the printed word has arrived at print perhaps through the intermediaries of secretaries, publishers, editors, printers, proof-correctors, and even, in some cases, alas, through censorship. It may even have come to the decoder through social and historical change from stranger and different habits of former epochs, and even, perhaps, through translation from a foreign language.

Nevertheless, for both encoders and decoders, and for any intermediaries there may be along the route of the communication channel, the language itself is there as a medium to be dealt with. It has certain intractable properties which eventually put up a firm and implacable resistance both to those who want to be as original as they can be and those who want to curb freedom of speech. If we want to speak or write English, then we have to use English words, English methods of sentence construction, and though we may be careless about the rules of grammar our carelessness is about something which undoubtedly exists, and which, in main outline at least, is known to all who speak English. So, in spite of human frailties at either end of the communication channel, or in spite of noisy interferences that may spoil the purity of the signal on its way, there is, embodied in the medium, in the language substance, a controlling influence which acts as an arbiter between the extremes of design and exegesis. It is here, presumably, that we must look for what is to be our guide to this third kind of meaning. For this controlling influence, a vague and in many cases by no means consciously apprehended knowledge of some insistent but insubstantial presence, must be somewhere in the norm of the language and in its grammar, for it is that which orders and directs morphemes or words into their proper places in utterance, and which, over many millions of language-uses, marshals the components of discourse into some kind of comprehensible arrangement. It is that which compels us to construct the pattern *he says* and not *he say*, and that which enables us to know the differences between aggressor and victim in *George hit Harry* and *Harry hit George*.

I propose to restrict the word *meaning* for applications to the larger units of language structuring, and to use the word *information* as a name for the smaller units which control the structuring in ways, good or bad, which eventually produce the finished signal, or what the encoder thinks of as the finished signal, which is what the decoder interprets. Thus, we can speak of the meaning of a sentence, but of the information provided by the parts – morphemes, words, phrases, clauses, subject and predicate, and so on – that make up the sentence. Or, we could speak of the total meaning of a literary work, say, even if it contained many sentences, but the information in the work, considered as a linguistic structure, would be what gave this total meaning; it could be both the sentences themselves along with their relationships to one another, or their cohesion, and the grammatical parts that make up each. Information, in this sense, is a quality of the norm, and its meaning is that of generally localizing and defining the total meaning in a sort of continuum of all possible meaning. It is as if all the sentences, say, or possible grammatical structures of the language, already existed as having been uttered, and were classified in the actually existing items of their use in everything that had ever been said or written.

2 Some Lexical Aspects of Information

In this sense of the word *information*, we can think of it as a kind of regulator or controlling influence in the linguistic apprehension of what is happening among speakers and writers of the language when they speak and write. We might define the word, when we use it here, as a property of the components of signals that can make them effective as conveyors of messages. And by *effective* we mean having a quality or property of stimulating an adequate response to the signals, – although what an adequate response to a signal might be is very difficult to say, since the adequacy of such a response can be decided only by a value-judgement on the part of somebody or other who looks at the response and the circumstances in which it occurs. It is impossible to be definite, for responses can differ not only according to what the signal stimulates in the decoder, but also in the decoder's ability to be stimulated. Such a response, of course, is the response to the stimulus of a sign. Outside language we can think of all sorts of responses to signs, and some of these we could regard as adequate. If somebody sees a black cloud approaching from the horizon, for instance, he might say that it was a sign of rain; or somebody might respond to a change in the direction of the wind by believing it to be a sign of a change in the weather; an unusual noise coming from the engine of a car might be a sign to the driver that something was wrong; or the smell that makes one's mouth water as one approaches a kitchen could even be a sign that a dish that one liked was being prepared. The believing in the coming of rain, in a change in the weather, in the wrongness of something in the engine, and even the act of salivating could all be adequate responses, in the sense that they would be agreed to as such by a very large number of people.

But responses to linguistic signs are not quite so simple. This idea of the meaning of information as being found in a response to a stimulus derives, of course, from the notion of information as an instruction to choose, which belongs to Information Theory, and also from what is called the analytical or referential theory of meaning, which belongs to semantics. However, the important point about a linguistic sign is that it is more than a sign – it is also symbolic, and at the same time quite arbitrarily so. All that this means, of course, is that language is used to refer to things or ideas, or to the ideas of things and ideas of ideas, and that sometimes different words stand for different things and at other times the same things. A man whose name is William Smith, for example, can be referred to by means of a vast number of linguistic units which are not *William Smith.* He could be referred to as *sir, daddy, darling, he, the man in the grey overcoat, the tall insurance clerk/prime minister/Sussex county cricketer/former trade union leader,* and so on; and yet any of these linguistic units could be used equally effectively to refer to somebody else. There is no special or necessary connexion between linguistic units themselves and what they stand for. This notion of the reference of words or linguistic units to things and ideas in general is a very loose one and often very vague. The word *bicycle,* for instance, is a much more precise one than the word *thing,* since it has a more limited range of reference, so that when we say that words refer to things it might be difficult to know if the word *things* means anything at all. To what extent words actually refer to things is a very difficult question to answer. The differences between primary and secondary intension on the part of the encoder and the actual understanding on the part of the decoder are not like differences between fact and fiction, but more like differences between comprehension and incomprehension. Outside the window of the room in which I am writing these words there is a tree. Having read that sentence, in which the words *tree, window* and *room* are given primary intension, the reader can have only the vaguest of ideas of what is meant by those words as the writer understands them. And even if the word *tree* is given secondary intension and changed to *sycamore*, the reader is not really given very much more information. Yet the sentence creates a fiction which the reader is almost as much the author of as the writer; all that the writer has done is indicate certain areas of significance in the great vastness of the universe, and from this great vastness the reader selects from his own experience of *rooms, windows* and *sycamores* a little nodule of recall and recognition. The words symbolize for him probably much more of his own experience than of the writer's. Then, again, there are some words whose symbolism, if it exists at all, must be extremely doubtful. Such words as *the* and *a* cannot be said to stand for things in the same way as words such as *tree* or *window,* and although words like *in* or *outside* may have some kind of spatial reference in some cases, it is difficult to see how being *in a room,* say, is quite the same sort of *in*-ness as being *in London* or being *in the mind* or being *in an emotional state.*

Such difficulties as these, of course, arise from assuming that words are the units of linguistic communication. It seems that it is not what linguistic units are so much as what they do that matters in this connexion. When we ask what linguistic units do, the answer that most readily springs to mind is that they combine together into syntagmatic relationships in structures. For those who like to think in mathematical terms, we can say that in this sense of syntagmatic relationships a total linguistic structure, the signal that conveys all the message, shows signs of having negative entropy, a measure of some order compared with a very large amount of disorder. A total linguistic structure, say, a book, a novel, an article in a magazine, is a partial ordering of the items of a code, which, before the ordering was complete, existed in a state of disorder; the gradual writing of the book, the novel, the article, or whatever it was, became a process of reducing part of this chaos to some kind of arrangement, which is the complete message. The cohesion of the work derived from the relationships of its parts will give it a meaning of its own as a total structure which tells somebody something, or at least, which can act as a stimulus to which somebody can respond in his own way. If we reverse the process, and analyse the completed message into its constituent parts, then we restore each of these parts to the positive entropy, or the disorder, of the code. For a chapter of a novel has less meaning than the whole novel, a paragraph less meaning than a whole chapter, a sentence less meaning than a whole paragraph, a word less meaning than a whole sentence, and so on, down to the individual grapheme, which has no meaning at all in relation to the whole novel, but of which it is, nevertheless, an integral part. In this descent, we pass from meaning to information, for, of course, each part, however small, certainly has information, and certainly helps build up the whole structure, even though, in relation to the whole structure, it has little or no meaning.

Considering language at the grammatical level, we can distinguish four kinds of information. We pass across the communication channel from encoder to decoder in talking about these kinds of information, which must exist, of course, both inside and outside actual language-uses.

First, we can have what might be called lexical information. The encoder of messages has his own stock of linguistic items which form a primary regulator for his ability to encode messages. He shares with some other speakers of the language a knowledge of what these items do and how they should be used. Not all encoders have the same sort of knowledge, of course, for some have only a limited stock and others a very large one. But unless an encoder is totally committed to malapropism, he will understand in a conventional way the usage of the main items of his stock; he will know the general area of reference of any of these items, and the general limitations of its use without any specific reference attached to it. The knowledge which the encoder has of this information is, like that in dictionaries and books on grammar, to a certain extent based on experience of usage. It is a record of his learning of the language and a sign of his ability in learning it. An encoder's or decoder's knowledge or awareness of some linguistic items may, of course, be sometimes rich with connotations derived from sensuous and participating experience in activity with actual things the linguistic items refer to, as, for example, a cabinet-maker may know and understand the feel and texture of different kinds of wood because of sensuous participation with them in the activities of his craft; but generally, one imagines, a close apprehension of the interpenetration of thing and idea cannot be much more than an elusive consciousness of existence. As a rule, we can say that this lexical information is rarely found in actual language-uses, except in dictionaries and discourse and books specifically about language. Nevertheless, both encoders and decoders bring whatever knowledge they have of lexical information to their interpretation of what they are doing when they encode and decode messages, for this knowledge, vague and tenuous though it often must be, is an essential and controlling part of the pre-arrangement of the language-code.

Second, every utterance in the language can be said to have some kind of content, to refer to some areas of supposedly real or actually imaginary human experience, or to exist in some register. The information that makes the decoder aware of this content, or the information that the encoder puts into the language-use in the hope of making the decoder aware of it, can be referred to as referential. This referential information defines in a general way what is the subject-matter of the language-use or what the language-use is intended to be about. Thus, in the sentence quoted earlier, 'The ancient Greek theatre had to be able to hold at least the whole male and free population of the city-state whose religious festival it housed', such linguistic units as *The ancient Greek theatre* or *the whole male and free population* give examples of referential information. In more ambitious uses of the language there can be several layers of referential information dispersed over the whole. If one asks, for example, what is the subject-matter of *Hamlet*, one can find that there are several interconnected localizations of experience which are indicated by several thematic distributions of referential information which is stated or implied. There is such referential information as that which refers to the revenge motif, that which deals with the intergenerational conflict, that which deals with the theme of incest, that which deals with the exigences of political power in opposition to individual freedom, that which deals with the exhibitionism of art, that which deals with the irrationality of human relationships, and so on. However, except to be noted as the basis upon which all other kinds of information in language-uses are built, as well as the total meaning, referential information is of not much stylistic interest, unless we arrive, as in *Hamlet,* at an exceptional work of literature in which the style, as it were, draws up the referential information into the total meaning, and thus produces some new creative activity in the language.

Third, there is what we might call functional information. There are some linguistic units in the language which in themselves have no direct means of making any reference to things or ideas or to the qualities of things or ideas, but which are necessary in the manipulation of those linguistic units which do have that means, or which are necessary in the construction of such units. Generally speaking, we can say that all the nouns, adjectives, finite verbs and adverbs in the language are capable of making this direct reference, and are the main units which carry the burden of referential information, and that all other words or morphemes are not. Thus, we can regard all pronouns, prepositions, conjunctions, modal operators of verbs such as *do, does, will, would, shall, should, may, might, ought,* and so on, all relative adverbs or subordinators such as *as, because, since, although, while, until, unless,* and so on, all interrogatives such as *how, when, where, while, what, why, whence, whither,* and so on, all determiners such as *a, an, any, the, this, that, those, all, some, no, my, his, her, their, our,* and so on, all inflexions of verbs which show contrasts of number, person, tense or finitude, all noun inflexions which show contrasts of number, and adjectival or adverbial inflexions *-er* and *-est* which show contrasts of comparison, as linguistic units which provide functional information. Such units as these can be used to construct other linguistic units, as when, for instance, we produce some such name as *the Board of Trade* or *the Duke of Wellington,* where the units *board, trade, Duke* and *Wellington* could be said to be suppliers of more general referential information. But in addition to such small units as these the language has other and more far reaching units of functional information which help to control the pre-arrangement of the code when signals are made. Such functional units as these are those which regulate and marshal the total deployment of morphemes in intelligible orders in sentences, as those which regulate the cohesion of paragraphs, or which decide on the formal characteristics of whole language-uses, which, after they have been used, enable the decoder to tell the difference between a sonnet and an epic, an essay or a novel. Once the encoder has been compelled or inspired towards language activity to encode a message, the formula $\Sigma \longrightarrow$ *Subject + Predicate,* producing a predicative or a relational sentence, begins to localize in the language substance the necessary referential information. What that supplied by the referential information is or does has to be marshalled into a conventional arrangement of functional information, which supplies the structural necessities of the eventual discourse. How conventional the arrangement may be is a matter for the individual encoder. If it becomes too unconventional it may baffle a large number of decoders, though it may fascinate a minority of them.

Fourth, we can distinguish what might be called contextual information. For as soon as it comes into its completeness the eventual discourse will begin to exist as a thing in itself, a newly created artefact in the world, crude or polished, primitive or sophisticated, made of breath or ink, and it will symbolize something. What it symbolizes will account for its existence, even though there may be some doubt about whatever it was that deserved the trouble of being symbolized. But in general, the area of human experience, real or imaginary, which it symbolizes will also account for its register; in particular, the aspect of that human experience which it symbolizes will determine in a more or less exact way how, within that register, the language substance is treated by the encoder and ought to be treated by the decoder. The components of sense, medium, tenor and style will spring from the context, and, in many exalted cases, in which the author was a stylist and not just a user of style, the language-use may call from the decoder sensitive responses and sophisticated appreciation beyond the ordinary. As a thing in itself, as a created artefact, the language-use will be structure made of its own parts, which will fit together in their own way, with all their own cohesive properties, and thus the language-use will be able to supply its own situational contexts for its own information and its own linguistic units. This is the source and nature of contextual information, which can be said to be the sort of information that any language-use supplies about itself or its parts. For instance, the very simple language-use *the Board of Trade* supplies its own contextual information about the way in which the decoder should treat the word *board*; it tells him, for example, what not to do – not to treat it as if it referred to a piece of timber, or not to regard it in quite the same way as he would if it turned up in the collocation *board and lodging*. Whenever contextual information is provided, and it is provided very often, a linguistic unit begins to take its life from its environment, which endows that unit with properties of linguistic sophistication it could never have else-where. Famous examples spring to mind. When Othello says, 'Honest Iago,' the word *honest* takes on a significance which it can only have in the context of the play *Othello*. When Henry James circles round the word he is seeking he seems to be creating a sport of spiral aspiration towards contextual information. When Burke said, 'But the age of chivalry is gone. That of sophisters, oeconomists, and calculators, has succeeded; and the glory of Europe is extinguished for ever', he provided scornful contextual characterization of economists and calculators that they have deserved ever since.

It should be clear that contextual information is of great stylistic interest. In fact we might say that the contextual information of a language-use both controls its style and allows its style to flourish. The matter needs more extended con-sideration.

A language always has its rules, the built-in redundancy of the prearrangement of the code, and these rules condition the language habits of all speakers and writers so as to impose re-straints upon such excessive originality as, in most cases, utterly meaningless utterance. When Ophelia said, 'They say the owl was a baker's daughter,' she was in her madness creating a linguistic structure, in which, also, the bringing together of the referential information provided by the words *owl, baker's* and *daughter*, and arranging it in the way it is arranged by means of the functional information of the nominal clause used as an object of *say*, and of the words *the, was* and *a*, produced a new thing in the world which had the potential of symbolizing the imaginative perception of some kind of extension of consciousness. To say that Ophelia was mad, and that in the reality of the world bakers don't have owls as daughters, is to miss the point. The important thing to remember is what Ophelia did not say: her utterance did not take on some such form as 'A they was daughter owl baker the 's say'; she put the words in the order in which she did put them, the order of a perfectly good grammatical English sentence. In other words, in spite of her madness, in spite of her quality of having different mental processes from other people, still she obeyed the rules.

Perhaps *rules* is not quite the right word to use. The word *rule* gathers round itself ideas which suggest other words, such as *regularity, regulation, uniformity, standardization, practice, custom, usage, habit, routine, observance, convention,* to say nothing of *order, precept, instruction, law, government, restraint, control, authority, command, domination, power, tyranny, absolutism, dictatorship,* as well as *injunction, charge, exaction, imposition, ukase, edict,* along with such adjectives as *rigorous, severe, exacting, harsh, austere, despotic, uncompromising, mandatory, compulsory, coercive,* and verbs such as *to check, to trammel, to debar, to shackle, to constrain, to subjugate, to enjoin, to confine, to prohibit, to refuse,* and so on.

In what we are speaking of here the general semantic field (as people call it nowadays) of the word *rule* has something to do with the idea of 'deprivation of freedom'. But the notion of checking and inhibiting too much nonconformity of self-expression is an enemy of the notion of style and a great supporter and encourager of the notion of anti-style. Perhaps, instead of using a word like *rules* to describe the conventional and social usages of the language, one could borrow from chemistry the idea of valence, and say that certain linguistic forms have a tendency to combine and cohere with one another, whereas others do not have this tendency. Thus, determiners and adjectives combine with the nouns they modify in the manner of some conventional patterning to form nominals which can, at least partially, be recognized as such because of the pattern. We naturally say *the ancient Greek theatre,* for instance, and not *theatre Greek ancient the* or *Greek the theatre ancient,* or even, except perhaps in an index, *theatre, the ancient Greek.*

What we discover when we examine this idea of valence is that it is largely a property of referential information which is used in the management and control of contextual information, and that it is in the valency of certain kinds of formulations of language substance that this property can be observed. I would suggest that there are five areas of language substance in which we can look to notice this control of contextual information taking place.

First, at what is probably the lowest grammatical level of this phenomenon, we have what are called paradigmatic relationships. A paradigm is a set of linguistic forms which are representative of a large group of forms because of some characteristics which all the forms of the group share. In English, as with many other languages, the paradigmatic relationships among groups of forms are shown by affixes, that is, morphemes which normally do not exist in language-uses by themselves (except in dictionaries and books on grammar), but which acquire a life and a usefulness of referential information when they are attached or bound to other forms. Thus, the English prefix *un-*, although it carries the general semantic reference to the idea of 'not, no, negative', is never used by itself, but appears in combination with other forms to give polarity of referential information to those forms, as in *unsafe, unhappy, unreasonable,* where the forms *safe, happy* and *reasonable* can supply referential information in their own right with, in this instance, what would normally be thought of as positive assertion. The existence of a large number of affixes in English can be looked upon as a method of controlling and managing referential as well as lexical information, since, if an encoder or decoder knows a particular cluster of forms made up of base and affixes, he can also know, with several exceptions nevertheless, the referential or lexical information of a cluster of other forms with a different base but the same affixes. Thus, in such a series as *report, return, refer, reject,* etc., the prefix *re* will always indicate some such notion as that of 'back' or 'again', as *reject,* for instance, carries the referential information of something like 'throw back', and could be contrasted with *inject* or *abject.* In a similar sort of way the suffix *-ion* or *-tion* produces nouns or words likely to have nominal referential information, although in Present-day English many words that started as nouns can now turn up in actual usages in the modifying position of adjectives, as in such expressions as *population problems* and *Information Theory*. It could be noted in passing that prefixes normally tend more towards referential information than suffixes, which tend to be more apt to provide functional information. The opportunities for stylistic deviation among paradigmatic relationships are not large, but they do exist. A good example can be found in Lady Macbeth's apostrophe:

> Come, you Spirits,
> That tend on mortal thoughts, unsex me here;

where the imperative of the verb *to unsex* is clearly a deviation of some kind or another. Presumably, Lady Macbeth did not wish to change her sex, as the *Oxford English Dictionary* seems to suppose, but to abolish it by becoming a devil incarnate; abolition of sex, but for a nobler purpose—

> Beat purer, heart, and higher,
> Till God unsex thee on the heavenly shore
> Where unincarnate spirits purely aspire!

—was recommended to George Sand by Elizabeth Barrett Browning.

Secondly, the language is capable of bringing together elements that already exist as morphemes which can supply referential information, and by compounding them to produce new morphemes, whose referential information, though different from that of the component parts, can nevertheless be deduced from them both, though not from one of them. Thus, the words *birth* and *place* both exist as separate morphemes, but when combined into *birthplace* make a new word which is understandable by decoders. Such compounds have their own rules, if that is the right word, for their formation, as can be seen from the two words *boathouse* and *houseboat*. It is the last element of the compound that normally assigns the word to its probable register. And even this rule is observed in the making of audacious compounds:

> Nor dare I chide the world-without-end hour
> Whilst I, my Sovereign, watch the clock for you;

or as with Browning's 'Ciphers and stucco-twiddlings everywhere',
though perhaps Browning's more ambitious effort—

> While, treading down rose and ranunculus,
> You *Tommy-make-room-for-your-Uncle* us!

—being so inclusive, may waive the rule for the moment. But
when adjectives result from the compounding, as with *hell-deep
instincts*, or as in—

> —what's the creature, dear-divine
> Yet earthly-awful too, so manly-feminine,
> Pretends this white advance?

—also from Browning, the rule still holds.

Thirdly, we can have what are known as syntagmatic relationships. It is the usual procedure for words to be arranged in
structures according to a conventional order, but they seem to be
put there, on many occasions, by a deliberate choice of the
encoder. However, sometimes the valency of certain words
brings them together into associations which acquire a life and
a lexical information of their own in particular registers, and
this lexical information seems to be reserved, as it were, for
special occasions. Such groups of words are called collocations.
The result of the use of a collocation is that, when a decoder
comes across one in decoding a message, he knows at least
approximately the area of reference of the combination of words,
and therefore, perhaps, if his knowledge of the language is wide
enough, he knows as well the register to which it belongs. Thus,
the word *high* has the general lexical information connected with
'great or specified upward extent', and this information is
neutral with regard to thousands of examples of its use. But,
combined with other words in habitual association, the word
high can help to form collocations which are normally used in
definite registers, as with *very high frequency*, which brings it
into the register of radio engineering, or with *High Treason* or
High Court, in the register of law, or *High Church* or *high altar,*
in the register of comparative religion. A distinction should be
made, perhaps, between what might be called lexical collocation
and what some linguists call, or used to call, grammatical collocation, for which a better name is probably *colligation*. In grammatical collocation, or colligation, which is always a matter of

structure, only certain types of morphemes habitually find themselves in some environments and are definitely excluded from others; as, for instance, *am* is found in close association with *I*, or *he/she/it* with present tense finite verbs ending with *-s* or *-es* (in the written medium), or the determiner *that* with singular nouns and the determiner *those* with plural nouns, and so on. Colligation of this sort, or grammatical collocation, restricts the choice of encoders very rigorously. Lexical collocation restricts choice in more or less the same way, but not so rigidly, since it does allow transgression of the rule for purposes of witticism or stylistic deviation. Thus, the following words all belong to the same semantic field: *new, fresh, recent, novel, up-to-date, latest.* But one could not apply them indiscriminately as modifiers in nominal segments and hope always to produce the same effect on decoders. We can talk about a *new idea, a recent idea* or *a novel idea*, but such an expression as *new news* seems odd, although *recent news, up-to-date news, latest news* are all quite permissible, and the question 'Is there any fresh news about so-and-so?' strikes one as normal. On the other hand *novel news* might run the risk of being ambiguous – it could be news about the latest novels, and the ingenuity of journalists has now surely been exhausted in the effort to provide novelty. At the same time, we can talk about *new bread* and *fresh bread*, but are hardly likely to say of bread just out of the oven that it was *novel* or even *up-to-date* or *recent*, though we could talk of the *most recent batch.* However, stylistic treatment of collocations can make them interesting, usually by endowing a word in an old collocation with a new contextual information. An unhappy and miserable sort of collocation is a cliché, and among clichés the expression *living beyond one's means* is an old one, but when Oscar Wilde said that he would have to die beyond his means, he did at least show that some clichés have some usefulness. He also demonstrated a well known method of stylistic deviation, that of taking something out of a linguistic structure or frame of reference of lexical information and putting something else in its place. One is smitten with a pleasant surprise to find something where it wasn't expected. The word *ago*, for instance, is one that cannot exist in usage unless it is part of a collocation. In millions of its uses it appears heralded by some time-measuring noun, as in *a year/week/month/century/day/*

million years/moment ago; such a usage has become an almost necessary cliché in our talking about past time. But the now famous example of Dylan Thomas's *a grief ago*, and the probably derivative example in a popular novel, *two Martinis ago*, show that kind of disturbance of the familiar and the sort of wit that can tend to make literature what it is.

Fourthly, it is possible to think of words in an aspect of their lexical information as occurring in sets. A set of words in this sense consists of a number of words gathered round a word of nuclear information, and all these words present allied but slightly different information, lexical, referential and in the end contextual. Those at the centre of the set, so to speak, are more general, or of primary intension, and those existing nearer and nearer to the periphery become more and more particular and peculiar to special registers. We have already given an example of a set on page 155, where we alluded very briefly to the word *rule*. The general idea or nuclear information of such a set is something like that conveyed by 'control' or 'regulation', although it is not always likely that everybody will agree about where among the words of a set the nucleus lies. In the particular set we were talking about, such words as *order, law, command, authority, government, tyranny, dictatorship, supervision, custom, usage, habit, restriction, routine,* and so on, would no doubt find a place, but exactly where that place would be in relation to the nucleus it is difficult to say. For the moment a word is taken out of a set, where it lies, of course, with only its lexical information to distinguish it as a thing to be usable, and is employed upon some business by an encoder, its mere lexical information, though still there in the language-use, is now enriched and decorated with contextual information. When Milton was at pains to point out that the husband was the dominant partner in the first and prototypical marriage, he said:

> For contemplation he and valour formed;
> For softness she and sweet attractive grace,
> He for God only, she for God in him;
> His fair large front and eye sublime declared
> Absolute rule . . .

and the word *rule* itself takes on the forbidding sternness of both an unbreakable precept and a reprimand. Wordsworth,

however, could make the word say something entirely different
and appropriate to a different kind of paradise:

> The creatures see of flood and field,
> And those that travel on the wind!
> With them no strife can last; they live
>   In peace, and peace of mind.

> For why? – because the good old rule
> Sufficeth them, the simple plan,
> That they should take, who have the power,
>   And they should keep who can.

The words of any set, of course, must spread out in many cases
and overlap with the words of other sets, for there can be no
really sharp division between any two sets; and if, somehow or
other, one tried to make such main divisions as one could, as
in a thesaurus, one could deal only with lexical information.
The existence of collocations and the possibility of imagery at
once preclude a rigid cutting off of the items of one set from
another. From the set we have looked at, for instance, we could
take the word *habit* and give it more or less the same contextual
information as *rule*, as in 'The good people of Königsberg made
a habit/rule of setting their clocks by the time of Kant's daily
walk.' Or, words can be made to cut across the categories of
information supplied by sets: the word *riding-habit* at once
springs to mind.

   Language is an activity that appears among the social relationships of human beings, who, because they live in societies, must
always try to make some compromise between order and
originality, between the needs of the community as a whole for
regular, undisturbed, uneventful social cohesion, on the one
hand, and the needs of each individual member for the free
expression of his own personality on the other. Because the
appetites and ambitions of most individuals are so strong, society
as a whole normally has the upper hand in this conflict, in
language as well as in political and economic affairs. Speakers
of a language attempt to hold the balance by imposing on the
language, in a presumably evolutionary process, a number of
patterns at every level, so that each individual user has to use
whatever portion of the code he is able to master in ways that
can be more or less predictable.

F

It is when originality wins and some gifted individuals use language in unpredictable ways that matters can become interesting.

The fifth area of language substance into which we can look to find control of contextual information is in imagery. An image is a use of language which provides instantaneous definition of the contextual information of the main lexical items by drawing freely on the redundancy of the language-code.

At any rate, that description or definition of an image will have to do for the time being. Imagery is also called figurative language.

In the past, figurative language was believed to be a kind of ornamentation deliberately added to what I have called referential information by speakers and writers for the purposes of pleasure and persuasion or to make what was said more vivid, vital and convincing. We realize nowadays that those who are specially skilled or gifted in the use of language, who are capable of creative construction of language-uses as things in themselves, and who are uninhibited by a compulsion to deviate into an anti-style, very often use figurative language as a way of thinking and feeling, and that a sensuous apprehension of reality can be communicated by means of a sensuous apprehension of the language's resources. It is in this way that one of the most important functions of language, that of its use as a means of sharing experience, rather than its use as a *soi-disant* means of making statements about the world, is transmitted.

Unfortunately, in our time a mystique has developed round the topic of imagery. A kind of existential philosophy is apt to creep unawares into any discussion of it, because, I suppose, imagery ultimately defies intellectual analysis. An image, in some respects, is like a joke, and a joke, of course, is something that exists for its own sake; either we see the point of a joke and laugh at it or with it and enjoy it immediately or we don't see it at all. And if we don't see it, then from the joke's or the joker's point of view that is just too bad of us; so far as we are concerned the joke was born to blush unseen, and whatever mirth-provoking properties it had were wasted on the desert air of our incomprehension. If, however, we seek to be enlightened, and ask for an explanation of the joke, bafflement is just as likely to ensue, for the joke will not respond easily to being treated in a logical way. It would disappear, and a new sort of joke emerge. A *lecture expliquée* of the joke which was intended to reveal its point to the uninitiated would be bound to fail, or at any rate, it does not seem probable that spontaneous and hearty laughter would attend its climax. This existential nature of certain kinds of language-uses, like jokes and imagery, is what makes them unlike the myth-creations of science. *They cannot be paraphrased.* Although, in the myth-creation of science, language and myth have become, so to speak, one flesh, this becoming one flesh is only a marriage of convenience, and is a marriage in name only, for it is hypothetical and replaceable. For instance, I can easily paraphrase the statement that the force attracting two bodies is proportional to the product of their masses and inversely proportional to the square of the distance between them, by saying $F = mM/d^2$, where F is equal to force, m and M to the masses of the two bodies, and d to the distance between them. And I can use any units of measurement to represent these quantities – I could measure d, for instance, in miles or inches, metres or millimetres, li or versts. But this is not so with an image, which is a language-use that exists free and responsible for itself in its own right, without the obligation of reference to anything except itself and its own uniqueness.

At the basis of every image is the notion, wise or foolish, of presenting the listener or reader of the language-use with a distracting analogue. This presentation combines both the process of making the analogy – which is purely linguistic – and the use of the imagination – which is far-ranging and referential, getting the language to do menial jobs for it and very often being a flamboyant and arrogant taskmaster. These two forces pull in different directions; and, since in the more fruitful images the language-use is pulled more strongly by the imagination than by the process of making the analogy, this distraction away from the referential information into the contextual is correspondingly the more powerful. The tendency is for the force to impel the language-use away from its structural or grammatical normality into the most deviant paths of deviation. The state of affairs is not unlike the mad Ophelia's sentence about the owl and the baker's daughter. The form of the utterance is straightforward enough, but the bringing together within that form of disparate elements, or bits of different lexical information from different and not obviously related sets, and making them harmonize and go like lovers hand-in-hand, can be the cause of all the bother. The powerful pull of the imagination is to be noticed especially in those worthwhile images which embrace the insight of a cosmic significance in the human condition, be it good or bad, favourable or depressing. At one level, the image,

> As flies to wanton boys, are we to the gods,—
> They kill us for their sport,

is a very simple one, of no great linguistic complexity. For as a structure of language substance it merely sets side by side a couple of sentences, one predicative and one relational (though admittedly the predicative one has an elegant inversion), which state the analogue and reinforce the statement with a statement giving a sample of the analogue's activities. But the point is that the simplicity of the language-use considered as a grammatical structuring is at variance with what it has to say.

And this is the point of imagery. The myth-creativeness of the author cannot function unless the resources of the language are strained beyond the limits of paraphrasable referentiality, since what an image says has never been said before, and the language is used, not to fasten its potential of referentiality firm on the earth outside the kitchen door where everything is familiar, already known, and explored, but to create, and one cannot create what has already been brought into existence. No doubt some learned exponent of English literature has endeavoured to expound to his students the following lines:

> The whole earth is our hospital
> Endowed by the ruined millionaire,
> Wherein, if we do well, we shall
> Die of the absolute parental care
> That will not leave us, but prevents us everywhere.

But the effort of exegesis will never produce an understanding equal to that of the first impact on the sensibility of one already prepared by some cultural environment or other to receive them. The language becomes not so much a vehicle for the transmission of ideas which can be communicated in a number of different media, as say Ohm's law can be stated mathematically or in ordinary language or translated from its original German into a very large number of other languages, but the language becomes a thing in itself *par excellence*. The experience of listening or reading becomes, through imagery, a different sort of experience from that of simply decoding; it is an experience in which the universe, or a portion of it, is not analysed but integrated.

However, we must be careful about the use of the words *imagery*, which is the name of a genus, and *image*, which is the name of a specimen of a species of the genus. The use of these words here has nothing whatever to do with any kind of artificial imitation of the external form of any object, for, in spite of the words *like* or *as* which sometimes turn up in some primitive images, there is very little, if any, genuine mimesis in the creation of pure imagery. Nor has the use of the words anything to do with such metaphorical uses as of 'a picture in the mind, or mental picture', whatever that might be, nor with any mental representation, nor necessarily with what the eye sees, nor necessarily with something used to illustrate or illuminate or make more clear or more vivid. An image is merely a way of using words in certain syntagmatic relationships. The fact, if it is a fact, that such a way of using words may suggest mental pictures or representations, or may stimulate the recall of miscellaneous memories, or odd nostalgias, or may even provoke the consciousness of exciting possibilities, is quite irrelevant. It is irrelevant, at any rate, to a linguistic discussion of imagery.

As we said, at the basis of every image there is what I have called an analogue. We can define an analogue in this sense, a purely linguistic one, as a word or expression of a different lexical set, and therefore of different lexical information, from some other word or expression. Thus, we can pick out any two words – that is, nouns, adjectives, verbs or adverbs – from two different sets and say that each is, or could be, an analogue of the other.

An image is a use of language which relates or substitutes a given word or expression to or for an analogue in some grammatical way, and which in so doing endows that word or expression with different lexical information from that which it has in its set. An image, in this sense, is merely a linguistic device for providing contextual information. The spectacular way, however, in which some images are now and then capable of doing this has given them an extra-linguistic prestige of great rhetorical and literary importance, which also, of course, makes them stylistically very interesting indeed, since they become markers of a style as opposed to an anti-style.

It is possible to make an approach to one aspect of imagery by considering scalar differences in different kinds of language-uses which produce what might be called virtual and real images. We can ascend from real to virtual images by moving, if not from the ridiculous, from the trivial to the sublime. For instance, at the lowest end of the scale, we might have some such utterance as that of the golf professional who says, 'Hold the club like this', where the pronoun *this* stands for the extra-linguistic actions which the professional visually demonstrates with his hands. In this case, the social usefulness of the message, in which the amount of language activity is very meagre, is supported by extra-linguistic signs, and these signs are the real analogue which influence the contextual information of the words *Hold the club*. Of all the numerous ways there are of holding a golf club they specify the particular one in question. Consequently, the word *this* in that utterance is a sort of imperative which directs attention away from the language activity. But if some one, in a situation which supplies the context for a great amount of language activity, and therefore calls upon the language to pay greater regard to the sense by specifying what that sense is, says something like, 'Plastic fibres in motor-car tyres are like the steel frames of concrete buildings', we have a tendency towards a less real and more virtual image. This is because the form of the utterance is more or less the same as the previous one, although within that form there is a greater amount of language activity. Even so, the analogue, *the steel frames of concrete buildings*, is again a sort of implied imperative directing the listener or reader to seek to confirm outside the language activity the contextual information which it bestows on the grammatical subject of the sentence. Suppose, however, that the writer of the sentence had said, 'Plastic fibres in motor-car tyres are like the steel skeletons of concrete buildings'. The word *skeletons* would have become the analogue of some unspecified word or expression, which might have been *frames* or some synonym, and the amount of language activity in the utterance would have become greater because the redundancy of the language would have been called on, and the analogue – the word *skeletons*, given its own

contexual information by the phrase *of concrete buildings* –
would have to do double duty since it also gave contextual information to *plastic fibres* as well. In this case the implied comparison becomes, as it were, more embedded in the language
activity of the utterance.

The point is that as we go up the scale and notice the
differences in the language-uses which produce images we find
greater and greater amounts, as it were, of contextual information
and correspondingly smaller and smaller amounts of referential
information. In this way, as we reach the top of the scale the
language-uses become more and more deviant, and consequently
more creative and more stylistically interesting. In a use of
language which is rich in imagery, we can see that this is so:

> Look, how the floor of heaven
> Is thick inlaid with patines of bright gold:
> There's not the smallest orb which thou behold'st
> But in his motion like an angel sings,
> Still quiring to the young-eyed cherubins,—
> Such harmony is in immortal souls;
> But whilest this muddy vesture of decay
> Doth grossly close us in, we cannot hear it.

On this scale of imagery, some images, of course, are quite
commonplace – *in his motion like an angel sings*, for example –
because the simile is the most elementary kind of image, and
the relationship between the analogue and that to which the
analogue gives contextual information is most dogmatically
explicit. The referential nature of the whole tends to limit the
genuine creativity. A good and creative image needs the assistance
of some added rhetorical necessity or embellishment to make it
worthy of being relished for its own sake as something new in
the world. A neat antithesis can help:

> Here lies Nolly Goldsmith, for shortness called Noll,
> Who wrote like an angel, but talked like poor Poll.

Or, better, some grace in the analogue and music in the
utterance:

> True ease in writing comes from art, not chance,
> As those move easiest who have learnt to dance.

Or a little gathering of analogues needs to be mixed with spices which give a little richness:

> She never told her love,
> But let concealment like a worm i'th'bud
> Feed on her damask cheek: she pined in thought,
> And, with a green and yellow melancholy,
> She sat like Patience on a monument,
> Smiling at grief.

Or the whole thing can be done in the grand manner:

> As when the Tartar from his Russian foe,
> By Astracan, over the snowy plains,
> Retires; or Bactrian Sophi, from the horns
> Of Turkish crescent, leaves all waste beyond
> The realms of Aladule, in his retreat
> To Tauris or Casbeen: so these, the late
> Heaven-banish'd host, left desert utmost hell
> Many a dark league, reduced in careful watch
> Round their metropolis . . .

Even when the image advances to the status of a metaphor, and the analogue and that to which the analogue gives contextual information become fused, there is not always what might be called complete linguistic assimilation. A distance exists, or is felt to exist at least in the *moeurs* of the time and in the currently common way of classifying ideas, between the sets of the words involved in the making of the image. At some periods this distance is felt to be greater than other periods, according to the notions of the age, the taste of those who regard the image, and their conception of what is fitting and appropriate. The conceits of the Metaphysical Poets were not to the taste of Dr Johnson, for instance, and he said that some of them were far-fetched. In Dr Johnson's view, that is, the distance between the sets was very great indeed. However, a personal view, even if representative of the epoch in which it is expressed, does not deny the validity of the objection for all time. But sometimes the distance is so great that the connexion between the analogue and the word or expression on which it is to bestow contextual information is not always clear. Sometimes a chronic weakness in the image shows that the journey to a distant set was ill-conceived in the first place. The encoder has to tell the metaphor to explain itself. Swinburne's lines, for example,

> The lilies and languors of virtue
>   For the raptures and roses of vice,

show this defect. Such phrases as *of virtue* and *of vice* lower the metaphors on the scale of value since they act in the quasi-imperative way of turning back the deviation from the norm into the contextual, before, so to speak, it actually gets there, and thus make the would-be contextual into something referential. The best metaphors are those which show a complete integration of the elements of the language's redundancy into the message:

> Now entertain conjecture of a time
> When creeping murmur and the poring dark
> Fills the wide vessel of the universe.

But the trouble with a large number of images is that they flow in and out of language-uses in such a manner that it is not always clear whether the encoder deliberately put them in any particular language-use, whether he was actually conscious of the figurative nature of the words he used, or whether the whole episode was a blunder or a happy accident. All images have a metaphorical aspect in which the analogue performs its task of contextualization with more or less definiteness. Some images thus achieve the heights, some are metaphors *manqué*, and some just lie about in the language as the debris of historical change and, perhaps, the happy spark from heaven that fell on some now forgotten encoder. Some kinds of words can be found to contain metaphors that are no longer regarded as such by encoders who use them. There must be millions of users of the word *complicated* who never think, at the back of their minds, that it once meant 'folded together'. On the other hand, some words clearly recognizable as metaphors, as when we speak of the *mouth* of a river or the *shoulder* of a motorway, are not, apparently, normally felt to be so; one certainly doubts if many people consciously think of such words as metaphors when they are used. Still less, one imagines, do many people nowadays, unless they self-consciously remember what they were taught in their youth, think of many of the familiar usages of metonymy and synecdoche as having pretensions towards metaphorical and analogic syncretism of linguistic information.

The built-in redundancy of the uses of language is a safeguard against excessive originality on the part of encoders; without the rules, or whatever one cares to call them, of the language, without the pre-arrangement of the code, there would be little or no means of linguistic contact between man and man. But at the same time, the existence of the redundancy can offer encouragement to those who wish and have the talent to be original. What the language has not yet been called upon to say deserves as much consideration as what has actually been said already. The kinds of ways of using language that we do not habitually use on our ordinary everyday communicative acts are just as important as the routine utterances, and usually far more exciting. What individual users of the language find in the connotations of the words which are their heritage, what new relationships among the complexities and still hidden resources of lexical and contextual information, and how they can be called upon to relate and to illuminate the relationships of things in the universe, what understanding of man's feelings and emotions for all that he can know about, must always be of interest to the rest of mankind. What the imagination can perceive in these relationships, what originality of language-use can express, and what the imagination can perceive, have in the past produced uses of language that men have always held in high esteem. The redundancy of the code, or that part of it which is of such apparently improbable use that it never achieves average use, is not for that reason of impossible use, and it is the source of literature. Poetry, drama and fiction rarely say anything that is new; they keep on repeating old ideas about man and his relations with the universe, and deal with perennial themes of his continually striving to assert himself, through love and hate, folly and courage, evil and death, disasters and triumphs, and all that makes him barbaric and civilized, cruel and compassionate, whatever he is; but all the time, poetry, drama and fiction speak on these themes with always renewed originality of insight that is obtainable only through language. It is only by means of repeated exploitation of the language's redundancy — 'raids on the inarticulate' – that literature is created. Poetry, drama and fiction combine into a whole three aspects of man's living: they represent language used as a form of playing, not working, of abandoning for the moment the responsibility of being alive; they represent language used as exploration, of prying into every nook and cranny of life that is to be found; and they represent language used as a kind of revelation, a way of thinking and feeling about man's apprehension of reality as an immediacy of one form of experience.

3 Subject and Predicate

We must now return to the grammar which we earlier gave in outline in order to examine it in more detail. What we have to try to describe is the way in which the grammar can control and manage the kinds of meaning it is possible for single sentences to express. These kinds of meaning, of course, can only be said to be kinds of meaning for each separate sentence, and the kinds of sentences we are dealing with are only those of the norm. There are two points which we have to bear in mind here. First, when single sentences are found in their normal environments they are not single sentences with a unique life of their own; they are parts of discourse; and as parts of discourse they are likely to have features of cohesion which can connect them to the other, or some of the other, sentences in the same discourse. In this manner they immediately lose whatever meaning they have when they are considered as separate sentences, and they become units of information or signs making up the whole signal, the total discourse itself. Second, and in spite of this, the whole discourse must begin somehow. This beginning can be said, in a rough and ready way, to be a conception in the mind of the encoder which is capable of being uttered in the form of a single sentence which can, somehow or other, be related to a prototype in the grammar of the norm.

For instance, Henry James's novel *The Portrait of a Lady* is undoubtedly a discourse, and a long one at that. James's own account, in his preface to that novel, of 'the light in which Isobel Archer had originally dawned', is long-winded but full of interesting information about this original conception in the mind of the encoder:

Trying to recover here, for recognition, the germ of my idea, I see that it must have consisted not at all in any conceit of a 'plot,' nefarious name, in any flash, upon the fancy, of a set of relations, or in any one of those situations that, by a logic of their own, immediately fall, for the fabulist, into movement, into a march or a rush, a patter of quick steps; but altogether in the sense of a single character, the character and aspect of a particular and engaging young woman, to which all the usual elements of a 'subject,' certainly of a setting, were to need to be superadded. Quite as interesting as the young woman herself, at her best, do I find, I must again repeat, this projection of memory upon the whole matter of the growth, in one's imagination, of some such apology for a motive. These are the fascinations of the fabulist's art, these lurking forces of expansion, these necessities of upspringing in the seed, these beautiful determinations, on the part of the idea entertained, to grow as tall as possible, to push into the light and the air and thickly flower there . . .

The 'idea entertained' is simply 'This is an engaging young woman', and that is that, a simple predicative statement of Type IIa.

So much by way of preamble: now for less exciting stuff. What we are setting out to do is examine the sources, in the language, of 'these beautiful determinations', for, no matter how tall it is possible for them to grow, it is they which provide the basic and controlling influences on the information which writers have to produce in order to make the total meaning, whatever it might be, of all their discourses. In other words, we are about to examine the limits of the kinds of information that can be put into discourses, so that from there it might be possible to see how deviation deals with these limits, and more or less where it is that deviation starts from.

Let us suppose that some tedious fact-finding and preliminary fieldwork among the data which can be found in some language-uses and in the central nervous system of the grammarian have been done, and that the grammarian's description of what he considers to be the norm can be set out in the form that follows, which is an extended version of the grammar given on page 64:

C1 $\quad\quad\quad \underline{\Sigma} \longrightarrow S + \text{Pred}$

C2 $\quad\quad\quad S \longrightarrow$

$$\begin{bmatrix} \text{pronoun}_1 \pm \text{mod}_1 & \dots (1) \\ \text{proper noun} \pm \text{mod}_2 & \dots (2) \\ \text{noun} \pm \text{mod}_3 & \dots (3) \\ \text{clause}_2 & \dots (4) \\ \text{phrase}_2 & \dots (5) \\ \text{verbal noun} \pm \text{mod}_4 & \dots (6) \\ \textit{there, it} & \dots (7) \end{bmatrix}$$

C3 $\quad\quad\quad \text{Pred} \longrightarrow$

$$\begin{bmatrix} V_1 \\ V_2 + \text{Comp}_1 \\ V_3 + \text{Obj} \\ V_4 + \text{Ind Obj} + \text{Obj} \\ V_5 + \text{Obj} + \text{Comp}_2 \end{bmatrix}$$

C4 $\quad\quad\quad V \longrightarrow \text{finite verb} \pm \text{mod}_5 \quad \dots (8)$

C5   Comp$_1$ ⟶

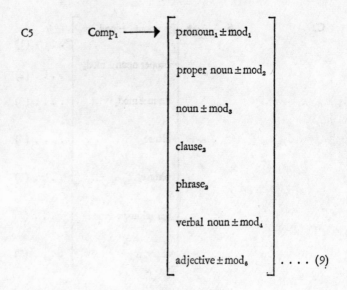

$$\text{Comp}_1 \longrightarrow \begin{bmatrix} \text{pronoun}_1 \pm \text{mod}_1 \\ \text{proper noun} \pm \text{mod}_2 \\ \text{noun} \pm \text{mod}_3 \\ \text{clause}_2 \\ \text{phrase}_2 \\ \text{verbal noun} \pm \text{mod}_4 \\ \text{adjective} \pm \text{mod}_6 \end{bmatrix} \quad \ldots \ldots (9)$$

C6   Obj ⟶

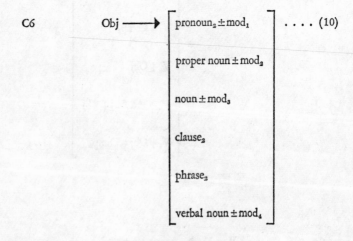

$$\text{Obj} \longrightarrow \begin{bmatrix} \text{pronoun}_2 \pm \text{mod}_1 \\ \text{proper noun} \pm \text{mod}_2 \\ \text{noun} \pm \text{mod}_3 \\ \text{clause}_2 \\ \text{phrase}_2 \\ \text{verbal noun} \pm \text{mod}_4 \end{bmatrix} \quad \ldots \ldots (10)$$

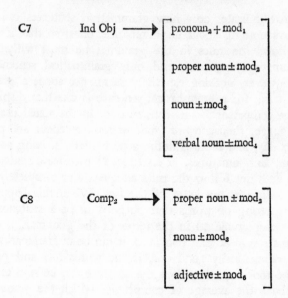

C7   Ind Obj $\longrightarrow$

$$\begin{bmatrix} \text{pronoun}_2 + \text{mod}_1 \\[1em] \text{proper noun} \pm \text{mod}_2 \\[1em] \text{noun} \pm \text{mod}_3 \\[1em] \text{verbal noun} \pm \text{mod}_4 \end{bmatrix}$$

C8   Comp$_2$ $\longrightarrow$

$$\begin{bmatrix} \text{proper noun} \pm \text{mod}_2 \\[1em] \text{noun} \pm \text{mod}_3 \\[1em] \text{adjective} \pm \text{mod}_6 \end{bmatrix}$$

C1

As soon as the mind of the creator of linguistic forms starts to embody thought or feeling in a signal of the language substance, somehow or other the formula $\Sigma \longrightarrow Subject + Predicate$ begins its work of selection and ordering, and sorts out from the mass of material stored in whatever kind of filing system exists in the brain those items needed to symbolize the message. The first choice of all, as we have seen, must always be a categorical one if what is to be uttered is to be a sentence. The encoder, having decided that he is going to make a sentence, must choose for it a subject and a predicate, for it would seem that in man's – or at least Western man's – perception of things and ideas what is talked about does something or exists in a perceptible or imagined state, and that it cannot be separated from its activity or its mode of being.

The grammar given above is supposed to indicate the repertoire of items from which the encoder can make his choices to embody his thought or feeling in language substance in a deliberately limited way. This limited way is that of the basic sentence forms of the language. At the same time, the grammar can be looked upon as a set of rules stating how the choices must be made if this limited range of grammatical sentences is to be produced.

The grammar indicates only how grammatical sentences can be made; it says nothing about ungrammatical ones; so that if the encoder follows the rules in the grammar he must willynilly make grammatical sentences, and only grammatical sentences. There is, however, nothing especially sacrosanct about a grammatical sentence, for a grammatical sentence is one that displays only average competence in its construction. In the actual usages of the language, thousands of grammatical sentences are produced every day, and there is nothing particularly striking about any of them. But sometimes, in an effort to produce a sentence, an encoder does not follow the rules adequately or completely or entirely according to the letter of the law. When this happens the resulting string of words that purports to be a sentence is likely to be ungrammatical in the terms of the grammar. It can be ungrammatical in at least two ways. It can be ungrammatically bad or ungrammatically good – or, if the words *bad* and *good* appear to be too subjective, then the sentence can be said to be below or above the average of competence which the grammar states. The grammar itself, of course, is in one sense a subjective measure of competence, because it is entirely a grammarian's grammar, even though it is based upon a code of practice which is found to be – again by the grammarian – generally acceptable.

As we now go on to give a commentary on the grammar and its rules, we shall look at each rule in turn to see how it can generate sentences or essential parts of sentences of different types which the grammar specifies to be basic sentences. The rules given in the grammar above are constituent-structure rules, and show all the constituent parts of, possibly, all the basic sentences in all their varieties. But some of the constituents will turn out to be essential morphemes or kinds of words which should, strictly speaking, need to be specified by different kinds of rules. These different kinds of rules are either morphemic or morphophonemic or else lexical. For instance, the grammar has got to account, somehow or other, for the fact that a structure such as *him is a wise man* or *they am three wise men* can be so ungrammatical or (in this case) so negatively deviant as not to be part of the language at all, or at least can only be a deliberately perverse deviation concocted either in immature ignorance or for some special purpose. The grammar hopes to give this account in a positive way. It says that if the rules are followed only grammatical sentences will result. The way to produce ungram-matical sentences is not to follow the rules. Nevertheless, every single one of the possible morphemic oddities cannot be decided here; this is not because such a decision is impossible, but simply because the amount of space needed to detail all the morphemic variations would need several volumes of millions of words. In the same sort of way, structures like *he is a wise* or *they are three wise* could be just as deviant as those previously given, only this time the deviation would be lexical and not morphemic. If the rules were completely developed they would have to account for the morphemic and lexical quirks and oddities of every word in the language. All the grammatical categories of all verbs, for instance, in their relations of tense, number and person along with the morphemic relations of some verbs with some pronouns would have to be described. And the fact, for example, that some nouns can turn up in adjectival positions while others cannot would also have to be described in detail at the lexical level. And all this, obviously, is a gigantic under-taking. Consequently, we propose to give here only the main constituent structure rules, and cease to penetrate into the language when problems become minutely morphemic or lexical.

C2

This second rule, C2, is a selectional one which specifies how to generate the subject of a basic sentence. Probably it can specify all possible subjects in English. It is a selectional rule because the rewrite part of it shows how many choices there are for an encoder who wants to construct a grammatical subject and because it says what each choice is.

(1) The first choice under C2 is

$$\text{C2.1} \qquad S \longrightarrow \text{pronoun}_1 \pm \text{mod}_1.$$

This means that once the encoder has made this choice he must rewrite S as a pronoun of the first category with or without, plus or minus, a modification also of the first category. This rule immediately implies the development of two more rules, one to describe what is to be understood by $pronoun_1$ and the other for mod_1.

The first of these sub-rules could be

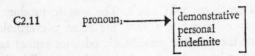

C2.11   pronoun₁ ⟶ ⎡demonstrative / personal / indefinite⎤

Then, at this point, we should at once leave grammatical description of generalities and come to actual morphemes of the language, and to a point also where we should have to develop morphemic rules to account for the peculiarities of each item. For instance, the morphemic rules belonging to sub-rule C2.11 could, for a start, be three:

C2.11 M1   personal ⟶ [*I, he, she, it, we, you, they*]

C2.11 M2   demonst ⟶ [*this, that, these, those*]

C2.11 M3   indef ⟶ [*all, few, many, more most, some, several, one, two, three,* etc.*]

We show that the items occurring in the square brackets are actual morphemes or providers of functional information in the language, and not statements of the grammar, by printing them in italics.

All the items thus listed, along with others which may be covered by the shibboleth *etc.*, can stand by themselves as subjects of basic English sentences – or at any rate, the grammar says that they can. They are all of the first category because certain other pronouns, those of the second category, such as *me, him, her, us, them,* cannot occupy subject positions by themselves – or, again, at any rate the grammar says they can't. If any of these pronouns of the second category were to turn up in subject positions by themselves, the sentence would be ungrammatical in some way or another, and interesting or uninteresting for that reason, – the context, presumably, would show what the interest was.

If the morphemic sub-rules were developed completely, we should have to take into account such features of grammar as number, and these rules would show that certain syntactic colligations, such as *he is, I am, these were, that was,* are grammatical, but at this point we stray out of the subject and into the predicate, and we are only concerned now with the generation of grammatical subjects.

One positive observation which we can make about the pronouns in the list of the morphemic rules is that they are all cohesive. That is, if we look at them from the point of view of their stylistic significance, we can see that they all carry functional information which refers them to other items in the language-uses in which they might occur, that this reference is beyond that of their immediate environment, and that it thus endows these pronouns with contextual information. Again, a complete grammar would be able to show how this is done, and should evolve rules to deal, for instance, with number and referential gender. And apart from dealing with the singularity of *he* (shall we say?), and the fact that *she* can refer only to feminine items, it would also specify what singular and feminine items were, and explain why it is possible to refer to ships and countries individually as *she*, but not, say, to computers and islands.

The second of the sub-rules of C2.1 could be

$$C2.12 \qquad mod_1 \longrightarrow \begin{bmatrix} \text{adjective clause} \\ \text{adjective phrase} \\ \text{participle} \pm \text{mod} \end{bmatrix}$$

We have to include this rule because of the possibility of such sentences as 'Those in authority bear heavy burdens' or 'Those who came to scoff remained to pray' or 'Those seen by the window were Spanish arc-welders, but those kneeling in prayer in the antechamber were Japanese psychiatrists'.

But this rule, if it is a true description of this portion of the language, shows that we can't have such subjects as *terrible I* or *unfortunate he*, or that if such subjects do turn up in any language-use, then they are deviant. In other words, the grammarian can say, if he wishes, that pronouns of the first category, which rule C2.11 and its attendant morphemic rules have defined, are not normally premodified in the same way that nouns can be. There is apparently one exception to this otherwise universal deprivation of pronouns, and that is the adjective *only*, as when we say, 'Only he knew the secret' or 'Only some among his retinue were allowed to share his confidences'.

Moreover, as we shall see afterwards, there has to be some account somewhere of the deictic nature of determiners, and of the fact, if it is a fact, that the premodification of some words that can sometimes behave as if they were pronouns turns them into nouns. In some such utterance, for example, as 'Many were admitted, but many more remained outside', *many* in its first appearance can be looked upon as a pronoun as defined in C2.11 M3, but in its second appearance it is a sort of deictic adjective premodifying *more*, which is not a pronoun but a sort of indefinite noun, so that the group of words *many more* becomes a nominal of comparative grammatical status to, say, *many people*.

A proper explanation of sub-rule C2.12 would need the development of other rules, and the derivatives of these other rules, to account for adjective phrases, adjective clauses, and participles and their modifications. There is no need to develop these rules completely. In the sentences given immediately after the rule as it was stated above, the items *in authority, who came to scoff* and *standing by the window* show the kind of structures that the rules would deal with.

However, there are one or two usages under this rule which are felt to be normal and others, which, if the rule were followed to the letter, might be thought of as deviations. For instance, the pronouns *I, he, she, it we, they* don't seem to be able to take to postmodification by adjectival phrases quite as readily as the other pronouns listed in rule C2.11. We can speak of, for instance, 'the Knight of the Sorrowful Countenance' or 'Our Lady of sorrows', and hence *he of the Sorrowful Countenance* or *she of sorrows* seem capable of becoming acceptable subjects, but such expressions are usually given currency by literary associations, and seem, on the whole, to be special cases. An expression like 'the Man in the Iron Mask' does not seem so readily to lend itself to the transmutation of *he in the Iron Mask*, in the same sort of way as that in which we can speak readily of *those in peril on the sea* (in spite of its liturgical association), or of *those in Africa, some in the United States, these in my pocket, those beyond the pale*. Such expressions as these have the quality of collocations or even clichés made acceptable and normal by habit and long usage.

Since, of course, the stylistic purpose of all modification is to delimit and to define and to reduce generalizations to selected particulars, there is a tendency for adjectival phrases to gravitate towards wanting to be adverbial. There is a different emphasis and assertion made by the adjectival phrases in 'I as chairman have the casting vote' and 'I in my capacity as chairman have the casting vote'. The tendency seems to be towards the dissociation of a particular in the role-playing of whoever is denoted by the personal pronoun, as with 'He in his capacity as chairman was able to dominate, but in his capacity as a husband had to submit'. However, Dylan Thomas's line, 'I, in my intricate image, stride on two levels', probably supplies a sample of the standard and interesting ambiguity. Presumably the phonological sign of the commas, separating the phrase *in my intricate image* from the pronoun *I* and from the rest of the utterance, is also rhetorical. Thus, *in my intricate image* becomes an adverbial modification of the whole sentence, indicating the locale of the striding in relation to the 'two levels'. The whole group of words *I, in my intricate image,* with the commas, therefore, has something of the same grammatical status as such beginnings of sentences as *I, however,* or *He, on the other hand,* and not something of the same status as *those in authority* or *we as delegates from the Boilermakers' Union.* Certainly, the caesura after *I* in Thomas's line is essential to both the rhythm and the semantic and rhetorical impact, as well as to the proleptic assonance of *I* in relation to the long heavily stressed syllable *stride*; and if the phrase *in my intricate image* were in any other place than where it actually is, the whole music of the line would disappear.

With adjective clauses as modifiers of pronouns of category one there is no real difficulty. It is easy to think of examples of standard-type sentences beginning with *I who, he whose, she to whom, that which,* and so on, whether the clauses are defining or non-defining. Although there seems to be discrimination among the pronouns listed in the morphemic rules of C2.11 about which can be modified by phrases in standard usage, this discrimination appears to be absent when adjective clauses do the modifying.

There is a blend from the modification by clauses to a modification by past participles in some cases where the antecedent of what could be the relative pronoun of an adjectival clause is the virtual object of the clause. This can be seen in such a sentence as 'Those interviewed stated they didn't know', where the past participle *interviewed* could be the vestige of some such clause as *whom our investigator interviewed*, or, perhaps more likely in Present-day English, *who were interviewed by our investigator.*

The complete statement of the third choice under rule C2.12 would have to account for both present and past participles and for the various ways in which each can be modified. For instance, in such a sentence as 'She, believing that all her lovers were really werewolves, decided to enter a nunnery', the participial phrase cut off by the commas could with equal propriety come before or after the pronoun *she*. However, in general post-modification is the rule for most kinds of modification of pronouns.

(2) The second choice under C2 is

C2.2   S ———⟶ $\left[\text{proper noun} \pm \text{mod}_2\right]$

Here again, problems of modification present interesting possibilities, as indeed does the whole rule itself.

If we assume for the moment that the encoder has made the minus choice, then we have to deal with the following rule for this sub-choice,

C2.21   proper noun ———⟶ $\left[\begin{array}{l}\text{all the proper nouns} \\ \text{in the language}\end{array}\right]$

And this, of course, tells us both everything and nothing, since we want a rule to tell us what the proper nouns are. At this point, therefore, we depart from constituent-structure rules and move into lexical rules, and presumably our lexicon, if we had one, would list all the proper names in the language and categorize them as

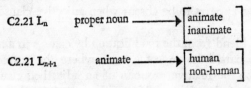

C2.21 L_n proper noun ———⟶ $\left[\begin{array}{l}\text{animate} \\ \text{inanimate}\end{array}\right]$

C2.21 L_{n+1} animate ———⟶ $\left[\begin{array}{l}\text{human} \\ \text{non-human}\end{array}\right]$

and so on, throughout a whole thesaurus of dichotomies of the lexical items known as proper nouns.

There is, of course, no actual reason to go to these quite startling lengths. As we said earlier, a generative grammar is a sort of analogue of a process, a reflection of the kinds of things that go on in the minds of fluent speakers of the language when they are making sentences. The two lexical rules just given, for instance, reflect and generalize some of the kind of knowledge about proper nouns which many fluent speakers of English can be presumed to possess. They know that the word *Socrates* is an animate human proper noun, and that the word *Athens* is an inanimate one, and that the first can enter into grammatical relationships – such as being replaced by *he* or *who* – which the second cannot enter into. Or at least, the grammarian can say that a fluent speaker knows this because the grammarian finds that he behaves as if he does. Of course, if one adds that the speaker behaves as if he does know that because he is a fluent speaker, the circularity of the argument is apparent. But one must also add that circular arguments are merely longwinded ways of stating intuitions, and if there were no intuitions about language-uses, the grammarian would never be able to get on with his job. In examining the language, the grammarian can only find examples of performance; the competence or incompetence of the performance can only be a matter of inference; and the competent speaker is in many ways the grammarian's invention, because, if there is a scale of competence against which performance can be measured, then any point whatever can be taken as the grammarian's norm. His choice is quite arbitrary; if James Joyce's *Finnegans Wake*, for example, had been taken as a sample of normal competent English usage, or the poems of E. E. Cummings had been taken as the norm, interesting results might have followed.

If, under rule C2.2, the encoder had decided to take the plus choice, then we should have to examine some new rules that explain what we are to understand by mod_2. We should have, first, some such rule as

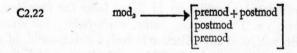

$$C2.22 \qquad mod_2 \longrightarrow \begin{bmatrix} \text{premod} + \text{postmod} \\ \text{postmod} \\ \text{premod} \end{bmatrix}$$

This rule tells us that proper nouns can be premodified, can be postmodified, and can be both pre- and post-modified at the same time. What is interesting are the conditions under which this can happen. We need two more rules to tell us what these conditions are :

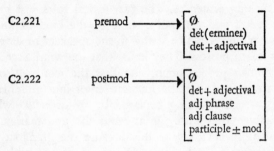

The symbol Ø means 'zero-morpheme' (the solidus through the zero distinguishes it from upper case O), and it stands for the absence of a functional or morphological element, where, in some cases, there might be one, and where the difference between two structures, or words, or whatever, can be detected only by means of the contrast of absence with presence, as the verb *walk*, for instance, can be distinguished from *walks* or *walked* only by the absence of the inflexion.

The normal usage of proper nouns is seen in some such sentence as 'Gladstone introduced the second reading of the Bill', where the proper noun has no modification at all – hence the symbol Ø in the rule above. But English proper nouns are not always properly proper, and we need the symbol Ø in the rules for particularizing and non-particularizing usages, as in the difference, for example, between 'Smith, who(m) we met in Pisa, manufactures waistcoat buttons' (non-particularizing) and 'The Smith who(m) we met in Pisa is not the same man as the Smith we met in Florence' (particularizing). There is, also, a sort of particularizing stylistic device in which a determiner and an adjectival are used. And adjectival may be an adjective by itself, an adjective preceded by an adverb, *very good*, or a string of co-ordinated adjectives as in 'Now fades the *long last* streak of snow', or 'That *joyous, sunlit, never-fading but irrevocable* day with you', and any adjective in such a string could, of course, be modified by an adverb. This particularizing stylistic device appears in some kinds of historical writing and in some kinds (children's? women's?) fiction. We can have, for instance, 'A resolute Disraeli now stood to address the House,' or 'The wily

Talleyrand . . .' or 'A very dejected and woe-begone Belinda sat in the window-seat counting the raindrops as they fell from the lintel'. We can also put here a form of postmodification of similar construction. In such expressions as 'Charles the Bold' or 'Louis the Fourteenth', which seem to occur only in historical registers in the first place, we see the same sort of deictic functioning. And, of course, in such titles as 'the Duke of Wellington' one supposes that *Duke* or *the Duke* is to be counted as the proper name and *of Wellington* as a postmodifying adjectival phrase. The contraction (back-formation?) to simply *Wellington* must be regarded as a disrespectful and democratic assumption of parvenu familiarity which resulted from a proliferation of dukes. How far such proper names as Winnie-the-Pooh or Jack the Ripper should be admitted into this category is a question that readers can decide for themselves, and some Welsh readers may be able to claim a different provenance for such expressions on the analogy of Owen the Post or Evans the Death.

Questions of postmodification by means of adjectival phrases or clauses are normally quite straightforward, except that adjectival phrases can sometimes show a blend into adverbial components, and it would seem that some kinds of prepositions cannot be used to make such phrases. A normal sort of preposition for the postmodification of proper names seems to be *of*, as in *John of Austria* or *Catherine of Aragon*, where the whole group of words becomes a proper name in its own right. But other prepositions, introducing phrases, seem to make the phrases adverbial except in some complicated phrases which also contain a clause. In such a sentence as 'Caesar in defiance of orders crossed the Rubicon', the phrase *in defiance of orders* presumably shows adverbial tendencies. But in such a sentence as 'Brutus, without whom the conspiracy would have lacked countenance, searched his conscience', the group of words *without . . . countenance* seem to belong more to Brutus himself than to his soul-searching. Sometimes an adjectival phrase can become completely incorporated into the whole proper name, as with Stow-on-the-Wold or Morton-in-the-Marsh. The use of phrases to distinguish two homophonous proper names is common – and when this happens a premodifying determiner is used: 'The Wellington in New Zealand is the one I mean, not the Wellington in Somerset'.

With adjectival clauses, which always appear in postmodifying positions in normal usage, there occurs sometimes the necessity for a distinction between defining and non-defining types, as they are called. In speech, intonation makes the distinction clear. In writing, the phonological signs of commas are used or are not used, as in 'Smith, whom we met in Florence, plays jazz on the harpsichord' (non-defining), and 'The Smith whom we met in Florence is not the same man as the Smith we met in Pisa'.

There is sometimes the same kind of blend into adverbial components with participial constructions as there is with phrases. Traditional English grammarians, no doubt influenced by Latin, where participles agree in gender, number and case with nouns which they modify, seem to have assumed that the participles of English are also always adjectival. This may be doubted, especially when the participles occur with pronouns or proper nouns and there is therefore not quite the same kind of defining necessity of the modification, since pronouns and proper nouns can hardly be thought of as universals. With participles there seems to be a dissociation of referential information except where common nouns are used. An artificial kind of particularization, of course, avoids or abolishes this dissociation, as in 'The terrified Amanda dared not face the consequences of her actions'; but as soon as the participle is separated from such an obviously adjectival function, it becomes less obviously adjectival, as in 'Terrified, Amanda dared not face the consequences of her actions'. With present participles the same kind of tendency is noticeable, as in 'Caesar disobeying orders crossed the Rubicon'.

There may be doubt in the minds of some about whether there is any need to make the distinction between mod_1 and mod_2 – as well, for that matter, between either or both and mod_3 – in the sub-rules of C2. In a complete grammar of English this distinction is necessary for each rule and sub-rule because it marks the limits of systems. A system, as we have said, is an area of language-use in which the encoder is presented with a small fixed number of choices, The symbol $pronoun_1$, for instance, is the sign of a system – a system which quite rigidly indicates that only a small fixed number of pronouns in English can stand by themselves as the subjects of sentences, and that the encoder of messages in English who wants to use a pronoun as the subject of a sentence must choose one of these if he wants to make that part of his sentence grammatically well-formed. This does not mean to say that if he makes a choice outside the system his sentence will not be acceptable. In the dialect of music-hall Cotswolds, for instance, 'Ur give it to Oi' (or whatever other phonetic transcription might be made) for 'She gave it to me' is acceptable in certain situational contexts. And such is the redundancy of the language that in most normal usages, if any speaker makes a mistake, as it is called, or a slip of the tongue, or if a writer does not always succeed in emulating the elegance and purity of the best models, most decoders have a good idea of what is being talked or written about. The symbols mod_1, mod_2 and mod_3 and all that they stand for are necessary as signs that the systems exist, or that the grammarian says they exist. These signs are merely reflections in the grammarian's grammar of what happens in the language outside it when speakers or writers perpetuate the process of making the language into an infinite number of sentences. One advantage of a generative grammar is that it can demonstrate the complexity of a language; another is that it can provide a means of organizing knowledge of that complexity.

(3) The third choice under C2 is

C2.3 $\qquad$ S $\longrightarrow$ $\left[\text{noun} \pm \text{mod}_3 \right]$

We now have to develop sub-rules to deal with this choice, and, again, it becomes necessary to leave constituent-structure rules and make for the lexicon. Even so, it may be a matter for discussion as to how far there is a rigid division to be made here. For there is a blend, of course, from one kind of rule to another, because some nouns can be subjects by themselves, and subjects are structural units, but at the same time nouns can be lexical units.

For the choice of noun without modification we might have

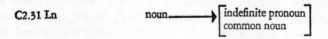

C2.31 Ln $\qquad$ noun $\longrightarrow$ $\left[\begin{array}{l} \text{indefinite pronoun} \\ \text{common noun} \end{array} \right]$

And this could be developed to

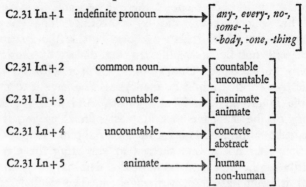

And so on. In the ultimate analysis all the subdivisions would have to be considered in relation to their possible kinds of modification, and new rules would have to be developed accordingly.

In those cases where the items are used by themselves as subjects there is no problem. But they cannot all be used by themselves, and the basis of choice of any particular item depends on whether it needs some kind of modifier or not, and methods of modification are not always the same. The variations on many occasions can be regarded as stylistic, since some of them are deviant.

It is doubtful, for instance, whether indefinite pronouns can normally have any premodification in the same sort of way as singular countable nouns can be premodified. Thus, we cannot normally start a sentence with a singular countable noun, and say, for instance, '*Motorway is . . .', but we must say, 'A/the/this/that/any/each/every (or, perhaps, my/his/her/our/your/their) motorway is . . .'; on the other hand we need no determiners to precede countable plurals, and can say quite grammatically, 'Motorways pose problems for civil engineers'. However, although we are free to make postmodifications of indefinite pronouns, as in 'Something good is bound to come of it' or 'Everyone who knows him likes him', we seem to be restricted to special cases in premodifying them, as with 'almost everybody' or 'hardly anyone' or 'a certain something'; and such an example as 'this despicable nobody', which conforms to a well known pattern of modification in making the general more particular, does in fact make the indefinite pronoun quite definite and gives it contextual information in an interesting way.

Indeed, another advantage of a generative grammar, in telling us what we can modify and what we can't, and the way in which we can modify one item but not another, is that it can give us some precise means of indicating finer semantic distinctions in different uses of the same word, or, if not the same word, then words which are homophonous. This is especially so, perhaps, in the relationships between countable and uncountable common nouns. In such a sentence as 'Imagination is essential to all novelists', the word *imagination* is uncountable and abstract; but in the sentence 'His imagination seethes with terrible fantasies', the word *imagination* is countable as one, and the word *his* – a possessive pronoun or adjective, or whatever you like to call it, belonging to the general system of determiners – is a modification which shows this aspect of *imagination* or which contextualizes it in a special way. A fair question to ask seems to be, What is the difference between *imagination*, in general, and *his imagination*, in particular? and have we here two homonyms or homophonous words which can be semantically distinguished by means of some grammar, and if so how can the grammar make the distinction? In other words, it is quite possible that changes of contextual information in items in the course of the development of the language are co-occurrent with the uses of them in different contexts, and that one of the aspects of this co-occurrence is the linguistic differentiation of 'shades of meaning' by means of different *ad hoc* usages.

It is clear, of course, that all questions of modification are of extreme interest to the student of style, for modification produces the creativeness of the language's myths by giving contextual information to what is modified. In general, there is a great deal of freedom for a writer in his choices of, say, adjectives and adjective phrases and clauses. The question, however, for the student of style is, Where does this freedom start? At what point is a writer able to free himself from the chains of the basic grammatical systems of the language and soar up into the empyrean of his own choosing? Presumably only a grammar of the norm can help us.

The choice $S \longrightarrow noun + mod_3$ is likely on the whole to be a more popular one than that of the noun by itself. The use of a noun without some kind of modification is normally forced on the writer by the conventions of the language. Without thinking very much about it, we can produce some such sentence as 'Allegory can be a literary formulation of religious or ethical conviction', because *allegory* belongs to the category of un-countable nouns and does not need a determiner. It is only when we come to acts of particularization, either of uncountables or universals, and to the effort to make more refined descriptions of the discriminations of experience, that modifications begin to creep in, as when we say something like 'The sophisticated allegory of Spenser can be contrasted with the more primitive allegory of Bunyan', or something like that, so that we are in the end talking about a quite different topic from the general topic with which we started.

Our rule for mod_3 could be quite a complicated one, embracing the compulsions of the language itself, as well as the dubieties, second thoughts, crossings-out, happy strokes of wit, sparks from heaven, and the most gratifying favours of the Muses that have been known to all who have ever seriously tried to put pen to paper. However, it need not detain us long, since most of it has already been dealt with. It is really a more comprehensive version of the sub-rules already dealt with.

The basis of the rule will be

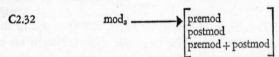

C2.32 mod_3 ⟶ $\begin{bmatrix} \text{premod} \\ \text{postmod} \\ \text{premod} + \text{postmod} \end{bmatrix}$

And from this we develop the two following rules

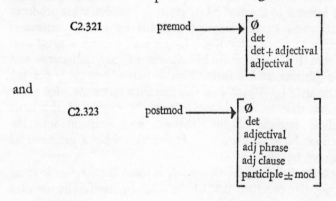

C2.321   premod ⟶ $\begin{bmatrix} \emptyset \\ \text{det} \\ \text{det} + \text{adjectival} \\ \text{adjectival} \end{bmatrix}$

and

C2.323   postmod ⟶ $\begin{bmatrix} \emptyset \\ \text{det} \\ \text{adjectival} \\ \text{adj phrase} \\ \text{adj clause} \\ \text{participle} \pm \text{mod} \end{bmatrix}$

Premodification presents no difficulties. All singular and count-able common nouns normally need the premodification of a determiner according to the degree of particularization that the encoder thinks he needs. Plural and uncountable common nouns need not have a determiner, but if some degree of particularization of some sort of deictic or demonstrative word is felt to be needed for some plurals to give them contextual information, as with 'These men, but not those men, should be liquidated', then a determiner is used. And every time a determiner is used it can, of course, be followed by an adjectival before the common noun is uttered. Adjectivals can also precede most plural and un-countable common nouns even when there is no determiner.

Postmodification becomes a little more complicated, but not very much so. When a determiner postmodifies, it is normally a numerical one, as in some such sentence as 'Page six has the relevant information'. How far the cardinal numbers are to be thought of as determiners, or adjectives, or determiners which are also adjectives, or adjectives which are also determiners, is not a question which seems worth asking or answering. One imagines, on the analogy of the sample of *page six*, that they are deictic or demonstrative, and cannot be thought of as a stylistic or semantic deviation. In the quotation,

Two nice little boys, rather more grown,
Carried lavender-water and eau de Cologne,

the word *two* seems to be more of a deviation into sense than one into attitude or conceit, while only the words *nice* and *little*, joined in collocation, represent stylistic choice.

One imagines, too, that there is a sort of deictic blend from these kinds of determiners into the kinds of adjectivals that can be used in postmodification. Just as the determiners in their usages display all the characteristics of a system which presents encoders with only a small fixed number of choices, so likewise there seems to be a fairly rigid range of choices here. We have first those pseudo-poetic samples in which the exigences of metre and rhyme force adjectival postmodification on embarrassed nouns – 'And did those feet in ancient time/Walk upon England's mountains green': although in some cases – 'Tasting of Flora and the country green' – there may be some ambiguity, since *green* here may be a noun of the same sort as that in

village green or even, perhaps, *Lincoln green*; and just
occasionally an irregularly postmodifying adjective may suddenly
and poetically justify itself:

> He pac'd away the pleasant hours of ease
> With stride colossal, on from hall to hall.

But poetic usages can be regarded as deviant anywhere, since
poetry is *ipso facto* a deviation from the norm. Postmodification
by adjectivals in the norm of the language seems to be very restricted to a few standard procedures and collocations. An obvious
example is *court martial*. And we can have instances or words
which might be prepositions or adverbs turning up as postmodifying adjectives, as in *the flat upstairs*. A fairly wide range
of infinitives can be used as postmodifying adjectives, as in such
expressions as *the will to succeed* or *his decision to do it*.

Postmodification by adjective phrases and clauses is so common
that it must be looked upon as part of the norm, and is so simple
that it needs no discussion. The two sentences 'Men in authority
bear heavy burdens' and 'People who live in glass-houses should
not throw stones' can provide easy examples.

With postmodification by participles there is the same tendency
of the participle to hover irresolutely between adjectival and
adverbial qualities which we have noticed already. It is quite clear,
of course, that when a participle premodifies a common noun
it loses completely whatever participle-like nature it had and
becomes utterly adjectival, as can be seen in such expressions as
the laughing man or *the terrified woman*. But when the
participle still shows something of its verbal nature, presumably,
and becomes modified itself adverbially or shows that it can have
an object, then it scorns to step into its complete adjectival role.
We can hardly say **the laughing at her foolish fears man*
or **the terrified by his menaces women*, though we can say,
'The man, laughing at her foolish fears, boldly advanced towards the unoffending mouse', or 'The woman, terrified by his
menaces, redoubled her hysterical caterwauling'. But in these two
sentences the participles seem to take on an adverbial role, or, at
least, more of an adverbial role than an adjectival one.

(4) The fourth choice for a subject under rule C2 is

C2.4   S———▶ clause².

Here we are concerned, not as we were in the previous rules with the naming of people, animals, things and ideas in general, but with providing a means for naming, in particular, ideas, thoughts, concepts, beliefs, opinions, and so on. For the rule which generates the subject here we might have

C2.41 $\qquad$ clause$_2$ $\longrightarrow$ $\begin{bmatrix} \text{clause}_2 \text{ morpheme} + \\ \text{pre-apposition} + \text{clause}_2 \text{ morpheme} + \\ \Sigma \end{bmatrix}$

Presumably the rule which describes a *clause$_2$ morpheme* would be a morphemic one which gave details of a limited range of certain functional units, something like this

C2.41 M1 clause$_2$morph $\longrightarrow$ $\begin{bmatrix} \textit{how, that, who, whom,} \\ \textit{whose, which,} \\ \textit{what, where, when,} \\ \textit{why, whether,} \\ \textit{whither, whence, etc.} \end{bmatrix}$

Thus the rule could account for such sentences as 'How this strange creature came to be among us is a mystery', or 'Who taught this stange creature to speak Hittite with an American accent has not been revealed', or 'Which of these remarkable structures is his home is not a question we can answer at the moment'. The rule should also, no doubt by some means which is hidden under the shibboleth *etc.*, have to account for clauses starting with such formulae as *to whom, from which, by whose, with what,* and so on, in order that it could deal with such sentences as 'By whose authority the statement was made is not revealed', or 'To whom he gave his confidences cannot be told'.

On the other hand, the rule for *pre-apposition* is presumably a constituent-structure rule of some sort, and one supposes we have to say for the second choice under C2.41

C2.411 $\qquad$ pre-app $\longrightarrow$ $\begin{bmatrix} \pm \text{det} + \text{noun from specified list} \end{bmatrix}$

And then a lexical rule would have to be developed to show what this list of nouns contained. The range would consist of such words as those which we have already said are, as it were, calibrations on the scale that we use to measure what we think

G

or believe about certain sorts of statements, such words as *fact, truth, belief, idea, feeling, certainty, conviction,* as well as words which are the names of kinds of utterance – more neutral words such as *statement, definition, verdict, conclusion, reason,* and so on. In this way the second choice under C2.41 accounts for such sentences as 'The fact that he made no answer to these charges does not prove his guilt', or 'The belief that strong sunlight puts out fires is an old wives' tale'. This rule, if written out in full, would have to include some indication of the ways in which the nouns from the specified list could be modified, so that the rule could be made to account for such sentences as 'This categorical statement, which has been so often repeated, that the government fully intends to continue with this plan, must be taken seriously'. The rule should also include something to account for the rather odd but well-established modification of *fact* or *idea* in sentences which begin with 'The very fact that . . .' or 'The very idea that . . .'

The symbol *clause$_2$*, of course, distinguishes noun clauses used as subjects from adjective clauses used in subjects.

(5) The fifth choice under rule C2 is

$$C2.5 \qquad\qquad S \longrightarrow phrase_2$$

And, surprisingly, this can become quite interesting and complicated. The symbol *phrase$_2$* is used to distinguish noun phrases which can be subjects by themselves from adjective phrases which can be used in the structures which can make subjects. A provisional means of identifying such noun phrases can be discovered in some such guide as 'a noun or nominal phrase is one which occurs in a nominal position', and since the position of a subject in a sentence is a nominal one, then a phrase which comes at the beginning of a sentence could be in many cases a noun phrase. But the matter is not quite as simple as that. In such a sentence as 'Through the woods is the path we should take', the expression *through the woods* occurs in a nominal position, though the expression *the path we should take* seems to have a more rightful claim to be the subject. Nevertheless, in such a sentence as 'From Tokyo to London takes fifteen hours by air', it seems that the expression *From Tokyo to London* is undoubtedly the subject. Even so, there seems to be some kind of conventional pattern of inversion which tends, in some cases, to make the encoders of some messages put the subject at the end. In such a sentence as 'Down in the forest lie three sleeping centaurs', the expression *Down in the forest* can hardly be a subject, and the inversion is necessary because to say 'Three sleeping centaurs lie down in the forest' seems to imply an unintended centauric somnambulism, and to say 'Three centaurs lie down to sleep in the forest' would, again, not convey the intended meaning. Moreover, the inversion seems to be rhetorical, and there is something, one feels, almost indigenous in it to the intonation of the English poetic idiom. The rhetoric is almost part of the convention of the language, and the feeling which produces it seems to be shared with that which has produced some of the greatness of our literature. A sentence like 'The path we should take is through woods' has a flat and unconvincing banality about it, and certainly it lacks the rhythm and slight poetic quality of the far from really poetic utterance, 'From Tamworth hither is but one day's march'. And the subject of that sentence, presumably, *From Tamworth hither.*

Another kind of subject that could be included here can be derived from infinitive verbal expressions that could occupy nominal positions in sentences. In such a sentence as 'He learnt how to tickle trout', the expression *how to tickle trout* is an object, but the phrase can easily be made into a subject by transposing it into some such sentence as 'How to tickle trout was all he learnt after three years at the university'.

The choice of $S \longrightarrow phrase_2$, therefore, can have its rewrite part expressed in the form

C2.5 $phrase_2 \longrightarrow$
$$\left[\begin{array}{l} prep_n + nominal + adverbial \\ prep_n + nominal + prep_n + nominal \\ phrase_2\ morpheme + intrans\ infin + \\ \quad comp \pm adverbial \\ phrase_2\ morpheme + trans\ infin + \\ \quad obj \pm adverbial \end{array} \right]$$

The symbol *nominal* can include in what it symbolizes any pronoun or any kind of noun with whatever modification is appropriate. The symbol *adverbial* can include in what it symbolizes not only adverbs themselves, but also adverbial phrases and clauses, all of which, in the completeness of the grammar would have to be described somewhere. And since, of course, infinitives are verbs as well as nouns in this rule they show the characteristics of verbs – such as having the property of being followed sometimes by complements or objects or of being modified by adverbials.

Lexical rules developed from C2.5 would have to specify a range of items for $prep_n$, because the first two choices under this rule are intended to deal with such sentences as 'From Tamworth hither is but one day's march' and 'From Tokyo to London takes fifteen hours by air', and it is difficult to conceive of all the prepositions in English having a use in the subjects of such sentences. Perhaps, too, only a limited range of nominals is in any way applicable. The third and fourth choices under rule C2.5 should be able to cope with such sentences as 'How to speak confidently and fluently in public is explained in this fascinating booklet' or 'When to beat his wife is a problem every husband faces'. Clearly, too, the symbol $phrase_2$ *morpheme* will need some kind of definition, since not all adverbs or subordinating conjunctions or whatever one likes to call them, like *how* or *what*, can be used in these subjects: for example, to say *that to say is ungrammatical, though *which to say/what to say* or *when/ where/how/why to say it* are all normal usages.

(6) The sixth choice under rule C2 is

$$\text{C2.6} \qquad \text{S} \longrightarrow \text{verbal noun} \pm \text{mod}_4,$$

and from this we can derive two further rules

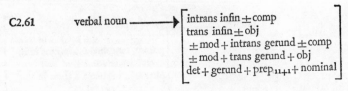

$$\text{C2.61} \qquad \text{verbal noun} \longrightarrow \begin{bmatrix} \text{intrans infin} \pm \text{comp} \\ \text{trans infin} \pm \text{obj} \\ \pm \text{mod} + \text{intrans gerund} \pm \text{comp} \\ \pm \text{mod} + \text{trans gerund} + \text{obj} \\ \text{det} + \text{gerund} + \text{prep}_{1141} + \text{nominal} \end{bmatrix}$$

and

$$\text{C2.62} \qquad \text{mod}_4 \longrightarrow \text{adverbial}$$

We have first to account for the differences in the subjects of such sentences as 'To err is human' and 'Seeing is believing'. This is easily done by means of the symbols *infin* and *gerund*. But a coarse distinction such as this is an anathema to the grammarian of generative grammars who seeks always delicacy and refinement, and so those infinitives which are intransitive have to be separated from the transitive ones. This takes into account not only such a sentence as 'To err is human', but also some such sentence as 'To write the perfect sonnet was all he wished'; or, if gerunds are used, it can distinguish between such sentences as 'Seeming to be wise is more difficult than being wise in fact' and 'Taming lions in the spare bedroom exasperated his wife'. Normally, of course, such a sentence as this last one would have its gerund premodified – *his taming lions*, for instance. There seems to be some kind of restriction on the ways in which gerunds used as the heads of subjects can be modified. For instance, *the taming lions* is not permitted, although *the taming of lions* is – hence the last choice under this rule, where $prep_{n+1}$ has to be a special symbol because not all prepositions can be used here.

Some gerunds seem to have utterly and ruthlessly deserted their parent verb and set up independently as nouns in their own right. Thus, in such a sentence as 'His hopeless yearning to write the perfect sonnet led him to nothing but disaster', one imagines that *yearning* has severed all connexion (except that of distant memory) with the verb *to yearn*. There is a small class of such gerunds, and these can be more freely modified than their less adventurous stay-at-home fellows.

These sub-rules would also have to develop, if stated in full, another sub-rule to deal with the choice of *comp* following an intransitive infinitive or gerund, and would have to point out that when a pronoun occurs in this role it very often appears in a reflexive form – as when the actress said, 'Being Lady Macbeth or Cleopatra is all in a day's work, but being myself needs effort'. In that utterance *being I* would have been so low on the scale of grammaticality as to be out of the language altogether, and *being me*, although no doubt acceptable in some situations, would have been coy and inelegant.

(7) The last choice under C2 is

C2.7 $\qquad$ S $\longrightarrow \left[\textit{there, it} \right]$

Here the constituent-structure grammar takes us right into the lexicon, and to a couple of special cases. For it is well known that there are in English a large number of sentences that can begin with one or the other of these two words occurring in subject positions, and behaving, indeed, as if they were subjects. On many occasions, speakers and writers do not want to specify that some definitely identified person, animal or thing does or is something, but merely wish to draw the listener's or reader's attention to the existence of some idea, state of affairs, or object (in the non-grammatical sense) that might be interesting. Thus, when we say 'It's raining', we have no idea what *it* might be, and in one sense one could say that in such an utterance *it* provides only functional information, so that we speak in the form of a sentence and do not merely respond to the existence of the rain by the utterance of the word *rain* alone. All sentences in which one or the other of these two subjects is used seem to be predicative. Unless the pronoun *it* has contextual information which it derives from its cohesive use to make it refer to some noun or other, it is never followed by a transitive verb in such sentences as we are considering here. And *there* as a subject cannot, of course, be followed by a transitive verb in these same kinds of sentences, because such a verb would immediately bestow upon it pronominal or nominal qualities and find new contextual information for it.

C3

Rule C3 is the general constituent-structure rule for the generation of the predicates of the basic English sentences. In one sense, the five subscripts to the symbol V are somewhat pleonastic, because in the basic sentence forms what distinguishes one kind of verb from any other is actually what follows each verb, and has nothing really to do with the verb itself as a grammatical entity; only in its stylistic function can what follows the verb bestow on it contextual information; in this sense, verbs have, generally speaking, only a vague lexical or referential information to differentiate them. There may, perhaps, be some excuse for noting a difference in the verbs of the first two choices and marking them off from the other three. This is because the verbs in the first two choices will always be intransitive, and their lexical or referential information will always be of a kind that could be called subject-oriented. This will be especially so with the verbs of the second choice, which, if they are not parts of the verb *to be*, will always have existential properties similar to those of the parts of the verb *to be*, such as the parts of verbs like *to become, to seem,* or *to appear.* These verbs, of course, are those which show linguistic myth-creativeness at its most ruthless efficient functioning.

Many of the verbs in English can be used both transitively and intransitively, and their contextual information – which is what gives them their stylistic importance – must, one supposes, derive from this state of affairs. However, transitivity does not affect morphology; the grammatical behaviour of verbs inside those segments of sentences which can be said to be exclusively verbal, and not nominal or adjectival, shows no differences whether the verbs are used intransitively or transitively.

If we consider three such sentences as (1) 'After the ceremony, Prince Philip left in a helicopter', (2) 'My secretary left a note on my desk', and (3) 'His grandfather left him all his estate', we can notice a sort of scale of transitivity, and see that these sentences are samples respectively of Types I, III and V of the basic grammar. But if we experiment with different morphological variations, such as those of tense and number, of the verb *to leave* in these sentences, we shall always find that, having made allowances for changes in the subject, we can replace any part of the verb *to leave* from one of the sentences in either of the other two, and though that part may suffer a change of contextual information, it will remain unchanged in its grammatical form. Thus, 'After the ceremony, they will leave in a helicopter' and 'His grandparents will leave him all their estate' are two sentences in which the segment *will leave* shows no grammatical difference.

C4

For the reasons just given, there is no need to describe the rule C4 in any great detail. Indeed, to do so would require a whole book. All we need say, for the purpose of the norm, is that only such-and-such is normal, and that everything else is a deviation. However, it is necessary to say what everything else is a deviation from, and where the deviation starts to be deviant.

(8) The rule C3, though a selectional one, specifies that each of its five choices must contain an element symbolized by V, and the rule C4 defines what V is:

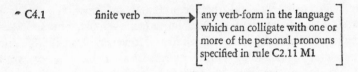

C4   V ⟶ finite verb$\pm$mod$_s$.

From this we can derive two sub-rules:

~ C4.1   finite verb ⟶ [any verb-form in the language which can colligate with one or more of the personal pronouns specified in rule C2.11 M1]

and

C4.2   mod$_s$ ⟶ adverbial

The sub-rule C4.1 consequently becomes a quite complicated lexical rule, although its main drift is fairly clear. Presumably such parts of verbs as the infinitive, the gerund, and the present and past participles have to be excluded from it, on the ground that they cannot colligate with the pronouns *I/he/she/it/we/you/they* in any direct manner. Thus, we can say *I speak* or *he speaks* or *you speak*, but not *she to speak or *we speaking or *they spoken, although, of course, with weak verbs whose past tense forms end with the morpheme *-ed* as well as their past participles, we should take the colligation as accomplished in the past tense, even though an encoder had written, say, *they waited*, under the impression that *waited* was a past participle and that the grouping of the two words was intended to be deviant in some way or another.

Nevertheless, present and past participles might occur in the verb-forms symbolized by V in the rule C3. For instance, 'He is waiting' and 'I have waited in vain for an answer' are not unduly abnormal sorts of utterances unless we make them so by our definition of the symbol V. However, to make them thus extra-normal by some such definition would also make *is* and *have* equally abnormal as they are used in those sentences, for it would exclude the possibility of auxiliary verbs, and imply that any tense other than the simple present was deviant. There is no reason why we should not behave in this manner if we wish, except that it seems unwarrantable to extend the concept of deviance into embracing niggling minutiae, and that the use of auxiliary verbs to form tenses in English is fairly normal practice, for tenses themselves are not usually thought of as deviant except in special cases which can speak for themselves. In any case, such excessive simplicity of such narrowly limited definition of finite verbs could hardly do justice to the rich variety of the language and would hardly show where deviation begins.

The rule C4.1, therefore, would be a part of the lexicon which classified finite verbs in some more or less arbitrary manner and which showed pretty extensively how, generally speaking, all the tenses, numbers and persons of verb segments in the active voice in English were formed. The first kind of classification that would have to be made would be that into the traditional dichotomy of strong and weak verbs, so that encoders could know the normal methods of forming the past tenses and be aware of the differences exemplified in, say, *I have spoken* and *I have talked*.

The second kind of classification, which is stylistically important as well as grammatically necessary, is that into what might be called grammatico-lexical kinds. This classification would distinguish certain kinds of grammatical features which are also providers of lexical and perhaps referential information in the functioning of verbs. A good guide to such a method of sorting out these features is one given by Professor F. R. Palmer[1]. He makes two main divisions of auxiliary verbs and full verbs, and then he subdivides the auxiliary verbs into what he calls 'primary' and 'secondary or modal', and the full verbs into catenatives and non-catenatives. This method of approaching the subject seems satisfactory, although, as apparently always with English, there are one or two examples which turn up in actual language uses which cut across categories without any sympathy for the grammarian's tidiness.

The primary auxiliary verbs are the finite parts of *to be*, *to have* and *to do*. They are primary, of course, because they have normal uses in the formation of tenses – *I was writing, I have written, I am writing, I shall be writing, I shall have written*. And the

[1] Palmer, F. R., *A Linguistic Study of the English Verb*, London, 1965.

primary auxiliary *do* turns up as an intensifier, *I do love pine-apples*, or less coyly and more functionally in negative state-ments, *I do not write while I am driving a car*. However, all the finite parts of these verbs can occur as full verbs on certain occasions. In sentences of the basic Type II, for instance, where finite parts of the verb *to be* are very often used as copulative verbs, their verbal fullness, one supposes, must be acknowledged, as in the sentence 'I am British', where *am* stands all by itself as a functional part which makes the sentence into a sentence and not just a group of three random words. The case is similar with *have*, one imagines, in its appearance sometimes in sentences of the basic Type III. Such a sentence as 'I have two cats' can be paraphrased as 'I own/possess two cats'; and in many sentences *have* can be contextualized to indicate ownership or possession, quite often in the nicest way, as in *to have and to hold from this day forth* in the alliterative and rhythmic beauty of the language of our ancestors. On the other hand, the verb *do* seems to have a more dependent kind of fullness, because, it would seem, of the vague generality of its lexical information. When it functions as a quasi-complete verb it appears to stand in a similar kind of relationship to another verb as a pronoun stands to a noun. It also very often has a conditional aspect, as in such a sentence as 'I should like to try to live without the bother of having to eat, but I should be foolish if I did so', and in many other sentences where a part of the verb *to do* and the adverb *so* form a collocation.

The secondary or modal auxiliary verbs are such words as *will, would, shall, should, can, could, may, might, must, ought*, and they are used before the infinitive to give contextual in-formation to the total verb segment. All of them except *ought* are used before the infinitive without its morpheme *to,* as in *I shall go, I may go, I must go*, but *I ought to go*. In the grammar of the norm this modalization is perhaps a luxury, but not too much of one. Certainly, one imagines that encoders are normally aware of it, and that deviations into it are not such enormous deviations as those, say, into the passive.

Syntactically, one can describe the normal usages of auxiliary verbs by stating the kinds of linguistic units which follow them in sentences. Thus, when parts of *to be* or *to have* are followed by present or past participles, then they simply form tenses.

When they are followed by an infinitive without its heralding *to* (or with it in the case of the deontic *ought* – stern daughter of the voice of God), there is the contextualization of mood. And mood is that property of verb forms which provides contextual information about such degrees of positive assertion or dubiety as indicativeness (*He went/He goes/He will go*), as probability (*That would be likely*), as possibility (*He might have said so*), as condition (*If I could do it, I would*), and so on.

Among the full verbs there is a quite large group whose members are also followed by infinitives with *to* or by some non-finite part of a verb. These are the catenative verbs, and perhaps we can notice something of a blend here from those modal auxiliaries to full verbs. There is, for instance, the odd case of the past form of the verb *to use*, as it appears in some such sentence as 'I used to see him often when I lived in Oxford'. Some catenative verbs can do without *to* preceding the following infinitive (*He helped build the boat*), but most that go with an infinitive need the morpheme *to* (*He wants to know the answer/ He likes to ask questions*). Others are followed by what is apparently a gerund (*He keeps thinking about it/He risked trying it/He remembered seeing it*). Sometimes there is the intervention of a nominal between the catenative verb and the infinitive that comes after, and in this case the infinitive abandons its *to* (*He made them do it*).

The non-catenative verbs are all the other verbs in the language. But, again, there is either a blend noticeable from one category to another, or forms simply cut across categories quite ruthlessly. There may also be different approaches to the analysis of structures. For example, a sentence like 'He keeps tropical fish' can unambiguously be said to be a sentence of the basic Type III, and if that sentence can be so thought of why cannot a sentence like 'He keeps brooding on his sorrows'? The answer, I think, is that the word *brooding*, which could be thought of as a verbal noun and the object of the sentence, brings with it something of its verbal nature and therefore gives contextual information to *keeps*, and does this by means of its non-perfective verbal aspect. There are some kinds of verbs which must have an infinitive after them somewhere or other, as in the sentence 'I persuaded him to see a doctor'. But there are other kinds of verbs, which seem to be able to influence the production of a similar type of structure on some occasions and quite different ones on others. For instance, 'I expected him to see a doctor' is a different sort of sentence from 'I expected rain', and one doubts whether *him to see a doctor* is a grammatical segment of the same kind as *rain*, even though it can be substituted for *rain* after *expected*. It is possible, of course, to do away with this distinction between catenative and non-catenative verbs, and to say simply that a sentence such as 'He remembered seeing it' is a sentence of the basic Type III with *seeing it* as an object, and that this is so because we have in the grammar already nominalized *seeing* when it occurs in subject positions and can therefore nominalize it in object positions too. There seems to be no real objection to this analysis, but at the same time the verbal aspect of infinitives and gerunds is preserved in the fact that they can, if transitive, have objects, and if intransitive, complements, and are modified adverbially. The preservation of this verbal aspect is often of great stylistic importance, since it tends to contextualize other words or expressions in the whole sentence. For example, in such a sentence as 'He remembered seeing it on Tuesday', it is apparent from the position of the phrase *on Tuesday* that the encoder thinks it is of some significance to point out that the seeing was done on Tuesday and not at any other time, and the position of the phrase, therefore, is clearly very important in contextualizing the information of both the elements *remembered* and *seeing*. On the other hand, in the more simple case of a non-catenative verb, as in such a sentence as 'He saw it on Tuesday', this kind of stylistic positioning has no possibility of occurrence.

As we have already seen, it is the verb which in general determines the form of the predicate of the sentences of the basic types. The part of the lexicon that deals with verbs under rule C4.1 would have to take this fact into account, and it would also have to take into account the ways in which the information of different and sometimes the same verb forms can be contextualized by the kinds of basic sentence forms in which they appear. It would have, first, to differentiate between intransitive and transitive verbs, for only the predicates of sentences of basic Types I and II, and the predicates of Types III, IV and V have, again in general, different sorts of transitive verbs. Many of the transitive verbs that appear in sentences of Type I are likely to be verbs of motion or of negative motion, although many of them may not be, but none of the intransitive verbs in sentences of Type I will have a complement; on the other hand every sentence of Type II will have a verb which is followed by a complement of some sort, and most of the verbs in the sentences of this type will be drawn from a comparatively very small selection of all the verbs in the language. Among the intransitive verbs there will be some, of course, which can also be transitive when they turn up in contexts other than those of sentences of Types I and II. Of the transitive verbs, those appearing in sentences of Type III are likely to be drawn from the largest class – probably the largest class of verbs in the language; while those appearing in sentences of Type IV – verbs which might be called 'donative', if a proliferation of technical terms is thought to be desirable – are members of a fairly small group. And sentences of Type V, it would seem, contain perhaps only verbs drawn from the membership of a group even smaller, for it is pretty certain that sentences of Type V are statistically of less probable occurrence than sentences of any of the other types.

One says 'probably' and 'perhaps' in the discussion of topics of this sort because one does not have accurate statistical data. Nevertheless, one is somehow convinced that one knows what one is talking about because of one's lifelong acquaintance with the language and one's awareness that one is a fairly competent speaker of it.

What one also knows is that fundamentally the modification of verbs is quite simple, though in practice the structures used for modification within sentences can become very complicated indeed. The rule C4.1, which comprehends all this modification under the symbol mod_5, says that in order to modify a verb the encoder must choose an adverbial. There is no need to go into the ramifications of the details of this rule. We can define the word *adverbial* in very much the same kind of way as that in which we defined the word *adjectival*, and say that an adverbial is a solitary adverb or a string of co-ordinated adverbs, an adverb phrase or an adverb clause. Without setting this down in the same way as the other rules of the grammar, we can ilustrate it as follows:

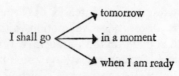

And it will be seen at once that the same kind of rule, that is, *phrase₃* ———→ *preposition + nominal*, is needed to generate adverb phrases as that needed to generate adjectival phrases, and that the only difference between them is that of position. In other words, a sentence like 'The man in the greenhouse picked tomatoes' is a different sentence, with different referential information, from the sentence 'The man picked tomatoes in the greenhouse'. In the same sort of way, the rule that generates adverbial clauses will be *clause₃* ———→ *clause₃ morpheme + Σ*. And so far as the norm of the language is concerned, the grammarian has only to state these rules in their completeness, and the job is done.

However, those structural units which we have called adverbials are capable of being used with great freedom in English. Very often an adverbial can become dissociated from the verb which it might be supposed to be modifying, and can assert pretensions to independence which give it a stylistic value. We have already seen (page 85) how differences in the positioning of adverbials can show subtle transformations of the basic structuring of sentences. In many of the utterances of the language, as indeed in the one you are now reading, adverbial modification can move as if it were outside the framework of the basic structuring so that it modifies not the main verb but the whole sentence.

C5, C6, C7, C8

The rest of the grammar can almost be said to be able to look after itself, for most of the remaining rules are repetitions of rules that have already been dealt with. Nominalization in English is basically subject to the same structural rules wherever it is found.

(9) Complements, for instance, in their general structure are the same as subjects. The only exception is that found in the seventh choice under rule C5, where an adjectival can turn up as a complement, as in the simple utterance 'These roses are red' or

'Charles Darwin is famous for his enunciation of the theory of evolution'. What differentiates adjectival complements from adjectivals occurring in subject positions is merely the feeling that speakers of English have that adjectival complements are still adjectival. In such a sentence as 'Red is a colour which I am fond of' the word *red* is without doubt a noun; or, in other words, we can substitute some adjectives in subject positions and thus turn them into nouns or give them the contextual and functional information of nouns, but we can't do this in object positions, except in some such isolated idiomatic collocation as 'He sees red', or in the language of some special register, as when in billiards some one can *pot the red*, where, of course, the determiner at once shows the word following it to be a noun. Professor Barbara Strang[1] refers to such examples as these as de-adjectival class nouns, and gives such examples as *the poor* as well as what she calls 'colour-adjectives'. But it seems simpler, on the whole, to say that some kinds of sentences bestow contextual and functional information on some words just by their being the kinds of sentences they are, and that the grammar of the norm can in some way or another show this. Certainly, it ought to be able to show it, for the grammar of the norm includes the lexicon, and when it comes to the full expression of its lexical rules it would be able to distinguish between those adjectives which can readily become nouns in special circumstances and those which cannot. It all depends on how much one can expect from a grammar and how far a grammar must deal with other than the merely functional information of the units of the language. In dealing with two units employed in an example which Mrs Strang herself gives – *the reds and golds of autumn* – the lexical rules could in some way indicate, one imagines, that the particular reds referred to were not Communists nor the golds different grades, say, of the same metal.

However, the rule $Comp_1 \longrightarrow adjective + mod_6$, selected from the seven choices under C5, seems to be a fairly straightforward one. The modification, of course, is adverbial.

(10) Under rule C6 the first choice is

C6.1 $\qquad$ Obj $\longrightarrow$ pronoun$_2$±mod$_1$.

[1] Strang, Barbara M. H., *Modern English Structure*, London, 1962.

This rule would be largely a repetition of C2.1 except that under the morphemic rules developed for that rule we should have something like

C6.11 M1   personal ———→ $\Big[$ *me, him, her, it, us, you, them* $\Big]$

And in the presumably following rule C6.11 M2 we should have to add the pronoun *them* to the list given under C2.11 M2, since *them* can contextualize *these* and *those* into objects in some circumstances, even though *these* and *those* can be used as objects in their own right.

4 Linguistic Artefacts

Technology is science applied to the production of artefacts, and among the earliest artefacts produced by man must have been swift and transient structures made of breath. But science is knowledge, pure and inviolate, without the marks of oily fingers; it is a fiction, a statement of the needs of the libido that becomes sacred to men who struggle for survival by imposing order on an apparently chaotic and hostile world. But before science can be applied it must be there, existing, in the mind (for presumably it can exist nowhere else), ready for application. Where does it come from? It comes, one supposes, from abstract ideas and from theories of thinking about them, the results of millions of observations and inferences from the noticing of similarity of events and their consequences, the common experiences of those who have to struggle to keep alive. Men have not carried this mode of thinking about in their heads since they first came down from the trees and started to hunt on the plains. It has taken them many thousands of years to learn it. Before abstract ideas can be thought, they have to come into existence. When men came down from the trees and began to hunt on the plains, if that is what they did, they had, one presumes, to learn how to walk before they could run; they had to have the experience of walking and running as experiences of motion, so that later this abstract idea of motion could be unconsciously generated as being a property, dimly perceived, of something else apart from the moving subject, who gazed at the world and thought about himself, brooding in silence.

The matter can be put another way – indeed, in several other ways. For instance, to believe that the universe exists is to impose some kind of order upon it, to endow it with being or existence in some kind of way. It can thus become an object of contemplation or recognition. Somebody imagined the universe, the entire unity of everything, and gave it a name, and people began to talk about what they imagined the name stood for, even though the universe itself was not a universal name like *tree* or *stone* or *man*. One can go even further. In addition to the universe's being an existing object, it can become an object on which one imposes order by one's imagining that it is doing something – such as exploding or being continually created – and not merely existing as a presence vaguely felt, or merely existing *per se*, in the purity of its essence. After that, almost anything can happen, for once you have started on this imaginative journey, it is difficult to tell where you are likely to stop. One assumption suggests another. Myths breed other myths. Fictions grow out of fictions. Men have invented systems of logic to convince themselves that one sort of assumption follows necessarily from another sort, and they have thus given to the linguistic structures which they have created a formal beauty of rigorous elegance which has satisfied their imaginations. For example, it seems to follow from the assumption 'that to believe the universe exists is to impose some kind of order upon it' that there are at least two entities which exist, the universe and the something which makes assumptions about it. At the same time, if I make this assumption, I also assume that I am part of the universe, that I am not outside it or separate from it, and therefore it follows that the universe and I are one, that without me the universe is incomplete.

To a new-born baby – as no doubt to the embryo in the womb, living though it is – the universe doesn't have any existence at all, one must presume. But one can imagine, as a result of the habits one's thought processes have acquired from sorting out impressions and perceptions as one has lived in one's environment, that to a new-born baby the universe must appear, if it appears at all, as a disorganized mess of unrelated sounds and colours and shapes and tastes and textures and smells. However, even to imagine that is quite gratuitous, and probably of no more ultimate validity than, say, some men's having at some time

H

imagined the existence of a god named Apollo. The new-born baby cannot recognize his unrelated perceptions as a mess. He has to wait until he is older, and then he manages to learn, perhaps, gradually to be able to sort out his perceptions and impressions and to be able in the end to distinguish chaos from organization. But that which, whatever it is, learns to do this resides in him; that which distinguishes and discriminates is his.

The idea of the universe presumably evolved among men over a very long period of time; and I am able to talk about the universe, I imagine, only because I have learnt about it from my ancestors, who discovered it as they lived through what we call history, gradually building up the idea over the years in a vast co-operative effort. I could hardly have thought up the idea all by myself. Even so, I believe that the universe exists, and I also believe that in holding that belief I impose some kind of order on the universe of which I am a part, but which is outside me as well as inside me.

Nevertheless, as I look round the universe, about which I can make these paradoxical statements, I behold a deplorable picture. The universe seems to be disintegrating, falling apart, breaking down, going out of business. Stone crumbles, iron rusts, timber decays; the fertile plain is eroded to a desert of sandy particles; the tidal seas bite into the land; plants wither, water evaporates, living creatures die and deliquesce. And beyond the range of immediate observation in the immediate environment (so the astronomers tell me) there is an enormous dispersion of the galaxies. In fact, everything seems to behave just as the Second Law of Thermodynamics says it should. The negative entropy of that which seems to have some kind of organization is always tending to become positive; the order of the system is being reduced to disorder; the tidy arrangement of molecules that makes up the speck of dust floating in the sunbeam that shines now in my room or that makes up the farthest supernova which I cannot see is moving always towards chaos:

Things fall apart; the centre cannot hold,
Mere anarchy is loosed upon the world,
The blood-dimmed tide is loosed, and everywhere
The ceremony of innocence is drowned.

Of course, the Second Law of Thermodynamics is only one of these imaginative linguistic constructions which we have to use to be able to interpret the world and our experience of it. The Law simply states a point of view. On the one hand we have entropy, chaos, disorder, which is, of course, no more than that which is not seen, not observed, not recorded, not described, not explained, not commented on by men. On the other hand we have the idea, the fiction, the comment, the statement, the explanation, the imposition of thought on that which is thought about.

A stone lies on the ground. It stays there for quite an appreciable length of time. It does not fly upwards to the zenith, nor does it jump about on the surface of the earth like a kangaroo. Man is capable of observing the stone as it lies upon the ground. He is also capable of making up fictions about it, which he may believe or not. He is capable of making up fictions because he has an apparatus of symbolism. He can say, for instance: 'This stone, naturally, cannot be said to know its relationship to its environment, nor can the piece of ground on which the stone lies be said to know that the stone lies upon it. But we, men, can *say* that the relationship of each to the other is there. We can also say, by merely extending the breath of our bodies to make structures of patterns of sound waves in the atmosphere, that the environment of the stone is the ground on which it lies, and, further, that the environment of the ground on which the stone lies is the stone. *A patch of earth and a stone – a stone and a patch of earth*: they interpenetrate and yet they are separate, they are one in two and two in one. Gravity (shall we call it?) keeps the stone where it is, and the place where the stone is kept (shall we say?) by gravity is also the place where gravity keeps the stone.'

When men came down from the trees and began to hunt on the plains, they had to learn how to stand erect, how to use arms which swung freely, how to extend the power of the hand at the end of the arm, and how to use the sharp focusing eyes in ways different from those in which they had been used before. As very primitive men gazed in the bright light across the distances of the plains, vistas appeared before them. Down from the trees, very primitive men found different things to see, different things to do, for men were living in a changing world, as always. It must have taken many thousands of years for men to get used to the feel of the change. But in the end – and the beginning – the sharp focusing eyes saw, the thumb and fingers at the end of the freely swinging arm grasped, and the stone was no longer lying on the ground. Clearly – or at least it seems clear to us now – the moment the stone was picked up, its environment was changed. So too was the environment of the patch of earth on which the stone had been lying. And so too was the environment of man. For the stone was, as we should say nowadays, eventually *useful*. This is because with the help of the stone men began to shape new surroundings that were extensions of themselves. They began to send messages to their fellows, to discourse among one another by means of artefacts, which were signals in physical substance. The first tools of the most primitive technology – pointed sticks, bits of flint harder than any metal except steel – were extensions of the power of the grasping hand at the end of the freely swinging arm. The stick can be cut with the flint, and a stick with a point can be shaped, and the pointed shape can be remembered. From a large number of pointed shapes men can not only abstract the universal notion of a pointed shape, but can also envisage the difference between a stick with a pointed shape at the end and a stick without one, and can learn the idea of intention. The act of cutting, if repeated over and over again for thousands of years, through one generation of men to the next and the next, can produce in the end the notion, the idea of the shape, the prototype of the information in the signal, which is the object, the aim, the intention, the hope, the aspiration, of the act after knowledge of it has become science as the result of abstraction during very long periods of practice.

This apparently is where science comes from. What appears to be shapeless, disordered, chaotic and without form, is only so because it is of a different shape from that which men imagine is the right one. What appears to be without form is only so because a different form can be imagined for a different usefulness. The comparatively large size of man's brain allows him the ability of association of ideas and of the creative imagination. This is only another way of saying that the human brain is a device which can sort out ideas, classify them, thus reducing chaos to order, and then make leaps across the classifications – or, as we say, make metaphors. The making of metaphors is the making of symbols of thoughts, the creation anew of perceived reality. When we make metaphors we bring together in thought and language those things which are never together outside thought and language. We think and talk of the 'mouth of a river', but rivers don't have mouths, and we only think and say that they have, for the symbolism of language is utterly arbitrary, and its arbitrariness is only controlled by lack of imagination. All metaphors need, however, the possibility of being structured in some communicative substance; they need the existence of a set of physical things that can be articulated together in recognizable patterns, although often, within these patterns, in new and un-conventional ways. In thus translating thoughts into physical substance men produce artefacts which carry messages. This chair I sit in, for example, tells me how to sit in it; or the typewriter on which I type these words has built-in instructions from its designer about how it is to be used – which keys to strike with the right-hand fingers and which with the left-hand, for example. And it is clear, I suppose, that even the most primitive technology – or the changing of the form of matter, the making of some-thing which is the right shape out of material which is the wrong shape – can become the prime activity of thinking. Or, as we say, practice makes perfect. The co-operation of hand, nerve, eye and brain, in changing the shape of matter, becomes able, when the thing has been done often enough, to produce also the idea of what is to be produced. And this same co-operation of hand, nerve, eye and brain can in the end, after many thousands of years of practice, also produce some such fiction as the Second Law of Thermodynamics. It can teach man that what he does during his existence in the universe is negative entropy, the opposite of disorder, the systematization of free-floating, un-associated and unharnessed molecules. It can also teach man that what is not done is entropy, the measure of disorder in the universe that his presence there tries to control, the enormous chaos that existed everywhere before he came and began to tidy up.

In speaking of the co-operation of hand, nerve, eye and brain, one must assume that the hand came first. It is apparently difficult for some people to think in this way, because, they assert, unless there is a brain to control the muscles and nerves of the hand, then the hand is dead and useless. But the hand which can touch and feel can also, one supposes, teach the brain to remember what it touches and feels, and thus to co-ordinate the sense-data. The hand and the eye, along with the organs of the other senses, we assume, by repeated explorations of environment, taught the brain to sort out and distinguish and discriminate eventually among what was available to be distinguished in the vastness of the great universe. The hand taught the brain to know the smooth from the rough, the soft from the hard, the aggressive from the comforting. There were crude hands before there were refined thoughts. We can assume, too, that the hands of the first men to walk upright were not very good at using bits of pointed stick to grub up roots or larvae or whatever they did with them. Only years of practice brought about an improvement. We can assume, in addition, that for many thousands of years after *homo sapiens* developed from *homo erectus* the hand became more skilled in extending its powers, first by using bits of stick, then bits of flint for cutting wood, then shaped and polished stones, then wood and stone together, and so on through the extensive Bronze Age to that of Iron, and through that of Iron to that of Steel, and then beyond into the Age of Light Alloys and Plastics, where we now think these thoughts.

When men come to live together in complicated social relationships that the mastery of technology eventually brings about, there is a dual kind of impositon of order on the apparent chaos of nature. The evolution of man in society can be looked upon as an effort, continuously exercised, to arrive at a satisfactory compromise between the needs of technology, which keeps the society in being, and the unrestricted appetites of each individual member of the social group. The demands of technology, which are necessary if the members of the group or nation or whatever it is are to be kept alive and society itself is to be maintained as a going concern; and as specialized techniques of doing work multiply in the division of labour as the social organization becomes more complicated, this effort needs more and more conscious control. Technology, primitive or sophisticated, is a constant bending and subduing of nature outside man to man's will. But there is also nature inside man, the libido, which is often regarded as dangerous and evil, capable, unless it is firmly controlled by social restraints, of destroying the society that maintains it, but which, nevertheless, has a powerful contribution to make to society if the species is to survive.

It is only by means of the continual externalization of extensions of the powers of each individual in society that social relationships can be sustained. Acts of externalization of the powers of individuals are normally directed towards the making of artefacts as structures of physical substances, and these artefacts have communicative value. Artefacts, things made by altering the shape of materials as nature presents them to man, are extensions of man's physical and psychic powers because they are expressions of man's efforts to come to terms with an apparently hostile nature outside him and inside him. Man is always in contact with nature – whether it is the familiar nature easily apparent to the senses, the nature of hills, woods, streams, wild plants and the singing of birds, or whether it is the nature of molecules and atoms and biological cells made apparent to the intellect by means of measuring devices and equipment used by scientists in laboratories. Man makes artefacts out of what nature supplies because he is hungry, naked and without a place to rest in until he does so; he needs them for survival. And artefacts become communicative because each man is alone, because no man can satisfy his hunger, clothe his nakedness or protect himself from weather and wild beasts unless he co-operates with his fellows. His artefacts, therefore, become media through which the messages needed for this co-operation are transmitted. They are signals of technological codes, defining and describing man in his environment, explaining man to himself.

One of the most natural things for man to do is breathe. Perhaps the very earliest of his artefacts, crude, coarse and savage, were made of noises built of breath; perhaps the first imposition of order on the apparent chaos of nature was that which made amorphous clouds of breath into an organized succession of sound-waves.

5 Anti-style and Style

The contemplation of style as a deviation from a norm can be viewed historically as a perpetual diversification and specialization of the technology of utterance. A vague and generalized apprehension of reality, occurring at a point where adumbrations of order meet disorganization or chaos, seeks to be realized as an artefact that can be understood by the senses and then interpreted as having some symbolism in its structure, some meaning in the way in which the elements that make up the artefact are arranged. For unless an artefact can have some semblance of form that can be related both to other artefacts of the same sort and to the notion of what such artefacts should be like, it is a useless artefact, one of nonsense, one that communicates either nothing or else an incomprehensible message. In learning the technology of utterance, speakers of a language learn not only what the norms of the basic kinds of utterances are, the chief signs of the code and the rules for their use, but they also learn part of the redundancy of the total code which is needed in any specialist activity. With simple codes, this learning is not at all difficult. But with a vast and complicated code, such as a modern European language, the difficulty is enormous, and nobody ever manages to learn such a code in its entirety. Indeed, one might regard a modern European language as a super-code which is made up of a very large number of smaller codes. Each individual who speaks the language has his own code which is a section of that language, and by means of it he communicates with his fellows in the common routine of matters of day-to-day living. Obviously, some people have larger codes than others in this respect, and obviously some people have codes closely connected with the practical activities which many other people never participate in. There are some codes which some people never learn, because such codes cover fields of experience in which not all people are specialists. Those of us who are not brain-surgeons, for instance, just don't bother to learn the code of neurology and relate it to the practical activity it stands for; and the technology of utterance in it for ever remains hidden from us.

The communications of men spread out into everything men do, for men can leave nothing alone, except the great and all-containing vastness of the universe itself. And men can leave nothing alone except this because they find, once they have started to impose an order on the apparent chaos of nature, that nature hits back and tries to control them. I cannot even express myself in language so as to make myself intelligible to others who speak the same language, unless I allow the messages I want to send to submit to the kind of code I use. If I speak, I can use only the speech sounds which the language has supplied; I cannot invent others, for those who hear these others will not recognize them as the speech sounds of the language they expect, and they will think I am mad, or speaking with tongues in a pentecostal or macaronic way. The very air I breath inhibits any attempt at utter originality of communication. And the intractable materials of the universe control me as I try to interpenetrate with them. The chair I sit in controls and dictates the way I sit; the objects in the world around me have an influence upon my movements; the materials out of which I try to make things decide the ways in which I shall make them. The life of man at every turn is dominated by the substances of the Earth he would like to conquer. We do not live in houses made of rose petals, or sit and lie on furniture made of marsh gas, or drink from vessels made of blotting-paper. This relationship between technology and environment is one in which man, the controller, discovers that he has to suffer the control and government of that which he tries to control and force to submit to him. This kind of relationship is not something which exists merely as a state of being; it is something which acts, operates, works, as a system which changes its states. It works on what people nowadays call cybernetical principles.

Cybernetics is a theory of the ways in which control and communication affect one another. If we accept that in performing a communicative act a man is also imposing some kind of order on the apparent chaos of the universe as he finds it, then he can impose that order only in ways dictated by the kinds of material he uses to make the physical substance of the signal in which he sends the message. In this manner, the controller of the communicative act is always controlled by what he seeks to control.

The kind of control which that which is controlled exerts over what controls it is called feedback, and feedback is an increment of energy derived from the actual working of some system. In the working of the system which we have described in the grammar of the norm, there is a tendency of this feedback to control communications, as social activities, so as to keep them within defined limits of their social usefulness. This produces an anti-style. The formula $\Sigma \longrightarrow Subject + Predicate$ has its own built-in recalcitrance. It will allow for deviations into sense and into structure and, in most cases, it will subdue attitude to the needs of sense and structure, but will resist, for the most part, deviation into conceit. When we think of style, in the first place, as a deviation from a norm, we think of it as deviating no further than these limits permit. The diversification of the total code into a number of specialized or institutionalized sub-codes is merely an accompaniment of the division of labour in social and economic history. Each facet of human economic activity has to develop its own style of the technology of utterance to deal, as human beings are busy in these activities, with the practical problems of getting jobs done; and the limitations of the activities themselves discourage any further deviation from the norm than sense and structure allow. But this feedback which produces an anti-style is static or negative; it is of that kind described by control and communications engineers and built into the hard-ware of servo-mechanisms, control systems and computers. In this static and negative kind of feedback we have simply the re-introduction into the system of the results of its own work-ing – as with a domestic hot-water supply, in which the ball-and-cock mechanism keeps on repeating its task of not allowing the level of the water to rise above a programmed height in the cistern by using that height as a control. It never allows the communicating device to communicate anything original, or use its medium in any way except a mechanical one, unless, of course, something goes wrong. But an anti-style is not supposed to go wrong. It is supposed to be utterly functional.

However, on a grander scale, in the feedback of social in-stitutions, we find that the controller is normally more and more dominated by that which he or it tries to control at each repetition of the task which the system has been brought into existence to perform. This can happen because the increment of energy which is sent back from the performance is an increment of a different kind from that which was sent out to initiate it, and was not numerically specified by it. Such numerical specification is – or at least, has been in the past – quite impossible in the feedback of social institutions conducted on a large scale, and this is be-cause of unforeseeable hazards – the future state of the weather, storms at sea, sudden death, failure of crops, and so on – which could affect the well-being of the whole or a part of society, and for which no kind of totally effective avoidance device could be built in to a human social enterprise. What happens in social evolution on a large scale is apparently something like this: as men sustain themselves in the place where they live, using their technology under the control of society's political and administrative components, they create artefacts by means of which the members of the society can communicate among themselves. But the messages which the artefacts carry teach the members of the society how to learn about the possibilities of the technology which they operate, even the technology of utterance in language; for those who give the orders in any social organization don't give them to machines whose performances can be more or less numerically computed and forecast; they give them to nervous systems which can learn, not only how to obey the orders, but also in obeying them how to change the pattern of doing so, and in that manner so change the kind of response to the order.

Three main components of social organization – the technological, the defensive and the administrative – do, it would seem, co-operate in social evolution to produce this kind of creative feedback by means of which society evolves. In giving its orders – such as 'pay these taxes' or 'defeat that enemy' – the administrative component sets in motion a series of activities which communicate states of awareness of actuality in the members of the other components to which the orders are given. But the response and the mechanism of the response are not easily predictable. If they were, the feedback would be capable of calculation, and things would go on, presumably, without major incident. Even so, something would have been learnt somewhere. Advances in social evolution, or, if not advances, changes, can become noteworthy and positive when that which is learnt alters the nature of the response. For example, the American colonists in the eighteenth century learnt an unforeseeable response to the order 'pay these taxes', and the administration in Britain, which ordered the defensive component to reply to this unexpected feedback with the order 'defeat that enemy', found itself confronted with an increment of energy which enabled that which the controller controlled to control the controller more powerfully. And the weakened controller, in these circumstances, had to make allowances for a new sort of development in the system; or – to put the matter another way – the system as a whole had learnt how to change itself.

In such circumstances, too, there will be what is nowadays, in a too well used cliché, called a failure of communications. The failure occurs in the nature of the feedback, which is learnt and fresh and was unpredictable in the initiation of the states of the system. It is not that anything new is actually said – merely that existing kinds of things to be said are uttered in a different style, or explained in new terms, or even through the exploiting of different kinds of media. There apparently always will be – or, to speak more precisely – in the past there always have been some members of society who prefer the old-fashioned to the newly invented, and who look upon differences as change and decay rather than advance and development. The failure of communication is merely a failure by one party or another, when there are different points of view or even differences of emphasis, to understand the terms and styles in which the messages are expressed; it is not necessarily a misunderstanding of the messages themselves. This is so because anybody who expresses what he has to say from whatever point of view has to express himself through myths, and if he expresses himself in language or any other media, has to use the symbolism of the substance out of which he makes his communicative artefacts.

Generally speaking, the truth of any statement thus made is only relative to the extent to which it is believed valid during the time in which the belief is held. And this is the sort of thing that continually happens in social development. The message remains in outline more or less the same, but the style of encoding it becomes different. For social evolution is not biological evolution. Although human social institutions may change, they can do so only within limits, for the species remains fundamentally the same. Some societies and social institutions change more rapidly than others, even though rapidity of change seems to be more often exceptional than usual. It would seem, for example, that the technological changes that have advanced western man's rapidity of development during the past four hundred years or so are quite extraordinary. Whatever the reasons might be, such spectacular technological advances tend to obscure, when oneself is a western man thinking about these matters, the notion of ultrastability. We can think of the ultrastability of a social organization as its power to persist in the main outlines of its structure while greater or smaller changes take place inside it. Society in Britain, for example, has shown some kind of ultrastability for the last thousand years. It has passed through stages of feudalism, mercantilism, capitalism and imperialism to the tendencies of the twentieth century towards the bringing about of a kind of totalitarian socialism – and all under the aegis of a monarchy and a class system of government with a tradition of unity perpetuated with only comparatively slight commotions now and then; while it was passing through these stages it preserved a cohesion of essential structuring; its form stayed very much the same while the content changed in increments of energy fed back into the system which was able to absorb them.

It would seem that there is an ultrastability in the kinds of things that men communicate to one another which is even more consistent. What men communicate through their myths expressed in their language is what their own collective point of view about reality and actuality is like. In making these communications men do, of course, learn cybernetically more and more about them as time passes. They are for ever accumulating knowledge of more and more detail. But what they learn today is that what was said yesterday was not quite adequate enough; and they will learn tomorrow that what was said today is not quite adequate enough either. The process is a continual refinement of the means of communication, and a continual probing into the details of general ideas. It is not that what was said in the past was untrue or wrong; it is merely that men find better, or more exact, or at any rate to them more satisfying, ways of probing into every facet of these general ideas so as to impose a more detailed pattern of experience on the apparent chaos of the universe.

In the basic grammar of the norm there were five ways in which the formula $\Sigma \longrightarrow$ Subject + Predicate could deviate into sense and structure, and then attitude and conceit; and it was suggested that all other kinds of sentence forms in English, such as sentences in the passive voice, or question, or commands, are but variations on these essential structural themes. Fundamentally, within the limits of the language, all that the language-using ego can say is 'I move' or 'I am' or 'I do something to something'; and then, as the power of language grows with use, and ego learns to discriminate and make distinctions by means of it, he can advance to the point of saying 'It moves' or 'It is' or 'It does something to something else', until it and its movement, its existence and its activities are given bit by bit their local habitations and their names. Each increment in the feedback of the learning process is gained by a new style of utterance, which, as soon as it is stabilized and moderately familiar, becomes expressed in conventional certitude of an anti-style, which, again, is the starting point for a new raid on the inarticulate, the emergence of a new style, and so on.

We made a distinction above between reality and actuality, because by the first we mean what is internal to men, and by the other what is external. Man himself makes this separation by his being the sort of creature that evolution has made him. One part of man is a complex of mechanisms which can receive perceptions of sense-data and classify and store them, and thus impose some kind of order on apparent chaos. This order can be looked upon as his point of view or what he thinks about the universe in which he finds himself. He can symbolize this order by means of artefacts which are extensions of his own body – the breath of his lungs on which he sends words into the atmosphere in structures of sounds, or the shaping of the material substances of the earth into all the things he needs or which he believes it is agreeable to have. Another part of man is that which can comprehend the existence of something behind or different from all that he perceives, and which makes him wonder at the incomprehensible when he brings his own reality into contemplation of the actuality that surrounds him. He diversifies this wonder into reverence and art, and because he has to live with his fellows or die, he has in the past given some of his reverence to his fellows: small men have made greater men into their heroes, priest-kings, sacred personages, who have governed the societies of those who have been unable to govern themselves or who have mastered and subdued those who were too weak to resist. For the raw, unschooled savage of reality has to be tamed and controlled in the everlasting effort to impose more and more order on the perceived actuality and to describe that order in more and more detail. Yet a third part of man is that which can make leaps across the classifications of what is perceived and stored of actuality, and which can thus produce the monsters and the glories, the horrors and the beauties, of the imagination, and which can see possibilities of creation in that which is uncreated – the form and line in the oily pigment before the brush takes it to the primed canvas, the shape in the three-dimensional space in the block of marble before the chisel chips away the dross, or the structure of words and their sounds that can fill the vacancies of silent air.

It is here, of course, at the point where the imagination can leap across the normality of the imposed order, that style of utterance can become interesting. For the leap is also one from the functionalism of anti-style into a new dimension. What makes the leap possible is the redundancy of the code. In the first place, the encoder may deliberately set out, when he plans his encoding, to draw upon the redundancy of the code and put more signs into the signal than are really needed to make the signal a functional embodiment of the message. Such conscious deviations produce, on the one hand, that kind of style which is admired by discerning encoders and to which positive value-judgements are attached, for these deviations usually show an original and pleasurable way in which redundancy has been used. In the production of imaginative literature and works of art this usefulness is obvious: a love poem can do much more than merely convey a declaration of love from encoder to decoder, and a Sheraton or a Chippendale chair can become something more than merely an object on which one can sit down. On the other hand, society occasionally needs messages in which encoders have put a special kind of redundancy: the report, in a schoolboy's history textbook, of what an Act of Parliament says whittles away an enormous amount of the deliberate redundancy of all the signals contained in the Act itself, and gives a more functional statement, in an anti-style approaching the norm, of what the Act is about. In the second place, there may be some decoders who see in a message more than was intended, or who may attach different sorts of value to a signal or series of signals than the encoder thought possible. Somebody once said that there were as many meanings of a poem as there were readers, and there must be many readers of some document like, say, the Book of Common Prayer, who can admire the beauty of the language and yet not find any great interest in the sentiment expressed. The kind of interpretation which a decoder puts on a message could endow the signal with a perverse, but nevertheless interesting, kind of style, for the decoder's subjective appraisal could give the mode of utterance something very far removed from its original function.

We could, in these concluding sections, have given some examples of the way in which the grammar of the norm can paraphrase different kinds of passages of prose or poetry. We could have noticed the basic statement that the norm produced, and could have compared this with the original, and we could have seen how this example differed from that. Then, no doubt, we could have classified kinds of deviation. But such tasks may be left to one's disciples, if one ever has any.

I prefer to conclude with a quotation from an account of childhood:

Radiating from that house, with its crumbling walls, its thumps and shadows, its fancied foxes under the floor, I moved along paths that lengthened inch by inch with my mounting strength of days. From stone to stone in the trackless yard I sent forth my acorn shell of senses, moving through unfathomable oceans like a South Sea savage island-hopping across the Pacific. Antennae of eyes and nose and grubbing fingers captured a few tufts of grass, a fern, a slug, the skull of a bird, a grotto of bright snails. Through the long summer ages of those first few days I enlarged my world and mapped it in my mind, its secure havens, its dust-deserts and puddles, its peaks of dirt and flag-flying bushes. Returning, too, dry-throated, over and over again, to its several well-prodded horrors: the bird's gaping bones in its cage of old sticks; the black flies in the corner, slimy dead; dry rags of snakes; and the crowded, rotting, silent-roaring city of a cat's grub-captured carcass.

Once seen, these relics passed within the frontiers of the known lands, to be remembered with a buzzing in the ears, to be revisited when the stomach was strong. They were the first tangible victims of that destroying force whose job I knew went on both night and day, though I could never catch him at it. Nevertheless I was grateful for them. Though they haunted my eyes and stuck in my dreams, they reduced for me the first intimate possibilities of horror. They chastened the imagination with a proof of limited frightfulness.

Were we to examine the grammar of the style of this beautiful passage, we would note, first, that the main deviations into sense and structure start with the intransitive verb *moved*, continue with the transitive verbs *sent, captured, enlarged, mapped,* that the deviations were held suspended by a major deviation of grammar and sense towards the end of the first paragraph, and that all this was delicately proleptic of what was to follow, in the next paragraph, after the change of point of view as the explored world comes back, so to say, and declares itself for what it is. We should note how these verbs were contextualized by the pre-modification such as that to be found in the first, second and fourth sentences, and how the sustained visual images were borne along on the premodification and postmodification, and how these images secured the generalizations into the particular realization of the explored world as well as the way in which these images showed deviations into attitude and conceit and thus produced the creativeness of the passage – that which makes such writing into a work of art, and not a mere utterance in some anti-style, no matter how good that may be. We should note too how the disposition of the modification round the basis of the verbs and the kinds of sentences the verbs insist on form-ing produces the firm and assured rhythms. We should note as well how, as the passage rises towards its climax, the normal words of the language are not sufficient for the author's creative purpose, and how new words, *dust-deserts, flag-flying, well-prodded, silent-roaring, grub-captured,* compound themselves from existing elements. We should note how the creation of these words stops when the climax is passed, and how the vocabulary becomes at once both more erudite – 'frontiers of the known lands', 'tangible victims', 'destroying force' – and more familiar – 'whose job I knew', 'could never catch him at it', only to become more erudite again in the last two sentences of the second paragraph. We should note the figurative uses of *radiating, acorn shell of senses, antennae,* and so on, and relate them to sense and conceit. We should consider such topics as the modification of *house* and the alliteration that forms part of it. We should note the intellectualization provided by the verb *were* in the second sentence of the second paragraph, and note how the whole myth of the passage thought of as a total structure moves towards that sentence. All this we should have to note and think about, and a great deal more as well, and the task would be an enormous one.

But what the style creates is ultimately most important of all. I can look upon the language of this passage, the signs and signals of the language substance, as the embodiment of an allegory, a thing in itself created out of language, and, in my opinion, beautifully created. It is an allegory of the sort of task that language has to do for man who imposes order on the apparent chaos of an apparently disintegrating universe, and whose imagination is chastened with the proofs of its own order and structuring.

REFERENCES

Many of the quotations used are taken from a corpus of samples of English usage made by the author from many kinds of printed matter published in Britain between 1960 and 1965. Since most of these sources are of only ephemeral interest, no references are given to them.

Page 12   HERRICK, ROBERT, *Collected Poems*, Oxford Standard Authors

Page 29   SHAKESPEARE, *Antony and Cleopatra*, IV, xii

Page 45   POPE, *The Dunciad*, IV, 652–5

Page 52   SHELTON, R. A. J., 'Vapour-phase Deposition of Copper by the Iodide Process', *Transactions of the Faraday Society*, Part I, January 1966

Page 53   AUDEN, W. H., Trinculo's Song, from 'The Sea and the Mirror', *Collected Longer Poems*, London, 1968

Page 108   DIXON, ROBERT M. W., *What is Language? A New Approach to Linguistic Description*, London, 1965, page 151

Page 111   STYAN, J. L., *The Dramatic Experience*, London, 1965, page 17

Page 115   ELSOM, JOHN, 'The End of the Absurd?', in *The London Magazine*, Vol. 4, No. 3, June 1964

Page 128   AGGAR, L. T., *Principles of Electronics*, Second Edition, London, 1955, page 155

Page 132   DE LA MARE, WALTER, *The Complete Poems*, London, 1969

Page 143   SHELLEY, *Prometheus Unbound*, IV, 236–45, Oxford Standard Authors

Page 157   SHAKESPEARE, *Macbeth*, I, v
           BROWNING, ELIZABETH BARRETT, 'To George Sand, a Recognition', *Poems*, (1844)
           SHAKESPEARE, Sonnet 57

227

Page 158 BROWNING, ROBERT, *Of Pacchiarotto, and How He Worked in Distemper*, xxvii

BROWNING, ROBERT, *Fifine at the Fair*, lii

Page 160 MILTON, *Paradise Lost*, IV, 297–301

Page 161 WORDSWORTH, WILLIAM, *Rob Roy's Grave*, 33–40

Page 164 SHAKESPEARE, *King Lear*, IV, ii

T. S. ELIOT, *East Coker*, IV

Page 167 SHAKESPEARE, *The Merchant of Venice*, V, i

Impromptu epitaph attributed to DAVID GARRICK

POPE, *An Essay on Criticism*, 362–3

Page 168 SHAKESPEARE, *Twelfth Night*, II, iv

MILTON, *Paradise Lost*, X, 430–8

Page 169 SWINBURNE, *Dolores*, ix

SHAKESPEARE, *King Henry the Fifth*, IV, Prologue

Page 172 JAMES, HENRY, *The Portrait of a Lady*, Preface, Collected Works, London, 1921

Page 191 KEATS, *Hyperion*, I, 194–5, Oxford Standard Authors

Page 210 YEATS, W. B., *The Second Coming*, in *Collected Poems*, London, 1950

Page 224 LEE, LAURIE, *Cider with Rosie*, Penguin Edition, page 14

BIBLIOGRAPHY

This list of books has been deliberately made short and highly selective, because I have thought it best to give only those titles most easily available to the student and general reader. For the same reason, articles in journals, though many of them are of undoubted interest and importance, have been left out; and in any case the specialist will already be acquainted with the more recondite items and will certainly know in what sorts of places to look for them.

I have tried to make the kind of selection given here serve two purposes. First, it can show what sorts of influences have, I think, been most important in shaping, over the years, the attitude to language and the ways in which language is used that is adumbrated in the main text. Second, it should help the student and general reader to discover, if they are not already known, some of the chief books likely to be of use in revealing the main principles of modern linguistics and the leading ideas of the revolution that has taken place in British and American thinking about the problems of language in the last forty years or so. I believe that this revolution would not have occurred had there not also been some other influences at work – in philosophy, in anthropology, and in the mathematical physics of communications engineering. I have therefore included one or two titles on these topics, so that the interested reader may look at them if he wishes; they have certainly been at least in the background of my own thinking about language.

Consequently there are three kinds of items on the list: those that are of linguistic importance and which ought to be read by all serious students of linguistics; those that are of secondary importance considered linguistically, but which are nevertheless interesting; and those which are of related interest. Items of the first kind are given without any asterisk; those of the second kind have one asterisk; those of the third kind have two.

* *AYER, A. J., *Language, Truth and Logic*, London, 1936

BACH, EMMON, *An Introduction to Transformational Grammars*, New York, 1964

* *BERLO, DAVID K., *The Process of Communication*, New York, 1966

BLOOMFIELD, LEONARD, *Language*, British Edition, London, 1935

CARROLL, JOHN B., *The Study of Language*, British Edition, London, 1954

—— *Language and Thought*, New Jersey, 1964

CHERRY, COLIN, *On Human Communication*, Second Edition, New York, 1966

CHOMSKY, NOAM, *Syntactic Structures*, The Hague, 1957

—— *Current Issues in Linguistic Theory*, The Hague, 1964

—— *Aspects of the Theory of Syntax*, Cambridge, Massachusetts, 1965

* *——*Language and Mind*, New York, 1968

CRYSTAL, DAVID, *What is Linguistics?*, London, 1968

CRYSTAL, DAVID and DAVY, DEREK, *Investigating English Style*, London, 1968

DARBYSHIRE, A. E., *A Description of English*, London, 1967

DAVIE, DONALD A., *Purity of Diction in English Verse*, London, 1964

DOBREE, BONAMY, *Modern Prose Style*, Second Edition, London, 1964

ENKVIST, NILS ERIC, SPENCER, JOHN, GREGORY, MICHAEL J., *Linguistics and Style*, London, 1964

FIRTH, JOHN RUPERT, *A Synopsis of Linguistic Theory*, in 'Studies in Linguistic Analysis', Special Volume of the Philological Society, Oxford, 1957

—— *Papers in Linguistics, 1934–1951*, London, 1957

——*The Tongues of Men and Speech*, London, 1964

* *FLEW, A. G. N., (Editor), *Logic and Language*, First Series, Oxford, 1952

FODOR, JERRY A. and KATZ, JEROLD J., (Editors), *The Structure of Language*, New Jersey, 1964

FOWLER, ROGER, (Editor), *Essays on Style and Language*, London, 1966

FRIES, CHARLES CARPENTER, *The Structure of English*, British Edition, London, 1958

*——— *Linguistics and Reading*, New York, 1965

GLEASON, HENRY A., JN., *An Introduction to Descriptive Linguistics*, Revised Edition, New York, 1961

——— *Linguistics and English Grammar*, New York, 1965

*GORDON, IAN A., *The Movement of English Prose*, London, 1966

HALL, ROBERT A., Jn., *Introductory Linguistics*, Philadelphia, 1964

HALLIDAY, MICHAEL A. K., MCINTOSH, ANGUS and STREVENS, PETER, *The Linguistic Sciences and Language Teaching*, London, 1964

HARRIS, ZELLIG S., *Structural Linguistics*, Chicago, 1960

HILL, ARCHIBALD A., *An Introduction to Linguistic Structures*, New York, 1958

HOCKETT, CHARLES F., *A Course in Modern Linguistics*, New York, 1958

HOUGH, GRAHAM, *Style and Stylistics*, London, 1969

JESPERSEN, OTTO, *The Philosophy of Grammar*, London, 1924

JOOS, MARTIN, (Editor), *Readings in Linguistics. The development of descriptive linguistics in America since 1925*, Second Edition, Washintgon D.C., 1958

——— *The Five Clocks*, Bloomington, Indiana, 1962

LANGACKER, RONALD W., *Language and its Structure: Some Fundamental Concepts*, New York, 1968

LODGE, DAVID, *Language of Fiction: Essays in Cristicism and Verbal Analysis of the English Novel*, London, 1966

LUCAS, FRANK L., *Style*, Second Edition, London, 1952

**MALINOWSKI, BRONISLAV, *Coral Gardens and their Magic*, London, 1935

MCINTOSH, ANGUS and HALLIDAY, MICHAEL A. K., *Patterns of Language, Papers in General, Descriptive and Applied Linguistics*, London, 1966

NOWOTTNY, WINIFRED, *Language Poets Use*, London, 1962

OGDEN, C. K. and RICHARDS, I. A., *The Meaning of Meaning*, Tenth Edition, London, 1949

*OLDFIELD, R. C. and MARSHALL, J. C., (Editors), *Language, Selected Readings*, Harmondsworth, 1968

ONIONS, C. T., *An Advanced English Syntax*, Sixth Edition, London, 1932

PALMER, F. R., *A Linguistic Study of the English Verb*, London, 1965

POTTER, SIMEON, *Modern Linguistics*, Second Edition, London, 1967

—— *Language in the Modern World*, Harmondsworth, 1961

**QUINE, WILLARD VAN ORMAN, *Word and Object*, Cambridge, Massachusets, 1960

QUIRK, RANDOLPH, *The Use of English*, London, 1962

—— *Essays on the English Language, Medieval and Modern*, London, 1968

*RABAN, JONATHAN, *The Technique of Modern Fiction*, London, 1968

RICHARDS, I. A., *Principles of Literary Criticism*, London, 1924

—— *The Philosophy of Rhetoric*, London, 1936

ROBERTS, PAUL, *English Syntax*, New York, 1964

ROBINS, ROBERT HENRY, *General Linguistics, an Introductory Survey*, London, 1964

**RYLE, GILBERT, *The Concept of Mind*, London, 1949

SAPIR, EDWARD, *Language, an Introduction to the Study of Speech*, New York, 1921

SEBEOK, THOMAS A., (Editor), *Style in Language*, Cambridge, Massachusets, 1960

*SHANNON, CLAUDE E. and WEAVER, WARREN, *The Mathematical Theory of Communication*, Urbana, 1949

**SMITH, ALFRED G., *Communication and Culture*, New York, 1966

STAGEBERG, NORMAN C., *An Introductory English Grammar*, New York, 1965

STRANG, BARBARA M. H., *Modern English Structure*, Second Edition, London, 1968

THOMAS, OWEN, *Transformational Grammar and the Teacher of English*, New York, 1965

ULLMANN, STEPHEN, *Semantics*, Oxford, 1962

—— *Language and Style*, Oxford, 1964

WARNER, ALAN, *A Short Guide to English Style*, London, 1961

WHORF, BENJAMIN LEE, *Language, Thought and Reality*, Cambridge, Massachusets, 1958

ZANDVOORT, R. W., *A Handbook of English Grammar*, Fifth Edition, London, 1969

INDEX

INDEX

INDEX